ESSAYS ON AESTHETICS

Perspectives on the Work of
Monroe C. Beardsley

Contributors

LARS AAGAARD-MOGENSEN is Visiting Professor of Philosophy at Saint Cloud University, Minnesota.

ANN BANFIELD is Professor of English at the University of California, Berkeley.

STEPHEN BARKER is Professor of Philosophy at the Johns Hopkins University.

SEYMOUR CHATMAN is Professor of Rhetoric at the University of California, Berkeley.

GEORGE DICKIE is Professor of Philosophy at the University of Illinois, Chicago Circle.

CHARLES DYKE is Associate Professor of Philosophy at Temple University.

BOHDAN DZIEMIDOK is Professor of Philosophy at the University Marii Curie-Sklodowskiej, Lublin, Poland.

JOHN FISHER is Professor of Philosophy at Temple University.

GÖRAN HERMERÉN is Professor of Philosophy at the University of Lund, Sweden.

SAMUEL HYNES is Professor of English at Princeton University.

GEORGE MCFADDEN is Professor of English at Temple University.

STEFAN MORAWSKI is Professor of Aesthetics at the Institute of Art, Polish Academy of Science.

ALEXANDER NEHAMAS is Professor of Philosophy at the University of Pittsburgh.

PAUL RICOEUR is Professor of Divinity and Professor of Philosophy at the University of Chicago.

FRANK SIBLEY is Professor of Philosophy at the University of Lancaster, England.

FRANCIS SPARSHOTT is Professor of Philosophy at Victoria College, The University of Toronto.

ALAN TORMEY is Professor of Philosophy at the University of Maryland, Baltimore County Campus.

ESSAYS ON AESTHETICS

Perspectives on the Work of Monroe C. Beardsley

Edited by JOHN FISHER

TEMPLE UNIVERSITY PRESS

PHILADELPHIA

Publication of this book has been assisted by a generous contribution
from Temple University's College of Arts and Sciences

Temple University Press, Philadelphia 19122
© 1983 by Temple University, except for chapters 1, 15, and 16.
All rights reserved
Published 1983
Printed in the United States of America

Library of Congress Cataloging in Publication Data
Main entry under title:

Essays on aesthetics.

Includes index.
1. Aesthetics—Addresses, essays, lectures.
2. Philology—Addresses, essays, lectures.
3. Beardsley, Monroe C.—Addresses, essays, lectures.
I. Beardsley, Monroe C.   II. Fisher, John, 1922–
BH39.E76   1983   111'.85   82-19666
ISBN 0-87722-287-8

To
Ruth Smith
who never got to read it
and to
Ruth Fisher
who did
In gratiis duplicibus

Contents

Acknowledgments   ix

Introduction   xi

The Philosophy of Art

1. Frank Sibley *General Criteria and Reasons in Aesthetics*   3
2. Lars Aagaard-Mogensen *Aesthetic Qualities*   21
3. Göran Hermerén *The Autonomy of Art*   35

Aesthetic Experience

4. Bohdan Dziemidok *Aesthetic Experience and Evaluation*   53
5. Stephen Barker *Kant on Experiencing Beauty*   69
6. John Fisher *Beardsley on Aesthetic Experience*   86

Art and Society

7. George Dickie *Art and the Romantic Artist*   99
8. Charles Dyke *The Praxis of Art and the Liberal Dream*   109
9. Francis Sparshott *Preservation, Projection, and Presence: Preliminaries to a Consideration of Pictorial Representation*   131

Narrative in Literature

10. Paul Ricoeur *Narrative and Hermeneutics*   149
11. Seymour Chatman *On the Notion of Theme in Narrative*   161
12. Alexander Nehamas *Mythology: The Theory of Plot*   180

Literature and Language

13. Ann Banfield *Linguistic Competence and Literary Theory*   201
14. Alan Tormey *Metaphors and Counterfactuals*   235
15. Samuel Hynes *On Hardy's Badnesses*   247

Tragedy and Comedy

16. George McFadden *The Quality of the Comic*   261
17. Stefan Morawski *On the Tragic: A Confession and Beyond*   278

Response to the Essays

18. Monroe C. Beardsley *Response to the Essays*   297

Index   307

Acknowledgments

All of the following essays were written expressly for this volume. It owes much to the College of Arts and Sciences of Temple University for financial support and to Dean George Wheeler for encouragement. The authors were longsuffering through unavoidable delays, and the editor acknowledges their patience and good humor. David Bartlett, Zachary Simpson, and Lynn Kendall of Temple University Press have been especially helpful. Grace Stuart gave countless hours to the preparation of the manuscript, a usually thankless task that in this case cannot be left at that, and Jane Barry helped immensely with the editing. The work is a tribute, and as such it owes most to the one it honors.

Introduction

The aging and unpredictable Ezra Pound once turned to a noted Johns Hopkins professor and uttered these words of wisdom for scholars to follow: "You have an obligation to visit the great men of your time." Not surprisingly, he did not enumerate the great men, but he did refer to a process that more than one scholar or would-be scholar has, to his great gain, initiated.

If we attempt to exploit Pound's advice, however, we will often discover that the great men have not been listening to him. The powerful, the statesmen, the professors, the artists, seldom recognize the implicit obligation to be visited that Pound's dictum placed upon them. Presidents reply with ceremonial and irrelevant printed notes of thanks; the secretary general is always in a meeting; the professor is out of town.

What has impressed a generation of acquaintances, strangers, colleagues, and students is that Monroe Beardsley has seldom been out of town, even when he *has* been out of town, for his door is always open, wherever he is. For many years my office has been adjacent to his, and many an afternoon I marveled at the patience of the man, who never turned anyone away, not students, not visiting firemen, not the curious, not the disaffected, not the exploiters. Nor did he ever highhandedly turn away their ideas, but gave each, as bizarre as the ideas often were, a fair, indeed sometimes more than fair, hearing.

I first heard Monroe Beardsley lecture when I was a student. The title was something like "Animadversions on Taste." I had never, in my innocence, heard a lecture with "animadversions" in its title before. I had always associated the term with censoriousness. It was my first encounter with criticism in the constructive sense in which aestheticians use the term. What I remember most about the lecture was that I understood it. To a beginning student that in itself was a mark of greatness in a professor.

Some years later I made my first visits to the office and the home of Monroe Beardsley and was immediately aware of the open door, and the characteristic generosity with his time, and the sense—as countless other visitors have noted—that to this professor all persons are equal in deserving his respect, his courtesy, and his spontaneous love for humanity; all are entitled to a hearing for their ideas. Since those days our paths crossed many times and finally converged into a collegial relationship that has been enriching to a degree that such efforts as this volume can only feebly suggest.

One of the primary difficulties in organizing this collection was the constraint upon size. Whose essays should be solicited? What criteria should be applied? The choice was a compromise. All of the contributors have had some significant working relationship with Monroe Beardsley. Many were post-doctoral fellows who came to Temple University to savor his ideas. Many other scholars, of course, have been deeply influenced by his work and his teaching, but the book had to have a focus. Thus, a number of former students who now hold distinguished posts at major universities, but have not worked seriously in aesthetics, do not appear; nor, for the same reason, do many other friends and colleagues who have been close to him throughout his career. I regret the exclusion of all those who, according to the criteria of influence, respect, and friendship, have every bit as much right to be part of this book as those whose writings are found on these pages. If the work included contributions from all those whose professional lives, whose ideas, whose attitudes toward the arts and aesthetics, have been influenced by Monroe Beardsley, it would have been a shelf of books, not a volume.

A year or so ago a rainy afternoon was suddenly brightened by a smiling face at the door. It was MCB, almost aglow with delight. "Let me show you something," he said. It was a letter from a distinguished American poet who had never met Beardsley, but had read a recent article and written to say that he enjoyed reading the piece and thought that the thesis was undoubtedly correct. The modesty, never mawkish or maudlin, that characterizes Beardsley was supremely evident: "He took time to write to me!" I replied with a laugh, in order not to embarrass him, but I meant it quite sincerely: "Great men often do that when they haven't time to visit great men."

So here in this volume seventeen friends and colleagues, in that special format sometimes called "essays in honor of," pay their visits to Monroe Beardsley. He has listened to them all with typical respect and, in at least some cases, admiration. He has responded briefly at the end, an act that, coming during a period of serious illness, is itself a mark of the man. He would never be comfortable with the term—indeed, if he had seen the proofs, he would have insisted on its deletion—but greatness does not seem too extravagant a label.

John Fisher

The Philosophy
of Art

1

General Criteria and Reasons in Aesthetics

FRANK SIBLEY

It is a somewhat daunting task to attempt to discuss the work of Monroe Beardsley, especially his work on aesthetics. Over a long period he has been more than prolific; he has pursued many issues with a wholly admirable pertinacity, developing and modifying his views bit by bit and in detail, with great good sense and sensitivity, not only as he has come to think his own positions need amending, but also in the light of criticism directed at him by others. There is a vast amount of his work with which I agree, and I doubt that I can say much that he has not already himself thought of, even if he may have rejected it as unsastifactory. Given the bulk, subtlety, and complexity of his writings, it is almost inevitable that at some point I shall misrepresent him or do him an injustice. It is likely that I may simply have overlooked or forgotten some important points he has made. I shall have to risk this and rely on his customary appreciation of those who tend to support views similar to his own from their own particular standpoint as well as his constant interest in and generosity toward those who either misunderstand him or attempt to oppose his views.

Throughout his writings Beardsley has steadily sought to uphold the view that in criticism there are and can be general reasons for aesthetic judgments. On this point I stand and have always stood on the same side as he does. Thus, basically, we face together those many writers over several decades—I dub them "particularists"—who have argued that in criticism there are no such general reasons. The dispute arises because both we and those we oppose agree that reasons, to be reasons, must have a consistency about them; but our opponents allege that any "reason" offered to support the judgment that one work has aesthetic merit may be offered to support the judgment that another work has an aesthetic defect. To debate this issue adequately would require several complex chapters; so in the space available I can indicate my defense of the "generalist" position only in the sketchiest way and with the simplest of examples. I shall argue that through not making certain distinctions adequately, Beardsley adopts an extreme and heroic position that is unnecessary even to dispose of the most serious of the denials of consistency just mentioned. Later I shall argue that the particular kind of heroic attempt he makes is inadequate to establish a deeper claim; that by means of it he can isolate ultimate criteria of aesthetic merit from ultimately negative aesthetic criteria. On the first question he attempts more than is necessary to defeat our common adversaries; and for the second question, the line of defense he adopts through the bulk of his work is unsatisfactory.

The line of defense that he employs for both questions consists in claiming that there are three primary or basic positive criteria—unity, complexity, and intensity of regional quality—that can never in any circumstances count otherwise than in a positive direction. These criteria he regards as ultimately "safe"; all other (secondary) criteria are "risky."[1] To make any of the latter safe in a given case, they must be linked to one or more of the primary criteria. I shall argue that a sharp distinction is essential within the criteria that Beardsley allows to be risky, a distinction he at times hovers on the brink of making. To take some of his examples, the presence of puns (or four-letter words) in a work may be either a merit or a defect; equally, he allows, may the presence of dramatic intensity (or a touch of humor).[2] Each is a secondary criterion. To show that either is, in a particular work, a merit, he maintains, ultimately requires a linkage to the primary criteria. But this, I claim, overlooks a vital difference. "X contains many puns" (I use x throughout to mean an artwork, not any specific kind of work like a tragedy, a pastoral poem, a sonnet, a statue, or a fugue) attributes to x a property or feature that is in itself entirely *neutral*. To claim that the puns are a merit in x, I agree, demands a linking explanation— they are striking, vivid, evocative, and so on. To claim that they are a defect also demands some such explanation—they are distracting, insipid, etc. So "X contains many puns (metaphors, etc.)," *tout court*, carries no implication of aesthetic merit or defect. But this is not so, I maintain, with "X has dramatic intensity." The attribution to an artwork of dramatic intensity, *tout court*, like the attribution of grace or elegance, is the attribution to it of a property that inherently possesses aesthetic merit. I would say that there are a whole host of properties that inherently possess a positive aesthetic polarity when applied to works of art, not just those I have mentioned, which seem to me aestheic *par excellence*, but many, like witty, balanced, and joyous, that have applications of another kind entirely outside the arts. Similarly there are a host of inherently negative properties, like garish, sentimental, bombastic, and ugly. If these properties are not themselves grounds of aesthetic value (positive or negative respectively) in the realm of the arts, I cannot conceivably see what could be.[3] They are like "honest," "conscientious," "considerate," in the realm of ethics. Whereas the neutral properties that can be offered in reasons for merit or demerit possess, without linking explanation, no inherent polarity whatever, these do inherently possess an aesthetic evaluative polarity. One cannot intelligibly say *tout court*, and with this Beardsley certainly agrees, "This work is bad because it is graceful," or "This work is good because it is garish." I would want to say that all these, not Beardsley's three, are basic or primary aesthetic criteria, some of merit, some of demerit.

But now the question arises why Beardsley should suppose them inadequate as basic or primary general aesthetic criteria and why he should regard them as "risky." The reason is clear. He is only too aware, as are the particularists, that grace or elegance or dramatic intensity need not necessarily be a merit, may even be a defect, in a particular work. And for this too, most certainly, an explanation is needed in each particular case. But this time it is not an explanation of why an inherently neutral feature (the presence of puns or metaphors) is a reason for merit in a work; it is an entirely different kind of explanation: why a feature, inherently a merit when taken *tout court*, is, in the context of a particular work, a defect. Beardsley, I think, never adequately distinguishes the two cases. He regularly lumps them together. He therefore tries the same sort of explanation with the second group, linking them again to his one-way criteria. But though an explanation is needed, it does not have to be of this sort. Indeed, it is here that the second crucial distinction not explicitly emphasized by Beardsley must be made. To save what I have called general evaluative criteria from the attack of the particularists, Beardsley supposes it necessary to perform what I called the heroic task of finding certain criteria to fall back on: not merely ones that, applied to a work *tout court*, inherently count one way, but ones that always, in every work, can count only one way.

It is clear that, and why, Beardsley makes this move. If there are genuine reasons, there must be generality; if generality, consistency; and if consistency, the reasons given must always count one way only. As he says about butchers' knives, "if a certain degree of sharpness is a merit . . . then to say that a knife has that degree of sharpness must *always* be a reason to support the conclusion that it is good, and it will apply to *all* knives of the relevant sort. . . . *It will, at least, never be a fault in a knife*" (my italics).[4] And so what I called his heroic task is to find primary positive criteria that are such that "the addition of any one of them or an increase in it, without a decrease in any of the others, will always make the work a better one."[5] But the distinction that must be made clearly here is that between overall judgments of things, like butchers' knives, where the relevant criteria are *independent* of each other, and overall judgments of those many things, including artworks, where the relevant criteria are *interacting*.[6] In the former, once the thing is discovered to have certain merit-qualities and if it possesses enough, the judgment that the thing is good is merely summative; the inherent merit-qualities do not interact. If the blade is sharp, the knife well balanced, the handle convenient to hold, and so on, then in the absence of overriding or defeating negative qualities (for example, that it breaks after one day's use), it is a good one. But with very many things, though we can set out criteria of merit, these are not independent; they can interact within the whole in various ways. What are merit-features *tout court* or *in vacuo* for that *sort* of thing may not work satisfactorily together with other such *tout court* merit-features in a *particular* thing of that sort. It is the sort of object sometimes spoken of as an "organic whole." This is not a case of defeasibility, inherent positive features being overridden or defeated by inherent negative features. With defeasibility, inherently positive features never become negative in a particular instance: duress may defeat a contract, but offer and acceptance never count against a contract. But where there is possible interaction in a complex whole, as in artworks, what *in vacuo* is inherently an aesthetic merit may *itself*, in conjunction with other inherently positive features in that complex, become a *defect*.

For this an explanation will be necessary, but it can be a perfectly intelligible, though special, sort of explanation. It will be a *reversing* explanation, not the sort that showed why the occurrence of puns or metaphors (neutral in themselves) gave merit to a work. And such reversing explanations are common. Indeed, the sorts of cases needing detailed discussion are legion. Here I can take only one of the simplest, suggested by one of Beardsley's examples. When someone has decided that certain parts of a work are highly comic and other parts intensely tragic—both *tout court*, or inherent, or, in my usage, primary criteria of merit—he has to judge for himself whether the comic episodes detract from or enhance the tragic character, or vice versa. If he decides that the comic elements do detract from and dilute the tragic intensity, *and* that the tragic element is predominant, the comic elements, though of aesthetic worth in themselves, will be defects in that work precisely because they dilute the predominant tragic intensity.

I have argued elsewhere that there are no sure-fire rules by which, referring to the neutral and nonaesthetic qualities of things, one can infer that something is balanced, tragic, comic, joyous, and so on. One has to look and see. Here, equally, at a different level, I am saying that there are no sure-fire mechanical rules or procedures for deciding which qualities are actual defects in the work; one has to judge for oneself. But if the critic does decide that the comic elements are defects in this work, a perfectly general reason can be given. A work that might otherwise have excelled by its tragic intensity is marred by certain (inherently valuable) comic elements that dilute and weaken that (inherently valuable) tragic intensity; or vice versa. It is a matter for deciding, judging, that one dilutes, rather than contributes to, the other, for deciding which of the elements is on balance predominant, and hence deciding that a feature, in itself valuable, is the detracting feature, or defect, in the context of that work. This is a built-in and unavoidable phenomenon, not only in artworks, but wherever inherent merit-qualities may interact, and not one we need or should regret.

Beardsley comes closest to this position perhaps in his article "On the Generality of Critical Reasons." There he adequately refutes several of the more simple-minded arguments of the particularists. But I think it is clear that by ultimately striving for what I called the heroic solution, he falls back on his three primary criteria, and in doing so fails to convince where conviction is possible. It is precisely in dealing with the most crucial case, where an inherent merit-quality constitutes a defect in a particular work, that he hovers on the brink of the right answer. He claims that "the General Criterion Theory [by "general" he means criteria that *always* count only one way] can easily take account of such variations."[7] Rightly he says, just as I do, that a general criterion theory "does not mean that this desirable feature can be *combined* with all other desirable features," or that "all plays that lack a high degree of [dramatic intensity] would necessarily become better by increasing it, for some plays might thereby lose some other quality that *especially* adorns them" (my italics).[8] But here his argument falters. In his Shakespeare examples (*Hamlet* and *Macbeth*), having agreed that humor is a merit in one context but a defect in another, he, in my view, wrongly concedes that a "touch of humor is not a *general merit*" (my italics), because something else, namely, high dramatic tension, is.[9] But he should not have given way thus on the generality of the merit of humor, especially as in the next sentence he in effect concedes equally that high dramatic tension is not a general aesthetic merit either; for some plays that lack it would, if it were increased, "thereby lose some other quality that especially adorns them." So by parity of reasoning dramatic intensity is not a general criterion either.

My claim is that humor and dramatic intensity are *both* inherently general aesthetic merits, though either may be a defect, given an appropriate explanation, in the context of a given work. Instead, Beardsley falls back onto his three "always positive" primary criteria, a position that I am arguing is unnecessary. (It is true that Beardsley then says that even secondary criteria are general "in an important sense," which may seem to coincide with the view I am espousing.) But his secondary criteria, though general, are "subordinate and conditional." "X is a *secondary (positive) criterion* . . . if there is a certain set of other properties such that, whenever they are present . . . the addition of X . . . will always produce an increase in one or more of the primary criteria."[10] I would deny that any such "set of other properties" can ever be specified.

Incidentally, if the particularist's fear is that the admission of general criteria of the sort I admit—grace, elegance, humor, subtle characterization, dramatic intensity, which I have called basic aesthetic criteria—would make evaluative judgments a mere matter of mechanically testing a work against rules, or that it would preclude the possibility of these inherently valuable aesthetic qualities being defects in a particular work, my answer to him has already been given. In fact, my answer amounts to a direct denial of the claim of one particularist, Mary Mothersill, who says that "there is no analogue in criticism to what in moral philosophy have been called 'prima facie duties'"—or, we might add, virtues.[11] The general qualities that, when mentioned *tout court* or *in vacuo*, I have called inherent merit-qualities are, in the context of a particular work, *prima facie* merits, but not necessarily *actual* merits.

The situation is analogous—I stress analogous, not identical—to that in ethics (and many other areas where criteria interact). If one accepts that promise keeping, truth telling, honesty, and so on are inherently moral virtues, it may nevertheless be necessary, even right in certain circumstances, *either* to lie or to break a promise.[12] Unless one accepts some fixed hierarchy of virtues or some plausible overriding principle like Utilitarianism, one is left to

a non-rule-governed decision, weighing, for example, the serious-
ness or relative unimportance of the lie against that of the promise
breaking, rather as one has to decide, in a hypothetical play containing both comic and tragic episodes, which are the defects and
which therefore ought to have been expunged. (The disanalogy
with ethics is that telling the truth may exclude keeping the promise, whereas the comic and tragic episodes are not mutually exclusive.) So I would call primary or basic those sorts of inherent aesthetic merit-qualities I have indicated, just as I would call the cited
moral virtues or general duties primary or basic. And this is to use
"primary" and "basic" in a way quite different from Beardsley's, for
in the context of a particular work these qualities will be only *prima
facie* merits, not necessarily actual merits of that work—though
they will be actual merits too if no appropriate reversing explanation is available.

I have said that Beardsley's heroic attempt to find (three) always-one-way basic criteria is not necessary to refute the particularist who raises the reversibility phenomenon. I can now say why. I
take three different kinds of examples. If we can say that x is hilariously comic *tout court* (being made so by the puns, etc., in it), if
we can say that x is exceedingly graceful *tout court*, or if we can say
that x has a tragic intensity (enhanced by its comic episodes) *tout
court*, we have thereby given fully adequate and sufficient reasons
for attributing aesthetic merit to x. Yet all of these fully adequate
reasons—being hilariously comic, being exceedingly graceful, and
having tragic intensity—cite Beardsley's "secondary" criteria, which
could, in certain circumstances, count negatively. But not here.
There is no necessity, when these reasons are given, to secure them
yet further by linking them to permanently one-way positive criteria.

I turn now to my second claim: that Beardsley's appeal to his
three basic criteria is inadequate for isolating ultimate criteria of
aesthetic merit from ultimately negative aesthetic criteria. Again,
to justify this claim fully would need lengthy argument. I can attempt only the briefest sketch. I shall have to concentrate on unity
and intensity of regional quality, saying little about complexity. It is
only fair to point out that Beardsley has always admitted the possibility that his three canons might not be adequate, and he has
frequently attempted to rebut possible criticisms. He admits that it
might be argued that "some [human regional] qualities are cited as
grounds for dispraise"; he regards the question whether "*all* Objective Reasons can be subsumed under these three Canons" as "a very
bold question"; but he is prepared "even to go as far as to say" that
they can, adding, "This may be too sweeping a claim," but "at any

rate, it is stated explicitly enough so that it can be attacked or defended."[13] It is certainly the case that through most of his work he has adhered to the claim and has not conceded any insuperable objections.

I shall consider unity first. Unity must be unity *of* something[14] and for some *purpose* or of some *kind*. Unity in itself is an empty concept. For, first, we cannot employ the criterion of unity except in a second-order way. We cannot just look for unity. If we have before us a simple poem exhibiting—to use one of Beardsley's examples—"heroic strength," we find this latter quality exhibited in the work either intensely or confusedly. If the former, we can conclude that the basic elements (words, rhythms, etc.) possessed unity; if the latter, they did not. If we are considering the play containing both tragic and comic episodes, we decide whether the episodes enhance or dilute each other. If the former, the work is unified; if the latter, it is not. So the judgment that the work has one or more of the qualities that I have called inherently aesthetic qualities is logically prior to the judgment of unity. Second, unity, unlike grace or elegance, is not a criterion that is inherently aesthetic at all. Almost anything may exhibit unity (organization, completeness, etc.): for example, a political rally. But even if we seek unity in what is in fact a work of art, that work may still exhibit a unity that is not an aesthetic or artistic unity. A very bad novel, its episodes thrown together haphazardly, could be unified in the sense that it preaches a single, coherent political doctrine throughout. It may have a unity, coherence, even a developing complexity of political viewpoint, but no artistic worth. But if we have to qualify unity by saying *artistic* or *aesthetic* unity, unity itself can hardly be an aesthetic criterion, and, *a fortiori*, it cannot be a primary aesthetic criterion. So as a basic one-way aesthetic criterion, unity cannot fill the bill. Somewhat similar comments can be made about complexity. We cannot necessarily decide independently that a work is complex or varied; this may also be second-order in the way unity is. And for complexity to be an *aesthetic* merit, the work must have a (reasonably unified) complexity that yields inherently valuable *aesthetic* properties. Like unity, complexity or variety can characterize political rallies and political points of view within an atrocious novel, as well as technical manuals, sporting activities, and so on.

If we now try to give appropriate content to unity, interpreting it, say, as unity of an intense regional quality or unity of a variety of such qualities, we come to difficulties over both intensity and regional qualites. "Intense" is ambiguous. The most common understanding of this term would be "extreme." A work may have an intensity of sadness, calm, tragedy, gaiety ("intensely graceful" and "intensely elegant" sound somewhat odd). But Beardsley cannot mean that regional qualities are, *ceteris paribus*, aesthetically better for always being intense in this sense. Some fine works are not intense in this way; they have a gentle humor, a hint of wistfulness, a faint suggestion of melancholy underlying a peaceful calm or quiet serenity. We value these regional qualities too and would not be without them. In the sense in which "intense" means "extreme," intensity is not necessarily what we seek in qualities of aesthetic value. So perhaps we must sometimes take "intense" to mean something like "pure," "quintessential," "epitomized," a clear expression of some regional quality. Intensity may mean simply that some regional quality has been securely grasped; characterlessness, insipidity, unclarity, and confusion have been avoided.[15] I shall say no more about this, but use "intensity" hereafter allowing it to take whichever sense is appropriate.

The far more serious question concerns regional qualities. Do we transform unity and complexity into clearly *aesthetic* qualities (and hence perhaps aesthetic merits) if we simply say unity (and complexity) of an intense regional quality? This question goes deeper than the one I began with, whether the "reversibility" of criteria emphasized by the particularists must always be met by a linkage to one or more of the three always-one-way primary positive criteria, of which intensity of regional quality is one. It calls in question the very claim that intensity of regional quality *is* a primary or always-one-way criterion of aesthetic value. And the reason it does this is that only some (intensive) regional qualities would seem to be aesthetic in character at all, and of those that are, only some are inherently positive, while others are inherently negative. In his various accounts and lists of regional qualities, Beardsley has given examples as different as triangularity, squareness, lyric grace, heroic strength, and dramatic intensity, as well as the qualities pompous, precious, subtle, garish; and I suppose we could add a few thousand more: mottled, pin-striped, leering, face-like, politically biased, ugly, sentimental, boring, and irritating (though I believe Beardsley would exclude the last three as "affective," not "objective"). All these, I think, could be (unlike perhaps insipid and characterless) more or less intense in one or another of the senses of "intense" indicated. But I would suppose that triangular, mottled, pin-striped, face-like, and politically biased are aesthetically neutral; and that while some of the intensive regional qualities listed above are aesthetically positive, others, like ugly, garish and sentimental are aesthetically negative. (Beardsley has been aware of these problems from the start;[16] at times he restricts positive regional qualities to "human" regional qualities, but he admits even then problems that I touch on below.) It would seem clear therefore that intensity of regional quality is far from being a primary positive criterion; only those regional qualities that are not aesthetically neutral and not aesthetically negative are positive. But, put thus, this is vacuous, and we seem forced to limit ourselves to some selected list containing only the sort of examples I gave earlier as primary positive criteria in my sense.

If the position I have presented so sketchily is correct, *some* (even "human") regional qualities possessing unity, complexity, and intensity are negative, capable of being "independently cited as a ground" of *negative* evaluations. Unless Beardsley can meet these objections, he fails to reduce the "very large variety" of positive reasons to his three primary criteria, a move that he regards as important—though I do not—to support a generalist position that in a broad way we equally accept. I believe that this kind of underpinning is not only inadequate but unnecessary. It is interesting to see how, characteristically, Beardsley has turned on several occasions in his more recent writings to these problems, which he recognized, as I have said, as early as the publication of *Aesthetics* in 1958. In all his relevant articles up till 1968, with one exception, he adheres regularly to the view that there are "exactly three basic criteria" that always count positively, never negatively. But in the 1966 article[17] the difficulty reappears, at least for the reader, though Beardsley does not tackle it: properties (like unity and intensity) are "instrumental"; they have the capacity to provide aesthetic enjoyment. But, the reader is forced to ask himself, "What if some instances of unity and intensity have the capacity to provide aesthetic revulsion?" In 1968 he returns again to face directly the question "Why are some aesthetic qualities artistically objectionable?"[18] He himself speaks of, and so admits, "defects due to negative regional qualities." He still tries to cope with them by reference to his three criteria, but with some lack of confidence ("Some of the other negative qualities are difficult to accommodate to this scheme. . . . But I hope that even those can be dealt with by dint of more sensitive and precise analysis").

I believe his attempt fails, as it did earlier. If intensity of some regional quality is to be a merit, then certainly, as he says, it is easy to see why *privative* qualities (e.g., insipidity, which entails lack of intensity) would be defects. Perhaps we can also admit that the qualities he calls *disruptive* (e.g., franticness) are destructive of unity (and hence of a pervasive intensity of desirable regional quality). But those he calls *reductive*, that is, lacking in complexity (crudeness, pomposity), along with others he finds hard to accommodate (grossness, preciousness), to which I would add bombast, garishness, sentimentality, and ugliness, seem to me capable of intensity (i.e., not privative), and not necessarily disruptive of unity or for that matter exclusive of complexity (i.e., reductive). A novel might contain a complex variety of kinds of sentimentality, not internally discordant but uniting, and so "enhancing" each other, to yield an overall and intense sentimentality. A vase might have a variety of ugly features—shape, decoration, color combinations—a uniting or mutually reinforcing complex of ugly elements adding up to an intensity of ugliness. Such works, it seems to me, would have unity, complexity, and a resulting intense regional quality—but a wholly negative one. If Beardsley cannot evade such cases, his position becomes similar to mine: some intense unified and complex regional qualities are defects, basic and primary defects. In what seems to me a tell-tale remark, he seems almost to concede this: for he speaks of a good poem as one that "generates a regional quality of aesthetic *interest*"[19] (my italics), where "interest" strongly suggests "value." But within a few lines he is resorting again to his three basic criteria: "the critic . . . must have the taste to tell how unified and complex a pattern is, how intensely it glows with regional qualities"—unless the word "glows" surreptitiously gives the game away.

The last relevant paper I know of fairly and squarely faces the difficulty.[20] He admits with his usual candor that he is left with a large problem, "how to explain why certain qualities, but not others, *can* be cited in reasons supporting judgments of aesthetic value." He refers us back to his previous attempt (just discussed) "to come to grips with this problem," but admits characteristically that "it is far from being solved." I feel this to be an admission that appeal to his three canons never solves (I should say, cannot solve) this problem. The "hint of a solution" he then offers is that certain value-grounding qualities, in particular "human qualities" (he concedes a possible difficulty about some others), are properties "naturally *interesting* to us . . . we can work up feelings about them. They touch us where we live." These are, of course, the ones that are positive, but I find this no more than a hint; and here, so far as I know, the discussion of this particular problem ends to date. One might hope that Beardsley had at last abandoned as unnecessary and inadequate the Three Canons view; but as we shall see in a moment, they reappear in another context even more recently.

Perhaps, with his customary persistence and ingenuity, Beards-

ley will yet offer an acceptable account of why some aesthetic criteria are inherently positive and others negative. This, as he has
always recognized, is an additional and difficult task. It is just as
necessary for him to show *why* his basic criteria (which, I have argued, fail to do the trick of collecting all positive criteria under
three heads) are aesthetically positive as it is for me to show why my
suggested host of inherent merit and demerit qualities are respectively positive and negative aesthetically. No doubt he would regard
it as an added difficulty for the position I have outlined "that there
seems no way of demonstrating that any particular list of qualities is
an exhaustive inventory of those that are aesthetically valuable."[21] I
cannot attempt to offer any suggestion here. Nor is it my present
task to discuss the persistent endeavors he has made to deal with
this problem, starting in chapter 11 of *Aesthetics* and continuing
through many more recent papers. Consistently he has adhered to
the view that positive aesthetic qualities are instrumental, capacities that provide, in certain conditions, a certain state of mind, for
which he has used, variously, the terms "aesthetic experience,"
"aesthetic enjoyment," "aesthetic interest," "aesthetic gratification," and so on. This state of mind he has in turn tried at various
times to isolate and define by reference to *its* unity, completeness,
complexity, intensity, and pleasure. To me it seems that these attempts result in difficulties, parallel to those I have discussed, breaking out again at a new level. Nevertheless, it strikes me as right that
of the two available kinds of moves, he should at least attempt this
one. The alternative, which Beardsley has several times rejected,[22]
is to discriminate the state of mind—aesthetic enjoyment, or satisfaction—by reference to the set of aesthetic criteria we employ and
the kind of properties we take aesthetic satisfaction in; instead, he
wants to distinguish an aesthetic experience "in terms of its own
internal properties," not by reference to the properties of the object
that are instrumental in giving rise to aesthetic experience. For the
latter course would be analogous to a moral philosopher's accepting
as not further explainable that honesty and considerateness are virtues and cruelty a vice without, as a philosopher should, continuing
to seek an explanatory principle. To do otherwise is to do what
Gilbert Ryle once said about "family resemblance," to accept a position that should be adopted only as a last resort. It is odd therefore
to find, though I must be misunderstanding him, that in one of his
later papers he looks as if he is reversing his position and reviving
his primary criteria: "Gratification is aesthetic when it is obtained
primarily from attention to the formal unity and/or regional qualities of a complex whole."[23]

I fear that in the foregoing my admiration for Beardsley's work may have been obscured by the fact that I have been critical, not of his staunchly maintained position that there are general aesthetic criteria, for I share this view and regard myself as an ally, but of the detail by which he supports the position. I can only say that this is because I regard his work as so important that it merits careful critical scrutiny. My regret is that I must inevitably have done him far less than justice in so brief a paper.

I shall end with the more congenial task of trying to strengthen Beardsley's defense against a criticism that would, were it sound, endanger any general criterion theory, whether his or mine. Again my account must be schematic in the extreme. The objection is that made by Michael Scriven: that in aesthetic evaluation the independence requirement is "difficult" to meet. This requirement "demands that we be able to know the reason or reasons for a conclusion without first having to know the conclusion; otherwise we can never use the reasons as a means of getting to the conclusion." [24] I shall ignore the word "difficult" and the temporal suggestion of "first." The only claim of genuine interest would be the logical claim that in aesthetics we cannot meet the independence requirement since we cannot know the reason for an evaluative conclusion unless we already know this conclusion. I shall assume Scriven to be making this stronger claim because he also says that reasons must be "such that we *can* know them without knowing the conclusion." I think Beardsley also understands Scriven's claim in this strong sense, since he says that if Scriven were right, "it would follow that critics *cannot* use reasons to arrive at their judgment." [25] Beardsley's reply to Scriven is somewhat complex, and I find it hard to assess it; but at one point (p. 83) it takes the form of reiterating his own view that "some reasons *must* be used by critics in arriving at" their judgments (which does not refute but simply denies Scriven's claim about aesthetic reasons) and that "therefore there must be some basic features . . . that are always merits or defects"—unity and intensity of regional quality again. I do not see this as an adequate reply to Scriven, nor do I see that Beardsley's appeal to his three basic criteria, already criticized, either helps or is needed, as he seems to suppose.

But I do think that Scriven's claim about aesthetic reasons is false, that nothing he says establishes it, and that it can indeed be refuted. We must, however, distinguish and set aside certain questions, important to discuss in their own right, but irrelevant to the central issue. We are not concerned, for instance, (1) with the ways in which, by various means, we can enable someone else to see for himself that a work is good; or (2) with the giving to someone of reasons that, if he accepts our statements as true, would require him to admit that a work must be good, though he cannot see that it is for himself; or (3) with the person who finds a work good and later looks for the reasons why it is, in order to justify his initial judgment. Our concern is with the critic who attends to the work for himself and in doing so finds in it qualities that serve as reasons for deciding or "concluding" that it is good (or poor, flawed, indifferent, etc.).

I shall concede Scriven's claim at its strongest: that a reason must be logically prior to a conclusion. I shall argue that, even so, Scriven's skepticism about aesthetic reasons fails at least in some cases, and possibly in all, and fails because of an easily committed confusion. The possible cases to consider for a full refutation are legion. I can here consider only one sort of case, though I think the general principle could be invoked differently in other examples. The case I discuss is in one respect an extremely simple one, but in another respect one of the most troubling, since it is a case where a *prima facie* merit is judged an actual defect. Scriven, I believe, is involved in an ambiguity involving two sorts of conclusions. For him, rightly, the ultimate conclusion is an evaluation that the work is good, perfect, flawed, and so on; that is, it is an overall judgment of *value*. But it is essential to distinguish this from an overall judgment of the *character* or *characteristics* of the work. (I deliberately use these terms rather than Beardsley's "quality" to avoid any possible suggestion of evaluation.)

The crucial kind of case to consider (though there are many others of interest) is that of the critic who approaches an artwork looking for the character or characteristics it has (elegance, grace, garishness, etc.) but who also actively accepts for himself (not merely on someone else's word) that some of these characteristics are *prima facie* aesthetic merits, others *prima facie* aesthetic defects. In the work he approaches (call it x), he finds predominantly a build-up of characteristic P (say, tragic intensity); he also finds in it episodes with characteristic Q (hilarious comedy). In the case under consideration, he decides that these latter do not heighten, but dilute (render less intense), the predominant character P. He therefore judges these to be defects. Note, however, that he did not simply judge the episodes with characteristic Q to be detractions from the *value* of the work. This *in vacuo* would be impossible; there must be some reason why he judges them defects. What he judges is that they dilute or weaken the predominant (tragic) character P, a judgment of the *character* of the work. But he also himself accepts, *ex hypothesi* in our simplified case, that *P* is a characteristic of inherent aesthetic value. So his overall judgment of the value of *x*—that *x* is not perfect, but flawed—follows from his judgment that the predominant character *P* is weakened (in Beardsley's terminology, made less intense) by the presence in *x* of episodes with the character *Q*. But this latter was a judgment about the overall *character* of the work. It is from *this* that it follows that, since he regards *P* as a characteristic of aesthetic value, *x* is less valuable than it would have been without *Q* and that *Q* is therefore a defect in the work. But he could not have decided that *Q* was a defect in its overall value, and that *x* was flawed, *without* having decided that characteristic *Q* in this case weakened the predominant characteristic *P*. The overall judgment of (somewhat defective) value rested on his judgment that *characteristic P* was weakened by *Q*. This, together with his accepted premise that *P* is a characteristic of aesthetic merit, yields the value conclusion that *x* is of less aesthetic value than it would have been without *Q*. Schematically, then, his overall judgment of value—that *x* was flawed, and that *Q* was its defect—rested on his judgments (1) that *P* is the predominant characteristic of *x*; (2) that *P* is weakened, not intensified, by the presence of characteristic *Q*; (3) that *P* is inherently a *prima facie* aesthetic merit; and (4) that though *Q* is also a *prima facie* aesthetic merit, its presence dilutes the intensity of *P*. In short, an overall judgment of character is distinguishable from an overall judgment of value and logically precedes it.

Beardsley in fact put the position exactly enough, without the trimmings, when he said, "A reason is some *descriptive* or interpretative proposition about the work. . . . Thus a reason always cites some *property* of the work, and we may say that this property is *then* employed as a *criterion of value* by the critic who presents that reason" (my italics).[26] This form of argument is in no way controverted by the fact that a person might, in temporal order, feel sure at the outset that *x* is flawed, without yet being able to say why. For when he does come to see why he initially thought it flawed, it will be because, in our simplified case, he realizes that *P*, the predominant characteristic, and one he accepts as aesthetically valuable, was rendered less intense by *Q*. Thus, though I have proved it for only certain sorts of cases, implicit or explicit acceptance of certain characteristics as being of aesthetic merit, and implicit or explicit recognition that *x* either intensely has, or in a diluted way has, some such predominant characteristic, function as the reason for, and have logical priority over, the overall conclusion as to the value of *x*. (This of course is only the simplest of cases; it has also to be distinguished from the sort of case already mentioned where hints of melancholy interposed within the gaiety, as in a Mozart movement, do not diminish or weaken the predominant gaiety, but unite to give the work a different and in itself valuable character, for example, the quintessence of a gaiety tinged with an underlying melancholy.)

One further point about Scriven's remarks. There is often a kind of absurdity involved in speaking, as he does, of reasons for a "conclusion." Ordinarily there need be no movement of inference to conclusion from reasons or premises. The critic does not normally say to himself, "X has strong and undiluted tragic intensity (or whatever); I regard this as aesthetic merit; so I must conclude that the work is good." When you already accept that the characteristic P is one with inherent aesthetic merit, in seeing or deciding that x has P you are *ipso facto* seeing or deciding that x has some merit, just as the butcher, finding his knife sharp, has, in doing so, found it, at least in that respect, good. He does not argue by a process of inference from premise to conclusion, "It is sharp; I accept sharpness as a merit; so I must admit that to that extent it is a good knife," even though an argument with premises and conclusion could always be constructed in this form. I cannot here deal with the many different and often highly complex examples that one can think of, but I am confident that an analogous answer can be made in most, if not all, cases to rebut Scriven's claim against the independence of reasons and evaluative "conclusions" in aesthetics. Thus, I think Scriven's charge is the result of inadequate analysis, a failure to distinguish overall character from overall value. I hope therefore to have at least sketched a strategy that any upholder of general criteria, Beardsley included, can successfully develop against one objection that, if true, would be serious for us all.

In this short paper I have tried to outline, and defend against certain criticisms, a General Criterion theory, a kind of theory to which both Beardsley and I are adherents. Though this has involved considerable criticism of the substructure of Beardsley's views, I cannot end without emphasizing again my high admiration for his range, variety, ingenuity, fertility, and persistence in pursuing, with subtlety and determination, what seem to me the central questions of aesthetics. The corpus of his work, which I hope will be added to for a long while to come, will inevitably remain a storehouse of important ideas and arguments for anyone seriously interested in the subject.

Notes

1. Monroe C. Beardsley, "The Discrimination of Aesthetic Enjoyment," *British Journal of Aesthetics* 2 (1963): 297.

2. Monroe C. Beardsley, "On the Generality of Critical Reasons," *Journal of Philosophy* LIX (1962): 484–85.

3. Beardsley, of course, constantly admits that there is a very large variety of reasons (see, e.g., *Aesthetics: Problems in the Philosophy of Criticism* [New York, 1958], p. 462, and elsewhere), but he thinks we can find room for them in his three main groups. He would probably reject my line of argument here as "a simple appeal to paradigm cases" ("On the Generality of Critical Reasons," p. 478).

4. "On the Generality of Critical Reasons," p. 479.

5. Ibid., p. 485.

6. Beardsley hints at this, but little more, in *Aesthetics*, p. 465, where he says, "It does not seem that the contribution of each feature of an aesthetic object can be considered in an atomistic fashion," and in several other places, including his remarks about secondary criteria in "On the Generality of Critical Reasons," p. 485.

7. "On the Generality of Critical Reasons," p. 485.

8. Ibid.

9. Ibid.

10. Ibid.

11. Mary Mothersill, "Critical Reasons," *Philosophical Quarterly* 11 (1961): 77.

12. Again Beardsley comes very close to this position in what he says about ethics in "On the Generality of Critical Reasons," p. 481.

13. *Aesthetics*, pp. 464–70.

14. This is implicit in various things Beardsley says, e.g., in *Aesthetics*, pp. 198–200.

15. Beardsley seems to note this point briefly, e.g., in *Aesthetics*, where he says, "The essential thing is that the work have some quality that stands out, instead of being vapid, characterless" (p. 298), and speaks of both "higher intensity and greater purity" (p. 382).

16. *Aesthetics*, pp. 463–64.

17. "The Aesthetic Problem of Justification," *Journal of Aesthetic Education* 1 (1966): 32, 39.

18. "Bad Poetry," published in *The Possibility of Criticism* (Detroit, 1970), pp. 98–100.

19. Ibid., p. 110.

20. "What Is an Aesthetic Quality?" *Theoria* 39 (1973): 65, 69.

21. *Aesthetics*, p. 509.

22. "The Discrimination of Aesthetic Enjoyment," p. 296, and "Aesthetic Experience Regained," *Journal of Aesthetics and Art Criticism* 28 (1969–70): 5.

23. "The Aesthetic Point of View" (1970), reprinted in *Philosophy Looks at the Arts*, ed. Joseph Margolis, rev. ed. (Philadelphia, 1978), p. 12.

24. Michael Scriven, *Primary Philosophy* (New York, 1966), pp. 57–59.

25. *The Possibility of Criticism*, pp. 77–85.

26. "On the Generality of Critical Reasons," p. 479.

2

Aesthetic Qualities

LARS AAGAARD-MOGENSEN

Philosophy is the pursuit of truth and *sui generis* in pursuing a transempirical order of knowledge—for example, knowledge about the probity of certain knowledge claims.[1] To say what we know in reply to a question like "What is an aesthetic quality?" thus requires philosophical thinking. Monroe C. Beardsley's reply is that he would not want to have to try to give an adequate philosophical defense of what is called "cognitivism" in aesthetics.[2] While I usually have a strong aversion to labels, I must all the same admit that I have at times flirted with this one, although my "defense" is rougher than tough and thus far less adequate than he or I should like.[3] Perhaps a defensive mode can serve an "ism" adequately, but it always serves philosophy inadequately. Consequently I would not be in the least inclined to insist on sheer opposition either to the "normative" (and emotive), or to explorations of an "unlimited variety of aesthetically valuable qualities."[4]

It seems to me that this is an aspect eminently favorable to the direction of Beardsley's expansive and argumentationally tight-knit series of definitional proposals,[5] an aspect afforded much less attention (even, perhaps, from himself) than it commands. A pull in this direction, I contend, mitigates some of the puzzles in his reply and therefore both contributes to a fuller appreciation of it and furthers this seminal issue in epistemology (including aesthetics).

Beardsley's reply, in the briefest of summaries, is that aesthetic qualities are (1) "regional" or "emergent"—that is, "qualities that a complex has as a result of the relation between its parts"; (2) "human"—"qualities similar to qualities found in persons, including their intentional states, their demeanor, and their behavior"; (3) "value-grounding"—"qualities that independently affect aesthetic value either positively or negatively."[6] He commits himself only to approximate extensional identity between these groups. This definitional proposal is thus a most versatile and powerful aid, as is demonstrated by Beardsley's employment of it in practically every

department of aesthetic analysis. And it is not its usefulness or theoretical powers I shall tend to, but its content.

Perhaps I had better start by putting my two puzzling clues
on the table. One is the most remarkable discovery that among the
approximately ninety qualities Beardsley mentions, "beautiful,"
"pretty," and "lovely" do not appear once ("dainty" appears once
in a quotation), an absence made much more conspicuous when
such unexpected descriptions as "wayward," "languid," "somber,"
and "swaggering" figure prominently; "ominousness," "funniness,"
"cheerfulness," "balance," and "delicacy" appear somewhat less
often, while "sadness," "grace," and "garishness" invariably appear
in discussion of other writers' examples.[7] Perhaps, you might say, I
brought the wrong expectations to the analysis; this is, of course,
not unusual in philosophy. I have considered this possibility, but I
still find it not at all odd to say that beauty, prettiness, or loveliness
is an aesthetic quality; nor is it odd to say that beauty is a central one (irrespective of its frequency in the human experience
and environment).

Perhaps beauty is omitted because Beardsley earlier gave a suc-
cint statement of his theory of "beauty," which he summarized as
follows: (4) "beauty is a simple regional perceptual quality, which is
a sufficient but not a necessary condition of aesthetic value."[8]
Beardsley also includes beauty in his plea for the autonomy of the
aesthetic in human lives: "the regular appeals to grace and vitality,
delicacy and energy, beauty and sublimity, strongly suggest that
however central a role in the aesthetic transaction we assign to
symbolic functioning, there remains an ineliminable kind of value,
distinct from cognitive efficacy, that is characteristic of artworks."[9]
And this bounces ineliminability back onto statement 4.

Checking statement 4 against statements 1–3 produces a more
telling reason why beauty is omitted from the comprehensive treatment of aesthetic qualities. The dissociating factor is simplicity:
beauty stays "simple," while the full-fledged aesthetic qualities tend
toward complexity. Beauty, being not quite a local quality and not
quite an admissible regional quality either, falls between two stools.
This leads to my second clue.

Beardsley's claim that utter simplicity excludes aesthetic quality gave me pause when I first read it, and, I confess, has left me
dissatisfied ever since. He has reiterated in later writings that it is
empirically obvious that local qualities cannot be aesthetic, precisely because they lack the particular sort of complexity awarded
by emergence.

As a token of this tenet, I choose a statement that is, perhaps, favorable to my purposes: (5) "A single sound cannot strictly be beautiful, I think, though it can be pleasing."[10] It does not seem to me that you can extricate yourself from the problem in the following way: "If a single note on a flute or French horn can be beautiful, it nevertheless cannot be beautiful music, for it is not music," a stipulation preceded by the argument that "some degree of complexity is necessary not only for being a good poem, but for being a poem—[and] similarly for other aesthetic objects." The landscape, however, is not music either.[11] Actually my point is not so much that this is a questionable argument as that it leaves open the possibility that a local quality can be aesthetic or, rather, can be beautiful. I agree that a single note on the French horn, say, can be beautiful, and in a much clearer sense than that in which it can have a "portentous air." And with "clearer sense" I connect "empirically obvious." But why its beauty should not be an aesthetic quality while the beauty of a musical piece is, is not equally obvious.

To my mind the two puzzles connect. I should perhaps again emphasize that identifying the connectors strengthens rather than weakens Beardsley's account. At this point some pressure must be exerted, and the degree to which his account resists it will be the measure of its strength. To do this I need to go over it somewhat like a minesweeper, determined to release and defuse every menace.

Let us start from a safe harbor. How obvious is the "empirically obvious"? Beardsley's answer is as tough as it is genuinely helpful: aesthetic qualities are perceivable on the grounds that "we may be able in an indirect way to persuade someone by argument that a sculpture contains a beauty he cannot see (by adducing the testimony of others, for example), but we regard this as somewhat futile unless we can point it out to him, make him see it for himself. It follows that any property of art that cannot be perceived—but must be felt or inferred—is something quite different from beauty."[12] The aesthetic judgment must face the inescapable facts that brook no denial; the recalcitrance of the aesthetic qualities possessed and hence ascertainable provides the ground for value. What better grounding can there be?

This sweeps part of the route. It does not seem plainly plausible, and far less does it seem true, that no color is ugly, or that no color is more beautiful than others, or that no colors are prettier than others. "Some colors are pretty" and "some colors are prettier than others" both seem acceptable. A deep blue, for example, tends to be prettier than a murky blue; a color is more beautiful the purer it is. Perhaps we can convey insight by ostension.

"Beauty," like "art," has provided philosophers with play-

grounds where they entertain themselves—without much thinking—over the absolute relativity of some concepts. Even Beardsley
had his share of fun with "beauty,"[13] although he also gets philosophical mileage out of it by pointing out that aesthetics contributes to the growth of philosophy, even if only by making these concepts work overtime as Horrible Examples.[14] And, of course, there
is something to this, particularly if you seize on the most mysterious
beauties (*Mona Lisa*) or the mythic ones (Garbo), but then you can
demonstrate fuzziness all over the conceptual repertory. And you do
meet with some unmistakable beauties. I should furthermore hesitate to line them up in one single dimension; it is not obvious how
to order radiant, delightful, ravishing, and voluptuous beauties, nor
where the order should lead from and to.[15] In other words, I cannot
make out beauty's simplicity.

Naturally I am not going to maintain that "beauty" is not a
human quality (2), though neither am I going to join Frank Gallo
in the extreme assertion that feminine forms constitute "the only
indestructible and inspiring resource of simple beauty left."[16] I do
not see that human beauty is obviously "similar to qualities found in
persons, . . . their intentional states, their demeanor, and their behavior." One has or possesses beauty; or one is beautiful. And there
are jarrings at the other end, too: I cannot see that sadness, somber-
ness, or stateliness in persons have much of an aesthetic aspect
to them, any more, I should say, than their somnolence, greed, or
skepticism have. There may be reasons, whatever their quality, why
such predicates enjoy aesthetic employments, but could they be
"similarities to sadness"?

And I take it these sorts of considerations prompt Beardsley's
reservations about regional qualities, such as his statements that (6)
they are "especially (*but not exclusively*) those qualities that are described by words taken over metaphorically from human contexts,"
and "I do not extend the aesthetic dimension to include sheer sensuous agreeableness or local pleasure; but *neither do I claim that the
lines of demarcation are sharp*" (my italics).[17] As long as you are citing
the qualities of being wayward, triumphant, and tortured as instances, this seems plausible enough. When you consider beauty,
grace, or prettiness as aesthetic qualities, the plausibility fades drastically. The problem seems to be one of metaphysical import.

Some might agree that "we must mean something different by
'warm' when we call a color warm and when we call a visual design
warm,"[18] though "to mean something different" is a slippery fish. I
should dissent to its companion that "we must mean something different by 'beautiful' when we call a sound beautiful and when we

call a piece of music beautiful" (the sense of "must" eludes me). I should particularly do so if the latter description is to be presumed to be a metaphorical importing (of the former?) into the critical vocabulary. To have the same predicate be an aesthetic predicate and an aesthetic metaphorical import is too much, for the following reasons. First, it permits a mode of thinking that by itself multiplies beyond reason the number of meanings or senses of a word. Second, it preserves the distinction between local and regional only enough for insinuating my judgment into these linguistic acrobatics.

Before proceeding let me point out that (5) paddles against obvious currents. Take "peep." A peep is a strident, feeble, shrill sound, high-pitched and piercing, like a whistle. Noises are a kind of sound too, especially those that lack agreeable musical quality or are noticeably unpleasant. A tone is a vocal or musical sound, and the word is especially applied to the quality of sound. Again, a note is simply a musical sound. This dictionary tour indicates the sort of distinctions we in fact do draw. It is clear that in order for (5) to be true, it should read "that a shrill noise cannot strictly be beautiful." And I suggest that there is no obstacle to deleting "strictly." It would be up to the dissenters to demonstrate that we employ these distinctions in unobvious ways, a position that could easily be denied.

Ahead lies the strait of dependency. Though Beardsley reminds us that the dependency thesis (1) has not received extensive investigation before,[19] he argues that it applies firmly to aesthetic qualities. Between locality and regionality in quality, he proposes this dividing line: that the former is, while the latter is not, directly manipulatable. "In the process of art creation, and in the performance of performable works, we can only get an A-quality through those it depends on. The waywardness of the composition cannot be corrected, nor the grace of a performance be achieved, by the simple direct process of removing a certain amount of waywardness or adding a certain amount of grace. The sculptor must alter his shapes and textures until some of the waywardness disappears."[20] However, the sculptor cannot simply remove a certain amount of texture or shape; he must add, remove, or change some clay, stone, or bronze. If a truck is stopped for being overweight, the problem cannot be corrected by the simple, direct process of removing a certain amount of weight; the driver must remove a certain amount of the goods with which his truck is loaded, and goods cannot be removed without a certain amount of beef, and beef cannot be removed without a certain amount of ———. Now texture, shape, and weight are presumably regional qualities, and, more interestingly, (at least some) local qualities seem dependent on this criterion as well. You cannot just take away a certain amount of red; you have to scrape off some paint or put on some paint of another color. In short, I do not see, on the one hand, how dependency circles can be avoided or dependency chains terminated.

On the other hand, even if we do not master them completely, we do engage in such processes as to grace, to beautify, to tidy, to adorn, to prettify, and to touch up things. Such activities are common enough, and when we decorate a room, say, we no doubt make it look better. It may not exactly be better looks we add or poor looks we remove. To decorate, however, is usually to make something more attractive by adding something beautiful or becoming. Not all trimmings are trinkets or fripperies. And I should think we could touch up a dull play or film script by adding some fun. We may not be as adept as film-music composers in all beautification programs.[21] Nor are all creative hairdressers masters of their trade. It would be an extremely odd requirement to demand that all operations succeed. Ordinarily we tolerate failures, and the kinds of effort we make to improve aesthetic qualities should not be excepted in this respect. Evidently we sometimes succeed. So perhaps we should admit that the grammar of "beauty" allows for manipulation.

What emergence is to dependence, supervenience is to the disappearance of aesthetic qualities. Obviously, there is something super about beauty, but whether it is *venire* is less obvious. Phenomenologically speaking, it may be right that some qualities have a slightly disembodied air,[22] but this seems to be true of all kinds of qualities in varying circumstances. If beauty is in some cases ethereal, it also, in other cases or to other persons, is very real. And while "local" qualities, such as colors perhaps, are for the most part real, rainbows and Op art demonstrate their air of disembodiment. It seems you can play this game either way; I know of no argument compelling us to one side or the other.

I am prepared to risk conflating several kinds of complexity now in order to sweep the deeper waters still, I believe, under Beardsley's pilotage. One distinction I shall largely neglect is that between ranges of simplicity and of locality; aesthetic qualities may depend on other aesthetic qualities—for example, the angularity of a silhouette is more localized than the portentousness of a sculpture—but even so the former need not be less complex than the latter. And although Beardsley does not say so, I believe the move toward localization does not lead us to simple aesthetic qualities like beauty. Certainly perceivability and complexity do not exclude one another.

That I am prepared to violate other distinctions is suggested by my guarded admission that beauty may be present in local qualities, but not in a very high intensity (which "defect" may be a reason for omitting beauty generally when dealing with critically useful aesthetic qualities; there is a threshold below which the grounds for value are not worthy of consideration). But it is evident that even if high complexity of relations of a complex's parts (tending toward indiscernible orders) does not correlate with high intensity in aesthetic quality, very low complexity, or simplicity, does correlate with low or no intensity in aesthetic quality.

Observance of the distinctions suggested by these asymmetries (localization/simplicity, complexity/intensity) will soon become unmanageable. But that is not all: the worst is still to come. Nevertheless, there are advantages that I wish to convey (rather than defend), and that will be the justification I offer for pursuing these distinctions. If we follow the lead of Beardsley's clause in (6), we reach what may be called the poverty of our aesthetic descriptive capacities. When he says that aesthetic qualities are especially but not exclusively those "described by words taken over metaphorically from human contexts," I take it he agrees that "the aesthetic vocabulary must not be thought wholly metaphorical. Many words, including the most common (*lovely, pretty, beautiful, dainty, graceful, elegant*), are certainly not being used metaphorically when employed as aesthetic terms, the very good reason being that this is their primary or only use, some of them having no current nonaesthetic use."[23] At most he would question the estimate of which words are "most common."

Of course we can see, or can be brought to see, any aesthetic quality; but we are still not very eloquent describers of them. And since even professional critical practice abounds in other than the primary aesthetic words, this poverty might be the reason. It is registered in the observation that the proportion in critical literature between the primary qualities and the metaphorical imports I have referred to is roughly 4:90. You may also put it this way: since beauty, say, is not a metaphorical import or merely similar to human qualities, there is something more positive and literal about beauty. Beauty is ———. There is something intransitive about our knowledge of aesthetic qualities; they do not easily accept linguistic dress. Of course this blank, which is not very well filled with "simple," poses a certain threat to the objectivity of aesthetic judgment; hence the urgency of establishing a connection between human qualities and aesthetic qualities. When they are in addition few and apparently ineffective in grounding value, their use is impoverished.

Consider additionally, first. Beardsley's suggestion that dependence relations typically are causal, and that their articulation
therefore "(partly) explains" the complex qualities. Second, aesthetic qualities are "infra-dependent" in the sense that they depend
on other qualities that occupy a spatial or temporal region lying
within their own regions, rather than being coextensive with them.
In other words, they exhibit self-contained relation nets. Third,
the chains are oriented from local qualities, or qualities that are
not dependent upon any other (perceptual) qualities, to the most
complex dependent qualities. The explanatory axis aligns with
dependencies.

Words from human contexts exhibit similar complexities, similar enough to capture the infra-dependencies of aesthetic qualities.
And obviously the poverty of primary aesthetic terms is abundantly
compensated for by our access to vast numbers of sufficiently complex terms from human qualities. The simple qualities do not readily lend themselves to such complex terms and seem to become the
exception. Of course, human qualities do not literally apply to
works of art, but by metaphorical transfer this application is perfectly permissible. The metaphorical import, so to speak, leases its
complexity to the intransitive aesthetic quality. The latter becomes
susceptible to explanation, and we do not have to rest satisfied with
merely seeing it.

Now, it might be suggested that this account still has a major
weakness. Since the primary aesthetic qualities resist the metaphorical transfer, they remain blanks as far as explanatory infra-
chains are concerned, and what the account achieves is not adequate compensation, but merely a massive restratification of the
aesthetic vocabulary to suit preferred interpretive purposes. In fact,
Beardsley has himself framed a concept for such an operation and
aptly named it "superimposition."[24] In this case the imposed interpretive scheme would not be a Freudian theory or the like, but
something comparable and certainly at least as comprehensive,
namely, a semantic theory assigning preconceived content to each
and (nearly) every aesthetic quality and phenomenon. In other
words, the account can be taken as just another look at the entire
aesthetic domain through the glasses of such a grand semanticizing
system. Obviously this, if true, would turn the threat into an anni-
hilation of the objectivity of aesthetic judgment. However, the
cogency of this suggestion remains to be examined after it is worked
out in detail, and I suggest that it loses whatever initial plausibility
it might present when the possession account's "weakness" turns
into a strength in the light of the following insight.

I do not think that we are always justified in expecting that a predicate must have an explicable net of infra-relations to enter the aesthetic domain legitimately or else be dislodged into neglect. We may settle for a real content—gladly, I should say. Nor do I believe that every metaphor functions like all previous ones, such that once it is acceptably introduced it either faces a descriptive death or, as a kind of aberration, a normative perpetual life.[25] Strangely enough, no one to my knowledge has given much scrutiny, let alone argument or justification, to why the complementation takes the form of metaphorical transfer. It has been taken for granted, I suppose, that its immense versatility also suited the aesthetic. I believe that there is a singularly compelling—deep, if you will—reason why metaphors unstrained assimilate, indeed well-nigh unite, with primary aesthetic concepts.

Metaphor is unique. It is widely recognized that linguistic theory can crack neither oysters nor metaphors (as Paul Ziff once strikingly put it). The reason is that linguistic competence alone is not enough for understanding metaphor.[26] It requires empirical knowledge to recognize that through the metaphorical predication a contingent property has become a sense (or part of one); a meaning has been created. The metaphorical predicates describe qualities that they thereby present for our apprehension, but do not refer to. The metaphor registers, and helps us to make, a discovery that some property is possessed by both (*in casu*) moral triumph and the musical triumph.

What this extralinguistic knowledge amounts to can perhaps be brought out by briefly touching on the deficits of common simile or comparison theories of metaphor as contrasted with a conversion theory like Beardsley's.[27] According to the former kind of theory, the metaphor merely expands the applicability of some predicate from its well-entrenched domain to another domain of discourse, as when we accept the court's expansion of a "ground for divorce" from cruelty to mental cruelty (but not mental infidelity yet) or of "criminality" from overt violence to certain kinds of economic transactions. But these are petty expansions, invoking merely some unobjectionable extensional similarity, which could hardly count as discoveries. Apprehension of qualities is quite a bit stronger—more direct you might say. The metaphor effects more than a realignment of a label, inasmuch as labels are rule-abiding, connected with their extension by a rule of some sort. But metaphors, on the contrary, are neither rule-abiding nor mere rule violations; they in fact genuinely transcend rules, which is to say that, engaged in this fashion, predicates do not bring the extension set of properties along with them through the transfer from their customary domain, but bluntly propose new ones. Failure to apprehend an offered metaphor is not failure to apply the metaphorical predicates' customary extensions to a new domain. It is failure to apprehend the created meaning. If communicative goals are to be achieved and humans (even if less often than we could wish) to achieve agreement by communicating, we necessarily have to invent, where we know our repertoire fails, suitable communicative means for the specificity and concreteness of apprehended extralinguistic knowledge. It could be a gesture, an explanation, but it almost always is a metaphor. "Obviousness," as quoted above, enters the communicative intercourse; and it is here clear how metaphor excels in bringing about the sharing of a discovery. The employment of metaphor is a locus in which the linguistic never gets into more robust betrothal with the real, a locus of interplay between discovery and apprehension, where the communicative endeavor climaxes in the unrestrained engagement of both.

But this directness is exactly where the primary aesthetic predicates have succeeded all along. What the metaphorical imports gain by virtue of being metaphors, beyond all other well-established communicative means, is in an inverse fashion accomplished by the primary predicates inasmuch as they register the very same sort of qualities (with perhaps varying success, just like metaphors). Metaphors, in other words, are a prime means we have or fashion on the spot for any sort of creative pursuit of the other's assent, sharing knowledge and insights resulting from our explorations. Artists were always thought of as creating new orders or intensities of qualities, and art as one way in which we legitimately, perhaps even valuably, add to natural ranges of qualities.[28] The primary aesthetic concepts—so puzzling, even fascinating and mystifying, to the learned and lay alike—are simple, direct, and concrete. They indisputably capture perceivable qualities with a veracity much more empirically obvious to most of us than the finer, critically introduced, complex imports.[29] They too exhibit the most obstinate cases against separating the normative from the nonnormative.[30] If you, to stick with the ultimate platitudinous case, see and say that a girl is beautiful, your judgment certainly cannot but describe her as well as ascertain her aesthetic value. And I think this paradigm summarizes my comments on aesthetic qualities throughout.

To see that both primary and metaphorical aesthetic predicates apply only where the obvious obtrudes to justify that a judgment shows insight and has truth to it, we need to notice a movement along another scale as well. Some philosophers incline to think that truth is (exclusively) the subject of principles. What does not submit to principled exercise enjoys a different validity, if any. The insight or relevance of instances depends on this subsumptionary activity. Neither aesthetic qualities nor metaphors seem to them to provide for discovery or insight, because at the concrete end of this scale, apprehension by ostension becomes so unprincipled that the insights they offer are afforded none but the most passing validity. But this is not so obvious. A gradual softening of this dogma is found in varying acknowledgments of paradigm examples, where the weight of insight and apprehension is shifted somewhat toward the instance. I attempt to disengage myself entirely from this dogma by stressing a telling difference between the paradigm case and, for want of a better term, the paradigm, where the applicable predicate takes on the task of espousing the discovery. As you can learn by example, as contrasted to learning by exercise or by experience, you can convey insight by ostension, and you can also learn something concrete. There is a long and often confusing debate on the uniqueness of intensely aesthetic objects, but I want to set it aside in this connection because the exact point I wish to get at is that the singularity as well as the particularity, precision, and concreteness of the aesthetic quality possessed is captured by the aesthetic predicate in a nonmetaphorical way. If this inversion (quality is to predicate as predicate is to quality) is tough enough to admit a continuum of the two, it surely is a strength; and if it is to this extent continuous, it is little wonder that there is a strong inclination to assimilate the two, and perhaps even to leave the primary ones behind in order to go on to the complex ones. Epistemically speaking, aesthetic qualities are then no less accessible, only livelier, than others not thought of as dis-possessed. Only you know them better. What better grounding can value possibly have?

Admitting descriptive poverty, we could say that discovery is the runway by which a mind can take off and become insightborne. To my mind this runway is built solidly of four main components—information, argument, metaphor, and paradigm—that concertedly pull in this direction. Or, using terrestrial imagery, you might say that they form the four-lane superhighway of insight, where information and argument are the outer lanes, and metaphor and paradigm are the passing lanes that enable your mind to overtake the big busses (ideologies, for example) that block your view ahead, even if they no longer carry any passengers.

But if I have scraped rock bottom with many of the statements with which Beardsley qualifies his account, it may be because the ground where a great many metaphors and other fine semantic constructions face denial or rejection is indeed rocky. That is why we often settle for less concrete talk. Our obvious constant need for metaphor, especially in the aesthetic, seems to signal that despite our refined and useful symbolic schemes, we all the same have lost neither sensitivity to nor gratification from the confrontation of our humanity: the ability to apprehend, particularly in the raw of life, the good of the truly beautiful. Nor have other philosophers— those, like Monroe Beardsley, who wholeheartedly join the pursuit.

Notes

1. Monroe C. Beardsley, "The Humanities and Human Understanding," in *The Humanities and the Understanding of Reality*, ed. T. B. Stroup (Lexington, Ky., 1966), p. 13.

2. Ibid., p. 13.

3. "On Cognitive Aesthetic," *Revue D'Esthétique*, forthcoming, and "Real Art and Constructed Reality," *Restant—Review for Semiotic Theories and the Analysis of Texts* 8 (1980).

4. Monroe C. Beardsley, "Beauty and Aesthetic Value," *Journal of Philosophy* 59 (1962): 628.

5. "When we ask a question about something, X, we do not always have to provide ourselves with a definition of the term 'X' in order to be sure we understand what we are talking about. But any reasonable suspicion that the term is obscure imposes an obligation upon us to try to 'clarify' it" ("The Humanities and Human Understanding," p. 4). Reduced in this fashion to an aid rather than a goal of inquiry, definitions are cleansed of several of their denaturing effects on philosophy.

6. Monroe C. Beardsley, "What Is an Aesthetic Quality?" *Theoria* 39 (1973): 50–70, and "The Descriptivist Account of Aesthetic Attributions," *Revue Internationale de Philosophie* 28 (1974): 336–52. This pair of articles, in the full sense of "pair," contains Beardsley's fullest account of the issue to my knowledge. Though other articles are referred to in passing, it is, I believe, fair to concentrate on these two.

7. Other descriptions include "anemic," "stately," "tortured," "tranquil," and "triumphant." It seems to me that the heterogeneity of the lot exceeds varying positioning in dependency chains (see below). Aesthetic qualities may make a forest, but hardly a jungle.

8. "Beauty and Aesthetic Value." None of the feature articles make reference to this work (nor does it make reference to *Aesthetics* [New York, 1958]).

9. Monroe C. Beardsley, "Languages of Art and Art Criticism," *Erkenntnis* 12 (1978): 116.

10. "Beauty and Aesthetic Value," p. 625. Compare the statement "We speak of 'garish colors,' too, but we do not suppose that a particular color can be garish," in "What Is an Aesthetic Quality?" p. 51; but supposition is not obviously decisive.

11. Compare Beardsley's rebuttal: "it is hard to see how the semantic definition of A-qualities would cope with the qualities of nature. A woody glen can be tranquil, too; and Wordsworth's daffodils were 'tossing their heads in sprightly dance'; but nature is not a 'character in a symbol system,' even if a string quartet is." "What Is an Aesthetic Quality?" p. 61.

12. "Beauty and Aesthetic Value," pp. 624–25; "The Descriptivist Account," p. 348.

13. "Beauty and Aesthetic Value," pp. 623–24.

14. Monroe C. Beardsley, "The Definitions of the Arts," *Journal of Aesthetics and Art Criticism* 20 (1961): 175.

15. "Beauty and Aesthetic Value," p. 625. It is not entirely clear why "going by a single quality to establish a single dimension" makes it known as a simple quality.

16. In *POP Art*, ed. Andre de Rache (Knokke, 1970), p. 42.

17. Monroe C. Beardsley, "Aesthetic Theory and Educational Theory," in *Aesthetic Concepts and Education*, ed. Ralph Smith (Urbana, 1970), p. 9; "Aesthetic Welfare, Aesthetic Justice, and Educational Policy," *Journal of Aesthetic Education* 7 (1973): 49.

18. "What Is an Aesthetic Quality?" p. 51.

19. "The Descriptivist Account," p. 338. There are some similar moves, however, in the debate about emergent evolutionary qualities; see, e.g., Paul Henle, "The Status of Emergence," *Journal of Philosophy* (1942): 486–93. Perhaps relativists are mainly productive of varieties of dependency theses.

20. "The Descriptivist Account," p. 338.

21. Ibid., p. 341.

22. "What Is an Aesthetic Quality?" pp. 52–53. The ancestry of physiognomic qualities, *Gestalt* qualities, expressive qualities, etc., surfaces here. Priorities in experiential vivacity have been variously pressed; for example, Rudolf Arnheim has been eager to emphasize that moods or expressive qualities are experientially primary because this order, he alleges, predominates among primitives and children (*Art and Visual Perception* [Berkeley, 1965], chap. 10). The days when primitives and children were held to tell us nothing but the truth are gone, and I consider even farther gone the days when they proffered philosophical wisdom. Besides, Arnheim's assertion seems not to be true; see Barry E. Moore, "A Description of Children's Verbal Responses to Works of Art," *Studies in Art Education* 14 (1973): 27–34.

23. Frank Sibley, "Aesthetic Concepts," in *Philosophy Looks at the Arts*, ed. Joseph Margolis (Philadelphia, 1978), p. 65.

24. *The Possibility of Criticism* (Detroit, 1970), pp. 43–44.

25. It probably could be made out to be another sort of poverty that aesthetic concepts are of only two kinds, viz., primary and metaphorical imports. Sibley, "Aesthetic Concepts," suggests a third possibility, quasi-metaphorical concepts of a sort, but otherwise says very little about them. I see no reason why there should be only two (or three) kinds, although I must set this point aside for another occasion.

26. The following metaphor notes are virtually a paraphrase of Beardsley's theory, raiding his sensitive analysis for the relatively few features I can bend to my purposes, without, however, misrepresenting them. It is found in *Aesthetics*, chap. 3; "The Metaphorical Twist," *Philosophy and Phenomenological Research* 22 (1962): 293–307; "Metaphor and Falsity," *Journal of Aesthetics and Art Criticism* 35 (1976): 218–22; "Metaphorical Senses," *Nous* 12 (1978): 3–16. In addition I employ two passages from "Semiotic Aesthetics and Aesthetic Education," *Journal of Aesthetic Education* 9 (1975): 19, 23.

27. Inasmuch as Beardsley unreservedly favors conversion theory and rightly finds obvious flaws in comparison theories, it is curious to note that "similar" in statement 2 has replaced "words taken over metaphorically" in statement 6 of 1970. This switch, even if unsustained, and the remark on musical and moral triumph curiously connect with the extensive discussions in aesthetics taking off from Wittgenstein's remarks on "seeing a likeness" in the last part of *Philosophical Investigations*.

Altogether I have only two reservations, inessential at that, about the conversion theory. One is the two-step development of language by metaphorical innovation, where the addition, according to Beardsley, always is from metaphor to literal standardization. It seems to me that this traffic is actually Parisian, to say the least, and not at all unidirectional. The other reservation concerns the aesthetic concepts directly. We should not endorse monopolizing the human qualities, because plenty of these human qualities are unsuitable (see Sibley, "Aesthetic Concepts"), while some qualities other than human ones do suit (see Beardsley, "What Is an Aesthetic Quality?" pp. 68–69).

28. Beardsley, "Semiotic Aesthetics and Aesthetic Education," p. 22.

29. Aagaard-Mogensen, "On Cognitive Aesthetic."

30. Beardsley basically agrees; cf. "I say 'up to a point,' because I do not believe that the two types of inquiry, normative and nonnormative, are completely separable, though they are distinguishable," in "The Humanities and Human Understanding," p. 9; and "perhaps it is impossible to make a clear distinction between predicates that designate grounds of value and predicates that designate value, when the context of judgment is widely understood and well-established," in "What Is an Aesthetic Quality?" p. 63. The latter clause takes some of the bite out of the critics' invention of fresh metaphorical ways of attributing aesthetic qualities ("The Descriptivist Account," p. 348) as value-grounding qualities; but again I should hold on to his indeed sensible general view of this: "Moreover, the varieties of discourse that pass for criticism are a discouragement to generalization, and some of the things that critics say are certainly as foolish and as useless as discourse of any kind can be. Nevertheless, my prevailing attitude toward criticism is respectful." *The Possibility of Criticism*, pp. 10–11.

3

The Autonomy of Art

Göran Hermerén

là, tout n' est qu' ordre et beauté
—luxe, calme et volupté.

Baudelaire

Introduction

What do Ezra Pound's *Cantos* have in common with Joseph
Heller's *Good as Gold*—apart from the fact that they are literary
works from our century? Or with Samuel Beckett's plays, Isaac
Singer's stories, James Joyce's *Finnegans Wake*, or Pablo Neruda's
poems? Is there any interesting sense of "autonomous" in which it is
correct or plausible to say that these works are autonomous? The
issue may be worth investigating, not least in view of a number of
recent works dealing with the autonomy of art.[1]

It may also be asked if all art forms are equally autonomous.
Or is it rather the case, as some theoreticians (Adorno, Werckmeis-
ter) have argued, that music is more autonomous than painting,
sculpture, and literature? Is this true of the operas of Rossini and
Mozart, the sonatas of Beethoven, the symphonies of Stravinsky,
and the compositions of Brahms and Rachmaninov? Is it also true
of Charlie Parker's solos on the alto, of Duke Ellington's famous re-
cordings from the forties, of the many compositions by Paul Mc-
Cartney and John Lennon? Is there a method by means of which
such statements about the relative autonomy of various art forms
can be tested? What is such a method like, if indeed it exists?

There is a vast literature that directly or indirectly is relevant
to a discussion of these issues. It is, I think, obvious that some kind
of assumption about the autonomy of art was taken for granted by
the New Critics. It also seems to be the theoretical basis for the
intentional fallacy, which is so closely associated with the name of
Monroe Beardsley. He has also recently stated and endorsed a principle of autonomy.[2] Several Marxists, however, are hostile to such
principles. If art is a part of the ideological superstructure, and

35

if this superstructure in one sense or other is, "in the last analysis" (as it is sometimes said), determined by the economic base of society, it becomes difficult to see in what sense works of art can be autonomous.

However, discussions about the autonomy of art are often confused and confusing. This is, in a way, what one might expect. It goes without saying that such discussions usually will concern ideologically loaded issues (e.g., arguments for and against various New Critical, structuralist, and Marxist doctrines about art). Often it is far from clear what is being discussed: the key words are used ambiguously, or several issues are discussed simultaneously. For example, one does not always distinguish clearly between the autonomy of art and our ideas about the autonomy of art, nor does one always keep the many meanings of "autonomous" apart.

Etymologically the word goes back to the Greek *autos*, "self," and *nomos*, "law."[3] But it has been used in different ways at different times and places, and it can be interpreted in many ways. The purpose of the present article is to outline a few distinctions by means of which it should be possible to discuss the problem of the autonomy of art in a rational manner. Having distinguished between a few theses about autonomy, I will also indicate briefly which of these theses in my opinion are plausible and which are not.

Autonomous Laws

Suppose that the thesis about the autonomy of art is interpreted in roughly the following manner:

Thesis 1. The development of art follows laws—for example, in the way supposed by Wölfflin and some of his followers—and these laws cannot be reduced to, or defined in terms of, nonartistic or nonaesthetic laws and concepts.

By drawing the distinction between artistic and nonartistic (respectively aesthetic and nonaesthetic) in different ways, a series of different but related versions of thesis 1 can be obtained. But if the laws of the development of various art forms are *sui generis*, and not, for instance, sociological or psychological, and if it could be demonstrated that there are such laws, it would be reasonable enough to talk about the autonomy of art, especially in view of the etymology of the word. But the problem is that, at least to the best of my knowledge, nobody has been able to give an uncontroversial (precise, true) and nontrivial example of such a law.[4]

Accordingly, if the thesis about the autonomy of art is interpreted in the way indicated above, I am inclined to consider it untenable.

Autonomous Origin

But it is possible to defend the idea of autonomy, even if it should turn out that there are no laws of the kind Wölfflin envisaged. Obviously this idea will then have to be given a somewhat different twist. For example, it can be interpreted as follows:

> Thesis 2. The origin of a work of art—or an artistic movement—can never be completely understood and explained, unless the explanation is given (a) at least partly, or (b) exclusively, in terms of artistic or aesthetic considerations (motives, events, actions, and so forth).

Version b clearly expresses a more extreme position than version a, but the more extreme version has been advocated recently, at least by art historians.[5]

A problem that immediately arises in the discussion of this thesis is that the criteria of "complete" explanations and understanding are notoriously unclear. Moreover, the meaning of "artistic" and "aesthetic" is, as already indicated, badly in need of clarification, to say the least. The distinctions between these terms and their negations have been drawn in different ways at different times and places. Even in our culture the arts have been classified in different ways, as Kristeller and others have shown.[6]

It is therefore easy to obtain a large family of interpretations of thesis 2. There are, however, good reasons to be skeptical about most of them, or at least about the more extreme versions. One does not have to be an expert in art history to find examples of works of art where the choice of motives, symbols, techniques, and so forth, cannot be explained and understood merely in terms of artistic or aesthetic considerations. But if the thesis above is taken only to mean that artistic innovations cannot be derived completely from, for example, social or psychic changes, there is no need to quarrel with it; art often transcends the conditions under which it has been created.

Needless to say, thesis 2 can be interpreted in still looser ways. But it then runs the danger of losing all interest. What is the point of talking about the autonomy of art, if all that is meant is that both artistic and nonartistic (aesthetic and nonaesthetic) considerations play an important role in the origin of works of art? If it is granted that social and psychological conditions influence art, and that art

influences both social and psychological conditions and our perception of these conditions?

Autonomous Qualities

A group of more interesting and sophisticated interpretations
of the autonomy thesis can be stated in the following way:

> Thesis 3. Interpretations as well as analyses and explications
> of works of art (paintings, poems, novels, etc.) (*a*) are always
> checked, or (*b*) can always be checked, or (*c*) can only be
> checked, or (*d*) should always be checked, against the qual-
> ities of the work of art in question.

Thus, one version of the autonomy thesis clearly entails that, for
example, the pictorial qualities of a painting are decisive in checking interpretations of that painting. The meaning of a work of art is
accordingly distinguished both from the intentions of the artist and
from the responses of the beholders; in that sense it is autonomous.[7]
It follows that interpretations and analyses cannot be verified by
studies in the biography of the artist, its social setting, or the history of its reception.

The problem with this thesis is, of course, that every work of
art is open in the sense that it can be described and interpreted in
many ways. Moreover, the qualities of the work are not given once
and for all; there is no "naked eye," as Gombrich and others have
pointed out.[8] It is therefore not *always* easy to distinguish between
what is in the work of art and what is merely in the imagination of
the beholder; the work is constituted by a dialogue of questions and
answers. (I stress "always" because I would obviously not want to
claim that such a distinction can never be made.)

Theses of the kind outlined above have been advocated by
scholars with very different philosophical backgrounds. As has already been mentioned, Monroe Beardsley has endorsed a principle
of autonomy that comes close to thesis 3. On the European conti-
nent Theodor Adorno has argued that art is autonomous in the
sense that it cannot be derived from its social setting; thus, facts
about the social setting of a work of art are not decisive in checking
interpretations of it.[9]

It often turns out to be difficult to keep the four versions of the
thesis apart, and some of them can easily be combined with each
other. But discussions of this thesis will only with difficulty avoid
normative issues, and this, of course, does not make it less interesting. Understood in this normative way, thesis 3 will say something

about what art historians or art critics should focus their attention on. The thesis of autonomy will then, naturally, be controversial, but it is likely to be taken seriously as long as we take art (literature, music, etc.) seriously. Especially in times when art is subordinated to political, moral, and religious interests, there are good reasons not to forget this thesis.

As I have already indicated, each of the versions of the thesis above can be clarified further by explicating not only the concepts of interpretation and analysis, but in particular the expressions "the qualities of the work of art," "the work of art in question," and their cognates. A central question is whether these expressions can be defined without referring to nonartistic or nonaesthetic factors (e.g., conditions). Is it, for instance, possible to decide whether a literary text is ironic without investigating the psychological, social, and historical situation in which the text was written? Monroe Beardsley and I have corresponded about this, and I have elsewhere argued that this is not possible.[10] If I am right, does this then mean that the irony does not belong to the qualities of the work, or that it is not in the work?

Autonomy and Reference

Another fairly common interpretation of "autonomous" is "nonreferring"; for instance, it seems quite obvious that Marcel Fresco and Gene Blocker use "the work of art is autonomous" in the sense "the work does not refer to anything."[11] This interpretation can be made more precise in different ways, in particular by clarifying what is meant by "refer" and by making explicit exactly what works of art do *not* refer to.[12]

Two versions of this autonomy thesis can be summarized as follows:

> Thesis 4. Works of art (*a*) do not refer to anything whatsoever—every work of art is a closed world without any connection with anything else; or (*b*) do not refer to any subjective or objective reality outside the realm of art—works of art refer only to other works of art.

Thesis 4*a* might possibly appear to hold for concrete (nonrepresentative) art and for certain kinds of music. But like Morris Weitz, I do not believe that even the alleged formalist Hanslick ("The essence of music is *sound* and *motion*) would agree. What about Debussy's *La Mer*? There simply seem to be too many counterexamples to this thesis.

Among the more conspicuous ones, Picasso's modern versions of the works of old masters could be mentioned, as well as literary allusions of many kinds (e.g., to mythological or religious works). The latter examples may well be compatible with the weaker thesis (4*b*). But here there are other counterexamples—religious art from the Middle Ages, Vanitas paintings, social criticism in literature (e.g., Zola)—which obviously contain references of various kinds to religious, philosophical, psychological, and social ideas and states of affairs.

It may be tempting to recall in this context that James Joyce is reported to have said that if Dublin was destroyed, it could be rebuilt after his book *Ulysses*. If there is some truth to this, the book must refer to Dublin in one way or other. Dickens' *Oliver Twist* is clearly a story from London, and in chapter 8 the author describes how Oliver walks to London. But why should one not be allowed to say that Dickens is referring to London, when he uses the word "London" in that chapter? It is not difficult to find other examples suggesting that even the weaker thesis gives much too crude a picture of the complex relations between art and reality.

The reason why many people have been tempted to accept these theses is probably the much discussed fact that literary sentences are "fictitious" or "fictional" (Beardsley) or "Quasi-Urteile" (Ingarden); they are not true or false in the same way as news reports or reports from the stock market. Suppose someone reads the line "I see a lily on thy brow" in a poem by Keats and asks: Was it one lily and not two? Was it really a lily and not some similar flower? Then he has clearly confused the poet with a botanist. It may well be the case that no singular statement in a poem or novel describes or refers to any subjective or objective fact or event. But obviously this does not prevent the novel or poem from presenting a model situation of human or social conflicts, which can be more or less universal. In that way a poem or a novel can, though in a roundabout way, refer to reality.

To sum up: neither of the two versions of thesis 4 appears to be tenable or plausible, at least not in the general form in which they are stated above; there are too many counterexamples referring to nonartistic events, ideas, and so forth, though the way in which these references are made is naturally very much influenced by artistic traditions and considerations. But if qualified properly, the thesis above may hold for limited classes of works of art. If, however, a sharp distinction is made between art and life, it becomes difficult to understand why art should be so important to us.

Autonomous Structures

But there are also other interpretations of the autonomy thesis. It can be argued that works of art are autonomous in the sense indicated below:

> Thesis 5. Works of art (and aesthetic objects) contain structures satisfying the following two conditions: (a) no element of such a structure can be eliminated, and (b) no element can be added to such a structure, without destroying the unity of the work.

Some aestheticians have argued that the presence of autonomous structures of the kind indicated above constitutes at least a necessary condition for something to be a work of art. But I doubt that this position is tenable. At any rate, it does not seem easy to apply this thesis to conceptual art, moving sculpture, and films. Can it be applied to Christo's *Fence* and his other projects? To Klein's monochrome blue paintings? Counterexamples can, of course, always be defined away as not being works of art, a well-known procedure in aesthetics, but such a strategy is not without dangers.

The thesis about the structural autonomy of works of art has been interpreted in a more sophisticated and interesting way by, for example, Stefan Morawski.[13] His main idea can be summarized as follows:

> Thesis 6. The work of art constitutes a microcosm, a closed world of its own, which in various ways is related to a macrocosm, a world outside the work of art. For example, the microcosm may depict, express, or be a model of the macrocosm.

If, however, at the same time it is argued tht this microcosm is genetically or causally dependent on the macrocosm, it is difficult to talk about the autonomy of art without being misleading, considering that one of the basic meanings of "autonomous" is "independent." This kind of autonomy can at most be called "relative," and that is also how Morawski refers to it.

It is not difficult to point to works of art that can be characterized in this way, and these characterizations may be fruitful and illuminating. But can this thesis be applied to all works of art? At this point there are in my view good reasons to be skeptical. Suppose thesis 6 holds for van Gogh's landscapes, Rembrandt's self-portraits, Hieronymous Bosch's *Hortus Deliciarum*, Magritte's surrealistic paintings, Baertling's nonrepresentative works, Calder's mobiles, and contemporary conceptual art. Or suppose—to choose yet another example from the visual arts—that it holds for Leonardo's *Mona Lisa*, for Duchamp's desecration of it, and for Andy Warhol's pop versions. Then I think it should be asked (*a*) if the macrocosms are not very different from each other here, and (*b*) if the relations between microcosm and macrocosm do not vary considerably in these examples.

If these two questions are answered in the affirmative, one would have either to accept that the thesis about relative autonomy is not very informative or to delimit its range of application in a way that is not too obviously ad hoc and that does not make the thesis circular.

Autonomous Institutions

If there is a strong and effective system of political censorship in a country, it may well be denied that art and artists in that country are autonomous. But then "autonomous" is being used in a slightly different sense than before, though it is related to the basic meanings of the word ("independent," "self-governing," etc.).

To begin with, let us consider the following new thesis of autonomy:

> Thesis 7. The institution of art is autonomous in the sense that there is no political, moral, or religious authority telling artists what to do and how to do it, or forbidding them to choose certain motifs, means of expression, and so forth.

This thesis is probably true of Denmark, and maybe also of Sweden and some other countries. But in many other countries the thesis is plainly false. There the avant-garde art and the literature critical of the dominant political, moral, and religious system has to go underground, as indeed it has in several European countries.

It must be acknowledged, however, that censorship can take many forms. For example, in the absence of any established political, moral, or religious authority trying to force artists to paint or write in a certain way, the situation may be such that only artists who take up certain subjects in a certain way will have a chance to survive economically. If, for instance, only certain kinds of works of art are bought, or subsidies to cover the printing costs are given only to certain types of novels, this may in practice have an effect similar to that of political, moral, or religious censorship.

Thus, it is possible to obtain a family of versions of thesis 7, depending on what kind of censorship one has in mind. To each of them corresponds a normative version of the following type:

Thesis 8. The institution of art ought to be autonomous in the sense that there ought not to be any political, moral, or religious authority telling artists what to do and how to do it, or forbidding them to choose certain motifs, means of expression, and so forth.

On the whole, I would be inclined to accept this thesis, both in its more limited forms, against institutionalized censorship, and in its more extended forms, against, for example, a system of subsidies favoring only works of art in a certain genre, in a certain style, or with certain contents ("message").

Of course, I am not against subsidies. I am also well aware of the difficulties in drawing precise boundaries here. In view of the high costs of printing, subsidies are necessary in several countries. Analogously, many theaters would have to close if they were not subsidized by the government or in other ways. But I am in favor of a pluralistic system in the sense that in no country should subsidies to the arts be handled by a single organization or a single board. Moreover, nobody should be a member of such an organization or board for more than, say, five or six years; it should not be a permanent position.

To avoid misunderstanding, I would like to stress that I have not said that I would be inclined to accept thesis 8 unconditionally or in all circumstances. On the contrary, it is not too difficult to imagine exceptions. Suppose, for instance, that works of art are created that in a persuasive way advocate fascism or the use of heavy drugs or encourage people to commit crimes or take part in racial discrimination. Considering the damages and tragedies that might follow—for example, fascism and the use of drugs—I would be inclined to say for moral reasons that there *are* important exceptions to thesis 8, but that these exceptions are rare. Moreover, I would—like Monroe Beardsley—want to stress that since the situations may vary considerably, each case should be considered individually and as a whole, and the aesthetic value of the work should be taken into account.[14]

The general argument in favor of thesis 8 is, of course, that a certain amount of freedom has proved to be necessary for the development of new and vital art forms. To put it differently, bad works of art are likely to result if artists are told what to do and how to do it by political, moral, or religious authorities. And good art is essential, since art is not merely a reflex of reality (the social, biographical, and historical conditions under which it was created); it transcends and changes reality by changing our experiences of the

world, by suggesting new possibilities and combinations, by presenting surprising connections. Art is not only something that
makes life more enjoyable or helps us to endure various hardships; it
is also a great source of mental and moral innovations.

However, two things need to be stressed at this point. First, in
theory but not always in practice (for obvious political reasons), the
problem of autonomy suggested by the theses discussed in this section is easy to solve. If censorship is abolished, art will be an autonomous institution, and artists will be autonomous. Second, suppose
the problem of autonomy in this sense is solved, as I think it has
been in several countries. This does not mean that the theoretical
and normative problems of autonomy raised in the other sections of
the present paper are solved. Thus, it is essential to distinguish between different problems of autonomy; there is no such thing as *the*
problem of autonomy.

Several arguments can be used to support thesis 8 in addition
to the ones suggested above. Some of them will be discussed in the
subsequent sections.

Autonomous Effects

So far, I have mainly concentrated on the genesis of works of
art and on what can be seen (found) in them. But according to a
different interpretation of the autonomy thesis, it can be argued
that works of art are autonomous in the following sense:

> Thesis 9. Works of art have (*a*) only aesthetic or artistic effects
> on the beholder's thoughts, attitudes, and feelings, and on so-
> ciety at large, or (*b*) no important nonaesthetic or nonartistic
> effects of that kind.

This thesis seems to be contrary to the most elementary studies of
the effects of art. But to deny that works of art have important nonaesthetic or nonartistic effects can, of course, in a difficult political
situation (or an extremely narrow-minded moral setting) be the
only possible way of trying to create freedom of artistic expression,
to defend art—or oneself—against accusations of being morally
subversive, of overthrowing current moral standards and the political system. In extreme situations such a defense may be the artist's
only chance, if he wants to survive socially, economically, and
sometimes even physically.

Oscar Wilde's aestheticism, as well as radical formalism in music, can probably be used to illustrate such defenses. Moreover, accusations against artists for undermining people's morals and the

current political system do not merely belong to the past. However, as I have already indicated, it is not difficult to find counter-examples to thesis 9. Consider some of the best-known works of Daumier, Balzac, Rivera, and Brecht, to mention just a few. These works had, and were intended to have, moral and political effects. It is therefore hard to take thesis 9 seriously as a general theory of art. At any rate, when this thesis is used to defend the freedom of art and of artists, it boils down to an argument for thesis 8 or to an attempt to change our views about what is important in art and what to look for in works of art.[15]

Autonomous Values

Suppose it is possible to single out conceptually artistic and aesthetic values, attitudes, interests, and so forth. A definition of any of these concepts may then be regarded as an ideal type in Weber's sense; and the values, attitudes, and interests we experience or cultivate may more or less approximate these ideal types.

Thus, it should be noted that the assumption made above should not be conflated with the assumption that artistic and aesthetic values, attitudes, and interests are experienced pure. The assumption above is, on the contrary, compatible with the statement that this is *not* the case. The fact that any pair of experiences, x and y, are conceptually distinct is a necessary requirement if it is to be possible to describe the way or ways in which x and y occur together when we contemplate works of art.

Given this assumption, it is, of course, possible to admit that works of art can have various nonaesthetic and nonartistic effects (political, moral, and religious) and yet argue that works of art are autonomous in the sense that the following thesis is true:

Thesis 10. The nonartistic and nonaesthetic effects of works of art (*a*) are, as a matter of fact, always separated from, or (*b*) can always be separated from, or (*c*) should always be separated from, the aesthetic and artistic value of the work of art.

In other words, the concepts of aesthetic and artistic value should be distinguished not only from each other, but also from whatever effects of a nonaesthetic and nonartistic kind a work of art may have.

Understood in this way, the thesis of autonomy will lead to a kind of critical puritanism, according to which the aesthetic and artistic value of a work of art has nothing to do with any political, social, educational, psychological, therapeutic, moral, pornographic, and other effects it may have. The autonomy thesis then becomes interesting and, to say the least, controversial. Its tenability depends upon the ability to single out conceptually artistic and aesthetic value (interest, attitude, effect, etc.), a project to which many distinguished aestheticians and philosophers since Kant have devoted considerable time and energy.

If this possibility is somehow taken for granted, the autonomy thesis can be given a slightly different twist:

> Thesis 11. Works of art (*a*) are, as a matter of fact, always evaluated, or (*b*) can be evaluated, or (*c*) can only be evaluated, or (*d*) should always be evaluated, without considering any nonartistic or nonaesthetic effects, values, or intentions.

According to one version of this thesis, the critic should thus concentrate exclusively on the aesthetic and artistic value of works of art, though critical practice seems to be compatible only with the weak version (*b*).

However, the situation may be saved by making a few changes in the thesis. First of all, it has to be admitted that in the practice of many critics moral, political, and religious considerations do play an important role when works of art are evaluated. Second, the range of application of the thesis of autonomy has to be restricted to conflicts between values or norms of the following type: the work, for example, is aesthetically good but expresses or supports (what are generally regarded as) bad morals; or it supports good morals, or what are generally regarded as good morals, in an aesthetically poor and uninteresting way.

After these preliminaries, the following thesis may be proposed:

> Thesis 12. In cases of conflicts between values or norms, aesthetic and artistic considerations should always be decisive and outweigh moral, political, and religious ones when works of art are to be evaluated.

Whether the last two theses are reasonable is not merely of a theoretical interest, since these theses also have obvious implications for cultural and educational policy.[16] What demands do we (readers, listeners, beholders) have a right to make on works of art and on artists? What demands do artists and works of art have a right to make on us? And what requirements should be satisfied if these demands are to be met in a democratic society?

Concluding Remarks

In this paper I have discussed a number of autonomy theses and tried to clarify them. For several reasons it is important to distinguish between these theses.[17] In the first place, some of them are clearly untenable, others tenable, still others unconvincing. The question "Is art autonomous?" does therefore not have a single, clear answer; distinctions have to be introduced before an attempt is made to answer the question. In the second place, the theses are methodologically different in the sense that it is not possible to use the same methods in checking their tenability.

To avoid misunderstanding, it should be stressed that my discussion makes no claim of completeness. Further comments could obviously be made on each of the twelve theses distinguished above, and still other theses could have been obtained by focusing on ideas or conceptions of autonomy, rather than on the autonomy of art. It is obviously one thing to try to find out whether art in one sense or other is autonomous, and something quite different to study the origin, meaning, development, and effects of various ideas about the autonomy of art.

Notes

1. See, for example, Michael Müller, et al., *Autonomie der Kunst: Zur Genese und Kritik einer bürgerlichen Kategorie* (Frankfurt am Main, 1972; 2d ed., 1974); Marcel Fresco, "Zur Autonomie von Kunstwerken," *Lier en Boog* 3 (1977): 15–28; Norbert Krenzlin, *Das Werk 'rein für sich'"* (Berlin, 1979); H. Gene Blocker, "Autonomy, Reference and Post-Modern Art," *British Journal of Aesthetics* 20 (1980): 229–36. The publication of a book on the autonomy of art by Cyril Barrett has also been announced.

It should be noted that there are interesting analogies between the controversies over the autonomy of art and the controversies between externalists and internalists over the autonomy of science. But I shall have to save a discussion of these analogies for another occasion.

2. Monroe C. Beardsley, *The Possibility of Criticism* (Detroit, 1970), p. 16.

3. See, e.g., *The Oxford Dictionary of English Etymology* and *The Oxford English Dictionary*, s.v. "autonomy."

4. For instance, in his essay *Art History and the Social Sciences* (New York, 1975), E. H. Gombrich mentions the following example of a law taken for granted in explanations in the humanities: "all cultural products have precedents." Among other things, however, this example raises the question whether it is conceptually possible to find instances of "cultural products" without "precedents."

5. For an example of a rather extreme version, which even denies that a sculptor can be influenced or inspired by a painting or drawing, see Rudolf Zeitler, *Uppsatser i Konstvetenskap* (Uppsala, 1977), pp. 41ff. Zeitler's idea in this paper (see p. 55) appears to be that an artistic achievement in a certain genre, e.g., sculpture, has to be explained by reference to other works in that genre only (sculptor A has reacted against and tried to surpass the works of sculptor B).

6. See Władysław Tatarkiewicz, *A History of Six Ideas: An Essay in Aesthetics* (Warsaw, 1980), chaps. 1–3; and the classic paper by P. O. Kristeller, "The Modern System of the Arts: A Study in the History of Aesthetics," *Journal of the History of Ideas* 12 (1951): 468–527; 13 (1952): 17–46.

7. For an elaboration of this point, see Beardsley, *The Possibility of Criticism*.

8. E. H. Gombrich, *Art and Illusion* (London, 1960), especially part 1.

9. Theodor W. Adorno, *Aesthetische Theorie* (Frankfurt am Main, 1970), pp. 334ff.

10. Göran Hermerén, "Intention and Interpretation in Literary Criticism," *New Literary History* 7 (1975–76), esp. pp. 71–74.

11. See Blocker, "Autonomy, Reference and Post-Modern Art," and Fresco, "Zur Autonomie von Kunstwerken." For a fuller exposition of Blocker's views on autonomy, the reader is referred to his *Philosophy of Art* (New York, 1979).

12. Consider the following possible criteria for a work of art, x, to refer to something else, y: (1) there is a code or convention according to which (at least some part of) x denotes or describes y; (2) there is a (not too small) group of people whom x makes think of y, e.g., because of similarities or analogies; and (3) x presupposes the existence of y, or x is pointless or incomprehensible. Debussy's *La Mer* probably refers to the sea according to criterion 2, but hardly according to 1 or 3. But novels expressing social indignation and protest, like, e.g., some of the works of Zola, refer to the social conditions they protest against, at least according to criterion 3. Obviously a work of art can refer to something according to several criteria simultaneously, and also refer to different things according to different criteria at the same time.

13. Stefan Morawski, *Inquiries into the Fundamentals of Aesthetics* (Cambridge, Mass., 1974), pp. 105–9.

14. Monroe Beardsley, *Aesthetics: Problems in the Philosophy of Criticism* (New York, 1958), pp. 577–81.

15. See my paper, "The Nature of Aesthetic Theories," in *Contemporary Aesthetics in Scandinavia*, ed. Lars Aagaard-Mogensen and Göran Hermerén (Lund, 1980), esp. pp. 212–14.

16. Of course theses 11 and 12 can be interpreted in such a way that they become trivially true. In an aesthetic evaluation, aesthetic considerations have to be decisive—otherwise it would not be an aesthetic evalua-

tion. However, in many cases people have to make an overall judgment about works of art. Then there may well be genuine disagreement about what relative weight should be given to aesthetic, moral, political, and religious considerations. For example, there are people who sometimes have to decide whether a number of works of art are to be exhibited, whether the exhibited works are to be bought, whether the exhibition is to be prohibited, whether the artist is to be prosecuted or get a gold medal. Since these situations vary considerably, however, it would in my opinion be unwise to accept the theses in the general form given here.

17. Attentive readers will no doubt have noticed in the twelve the-ses distinguished here both that "autonomous" is not always used in the same sense, and that what is said to be autonomous also varies.

Aesthetic Experience

4

Aesthetic Experience and Evaluation

BOHDAN DZIEMIDOK

A belief in the existence of a close relationship between aesthetic experience and aesthetic evaluation has had a wide currency ever since the problem of aesthetic evaluation became the object of study and systematic analysis. Those who shared this conviction believed that every aesthetic evaluation of an object, including a work of art, is based on a prior aesthetic experience evoked by that object. Someone who is incapable of having a positive or negative experience in relation to a given object cannot acquire the data constituting the basis for a valid evaluation. Thus, the ability to have an aesthetic experience was regarded as a necessary condition of aesthetic evaluation. For example, someone incapable of experiencing music does not have proper qualifications for passing judgments about it as he does not satisfy the requirement that gives one authority to evaluate music. Many theoreticians maintained not only that evaluation is based on aesthetic experience but also that it has its beginning in that experience. In its opening phase, in its initial and elementary form, aesthetic evaluation is a component of that experience and imparts a positive or negative coloring to it.

In recent years both these views—that aesthetic experience is the basis and the necessary condition of aesthetic evaluation and that aesthetic evaluation appears not only in the form of value judgments but also as direct emotional experience constituting an essential component of aesthetic experience—have been questioned more and more often. The aim of this paper is to give a brief survey of some of the conceptions of the followers of the traditional belief in the existence of a necessary relationship between aesthetic experience and aesthetic evaluation and to discuss the arguments of representatives of the opposite position. In the final part of the paper I would also like to suggest a compromise solution of this controversy on the basis of Stanisław Ossowski's findings and differentiations.

Empiricist and Instrumentalist Conceptions of Aesthetic Evaluation

One of the classic representatives of the traditional attitude toward these problems was David W. Prall, who maintained that aesthetic judgment is always a record of direct aesthetic experience.[1] Aesthetic judgment is a secondary, derivative, and purely intellectual phenomenon, and as such it is not involved in the process of value formation.[2] However, direct emotional intuitive evaluation, which is a component of aesthetic experience, is a value-constituting factor. According to Prall, criticism begins with the record of this direct experience of value in aesthetic judgment, and "without this starting point in direct perception and felt appreciation, criticism is ungrounded, unreliable, and perhaps dishonest, if not altogether irrelevant and meaningless."[3]

Among Polish aestheticians contemporary with Prall, similar views were held by Mieczysław Wallis.[4] Prall's and Wallis's opinions concerning the role of aesthetic experience in the process of aesthetic valuing are connected with a certain conception of aesthetic value as the object's capacity to evoke aesthetic experience. Such definitions are as a rule formulated by representatives of different varieties of empiricism, naturalism, and instrumentalism in aesthetics. The representatives of these orientations do not regard the work of art as an autonomous value but treat it as a means of evoking valuable experiences, as an instrument of enriching man's experience. This is the position of such philosophers and aestheticians as John Dewey, C. I. Lewis, S. C. Pepper, Thomas Munro, D. W. Gotshalk, and others.[5] The overwhelming majority of these theoreticians distinguish two forms of aesthetic evaluation: direct valuing, which is a component of aesthetic experience, and intellectual valuing, which is expressed in evaluations or, in other words, in value judgments or evaluative judgments.[6]

John Dewey's views are exceptional in this respect. Dewey held that valuing as a cognitive and reflective act cannot appear in the form of direct and subjective experience of value, but exclusively in the form of value judgments.[7] Only direct perception provides the basis for the formation of value judgments and determines their character. Dewey wrote, "Since the matter of esthetic criticism is the perception of esthetic objects, natural and artistic criticism is always determined by the quality of first-hand perception; obtuseness in perception can never be made good by any amount of learning, however extensive, nor any command of abstract theory, however correct."[8]

The empiricist conception of value and evaluation has found its fullest as well as its most elaborate and consistent expression in the works of Monroe C. Beardsley. Beardsley consistently and persistently attempts to isolate the sphere of aesthetic phenomena, particularly values and aesthetic experiences, and to grasp and define their specificity. Object x has a greater aesthetic value than object y when it is capable of evoking an aesthetic experience of greater magnitude than that produced by object y.[9] Aesthetic experience is thus not only the sole test of aesthetic value, but also its measure.

Beardsley developed and clarified this position in his works published prior to 1970. The most essential addition was the attempt to explain and concretize the suggestion that aesthetic experience is a measure of aesthetic value. Less important—and in view of his later works only temporary—was the replacement of "aesthetic experience" by "aesthetic gratification." Aesthetic value became defined as the capacity of an object to provide aesthetic gratification under suitable conditions.[10] He stressed that the aesthetic value of an object is not a function of the actual degree of gratification obtained from it in any given case. It is "measurable" neither by the mean degree of aesthetic gratification obtained from the object in all possible instances nor by the total aesthetic gratification that it provides in the course of its existence. Rather, "aesthetic value depends on the highest degree obtainable under optimal circumstances."[11] Optimal circumstances occur when the object is experienced correctly and completely. The aesthetic evaluation of the work of art should be based on the aesthetic experience that occurs in optimal circumstances. A critic, in evaluating the work of art, usually relies on his previous aesthetic experiences and those of other people. He can "say that he knows his judgment is true by direct experience."[12] In certain cases, however, he can also take into account future aesthetic experiences that can achieve a more complete actualization of the aesthetic value of the work.[13] Beardsley stresses that the critic should substantiate his value judgments in each particular case, and "the only way to support such a judgment relevantly and cogently would be to point out features of the work that enable it to provide an experience having an aesthetic character."[14]

This brief account of the views of American aestheticians on the relationships between aesthetic evaluation and aesthetic experience has, of necessity, involved some omissions. It has not been possible to give a complete survey of the works of the authors under discussion as far as the theory of aesthetic evaluation or the theory of aesthetic experience are concerned. I have not offered here a detailed critical discussion, as that would require a separate full-length study. My reference to the ideas of American aestheticians had a purely instrumental character: I wanted to demonstrate that all these authors representing a definite methodological approach (naturalist/empiricist) shared, despite certain differences of opinion, the belief in a close connection between the aesthetic evaluation of the work of art and the aesthetic experience evoked by that work. Another reason for the conciseness of my presentation is the fact that the above conviction is not something extraordinary among the adherents of naturalism and empiricism in aesthetics. These theorists are often accused of psychologism, and many opponents of psychologism in contemporary aesthetics therefore find it much easier to belittle the views of those subscribing to naturalism and empiricism. But are the supporters of psychologism the only ones who believe that aesthetic evaluation is connected with the aesthetic experience preceding it and that aesthetic evaluation should rely on aesthetic experience?

Ingarden on Evaluation and Experience

In order to answer the preceding question it will be helpful to turn to the views of the philosophers who consistently opposed naturalism, empiricism, and psychologism in aesthetics. Consider Roman Ingarden, the most outstanding of the founders of phenomenological aesthetics.

Roman Ingarden distinguishes aesthetic and artistic evaluations. This distinction is fundamentally based on the differentiation of artistic values, which are connected with the work of art as a schematic artifact that in this particular form is aesthetically neutral, and aesthetic values, which appear in the aesthetic concretization of the work of art: that is, in the aesthetic object.[15] In aesthetic experience we can have direct and intuitive contact with aesthetic values, which are qualitative in nature. Artistic values, on the other hand, are not qualitative phenomena but, according to Ingarden, specific capacities of the work of art that cannot be discovered in direct aesthetic experience; nor is it possible to have intuitive contact with them. However, it may be concluded that they exist as a definite capacity of the work of art on the basis of a series of aesthetically valuable concretizations of the work.[16] Artistic values are reducible to the twofold capacity of the work of art as a schematic artifact: (1) the capacity to evoke aesthetic experience; and (2) the capacity to form the basis for constituting the aesthetic object and the aesthetic values connected with it. Thus, artistic values are instrumental in nature, like the work of art itself, which, according to Ingarden, is only a tool used in the constitution of a valuable aesthetic object. The artistic value of the work of art is proportionate to the aesthetic values of its possible concretizations, which occur under suitable conditions, and, perhaps, to the heterogeneity of those concretizations.[17]

The differentiation of aesthetic and artistic evaluations is the consequence of these fundamental discriminations in Ingarden's aesthetics. The difference between the two types of evaluation can be briefly formulated in the following way. Aesthetic evaluation concerns the aesthetic values of a definite concretization of the work of art and is inseparably correlated with aesthetic experience as it finds its primary expression in a direct emotional reponse to value; intellectual aesthetic evaluation is only its secondary expression.

Artistic evaluation is not directly connected with aesthetic experience, even though it usually relies on aesthetic experience or, rather, experiences. It is only expressed in the form of artistic judgments and ought to serve the grasping of the artistic value of the work of art itself. The formulation of a valid artistic judgment is, according to Ingarden, a more difficult task than passing a judgment on the aesthetic value of a given concretization. "A valid artistic evaluation can only be made by someone who possesses a survey of possible concretizations of the work."[18] Because we can never take all possible concretizations into account, artistic evaluations are always only approximate. Their validity is limited, since artistic evaluation is as a rule only partly substantiated.[19]

In this situation, according to Ingarden, the immediate aesthetic evaluation is more important. The most elementary and basic form is the "response to value" (*Wertantwort*), a concept introduced by Dietrich von Hilderbrand to denote the direct emotional evaluation that occurs in the final phase of aesthetic experience. On the other hand, aesthetic evaluation or aesthetic value judgment (in his postwar works Ingarden prefers the latter term) is a linguistic/conceptual expression of value response.[20]

Aesthetic value judgment is, and should be, an expression and result of value response. However, this judgment, as a purely intellectual act (formulated in terms of cognitive rather than aesthetic attitude), is characterized by a certain autonomy and need not always be based on actual aesthetic experience. Such cool judgments, abstracted from a definite aesthetic experience, are frequently passed by some critics employing learned, professional criteria. People who have a great deal to do with works of art sometimes lose the faculty of direct emotional response to the work of art and, in the words of

Ingarden, "develop a technique for orienting themselves by certain secondary features of the work of art, whether or not it possesses a value, without ever having beheld this value and without ever having known the value quality at all. From the secondary features they notice, they infer purely intellectually that the work of art in question can lead to the constitution of a valuable aesthetic object."[21] Such evaluations have a purely intellectual character, and only through a misunderstanding can they be regarded as aesthetically valuable. An inferential value judgment may even be correct, as Ingarden admits, "but the experience which essentially grounds it, which shows it to be legitimate, lies in the final phase of the aesthetic experience and is in particular contained in the emotional acknowledgment of the value of this aesthetic object, which is based on the beholding of its qualitative harmony. Only judgments grounded in this emotional acknowledgment are actually substantiated, confirmed, demonstrated. The judgments passed, often with great skill, by professional critics are in general only indirect judgments, not of the value of the aesthetic object, but of the work of art as a means (tool) which, given the aesthetic experience, can lead to a positively valuable aesthetic object."[22]

Thus, neither artistic nor aesthetic judgments are in Ingarden's theory totally autonomous, if evaluation proceeds correctly, nor are they dependent on the whim of the person pronouncing them. Both require substantiation by the "more primary" stages of evaluation. Both find their direct or indirect substantiation in the primary response to the aesthetic value of the concretization of the work of art. In his report delivered at the Third International Congress of Aesthetics in Venice in 1956, Ingarden states explicitly that "aesthetic value judgment is only a derivative and secondary formation and in the process of grasping the value of the aesthetic object plays a secondary role."[23] Ingarden expressed his strong and consistent belief in a close relationship between aesthetic evaluation and aesthetic experience on other occasions as well: for example, when considering the problem of the validity of judgments and in his polemic against extreme relativism and subjectivism in the theory of valuing.

The problem of the validity of aesthetic and artistic evaluation is discussed by Ingarden in *The Cognition of the Literary Work of Art*. The question is whether the evaluation of a given literary work passed by a reader is "binding and valid" for other readers, or whether other readers have the right to reject it.[24] Having discussed this problem, Ingarden concludes that not everyone has the right to reject the evaluation made by someone else. In his opinion two groups of readers do not have this right. The first consists of those readers who are "incapable of completing an appropriately qualified aesthetic experience and accompanying objective aesthetic cognition," and the second of those who "have not been able to complete those operations up to the time when they question an evaluation."[25]

One of the main polemical currents in Ingarden's works is his opposition to those subscribing to the formula *"de gustibus non est disputandum."*[26] The followers of this formula point to the discrepancies in aesthetic experience and evaluation, which in their opinion sufficiently support the view that all evaluations are equally justified in purely subjective terms and that no discussion of this matter can produce a meaningful result. Ingarden does not question the existence of discrepancies in preferences and aesthetic judgment but maintains that extreme (subjectivist) relativism is not sufficiently justified: the argumentation of its adherents does not withstand criticism and is either based on false premises or springs from such misunderstandings as its failure to acknowledge the fundamental discriminations introduced by phenomenology. In Ingarden's opinion the reasoning of the extreme relativists is based on two erroneous premises: (1) the belief that the work of art itself is the object of evaluation whenever an aesthetic judgment is made; and (2) the assumption that when there are divergent value judgments referring to a single work of art, the object of evaluation is always the same—that the same thing is evaluated in all cases.

Extreme relativists—and they are not alone in this respect—do not take into account the fact that the work of art as a schematic configuration is capable of giving rise to a set of different concretizations that possess equal validity. In such cases not only are evaluations of the work of art different, but the objects of evaluation themselves—the particular concretizations of the work—are different, and so there is no real divergence of evaluation concerning a single object. If this is true, the difference in evaluations not only does not express discretion and anarchy in the sphere of aesthetic evaluation, but, on the contrary, is perfectly justified.[27]

Ingarden, however, does not limit himself to demonstrating that the generalizations advanced by subjectivist relativism and aesthetic skepticism do not survive criticism. He believes that the very problem constituting the object of the dispute is incorrectly posed. The problem of the validity and justification of artistic and aesthetic evaluations is in fact a secondary, less essential issue. The fundamental question is the following: is value response to a definite concretization of the work of art conditioned by that value? First of all, in his opinion, it is necessary to find the answer to the following question: are different emotional value responses possible with respect to a definite concretization constituted in a certain aesthetic experience?[28] Only an affirmative answer to this question would justify the saying *"de gustibus non est disputandum."* This possibility seems to be highly unlikely, to say the least. Ingarden believes that there exists a close, sensible rather than causal, relationship between evaluation and the value quality that this evaluation refers to. We respond with enjoyment to the beautiful, with pleasure to the pretty, and with repulsion to the ugly. "Here we always deal with something sensible, one could say that reasonable behavior towards something that is grasped and felt. . . . The sensible relationship between value response and value quality is so close and obvious" that responding with an improper value response would be, according to Ingarden, "a senseless behavior."[29] Pathological or perverse cases—for example, of the ugly, cannot undermine the proper aesthetic evaluation, just as errors in reasoning do not undermine the laws of logic.

It appears from Ingarden's remarks that although he is an opponent of psychologism, in the matter we are dealing with here his views are to a large extent similar to those of American empiricists and naturalists.

Aesthetic Evaluation without Aesthetic Experience

To present the arguments of the opponents of the thesis that there exists a necessary and proper connection between aesthetic evaluation and aesthetic experience, I shall rely primarily on two papers by John Fisher and Piotr Graff, published at the end of the sixties.[30] Both authors explicitly question the existence of the relationship between aesthetic evaluation and the aesthetic experience of the work of art. Fisher admits that some degree of aesthetic enjoyment accompanies nearly every case of positive aesthetic evaluation but maintains that evaluation of the work of art is also possible without aesthetic enjoyment. In actual cases of evaluation, that is, value may be ascribed to the work of art and its place in the existing artistic hierarchy determined without prior aesthetic enjoyment. Sometimes lack of enjoyment is compensated for by the perceiver's general sensitivity to the formal qualities of art and acquaintance with current artistic norms. In actual aesthetic valuing we often encounter statements of the following kind: I do not like *x*, though I must admit that it is aesthetically valuable. If the experience of aesthetic enjoyment were the necessary condition of aesthetic evaluation, such a statement would not be possible. The view that enjoyment is necessary for aesthetic evaluation results, according to Fisher, from the confusion of cause and effect in the following reasoning: "If certain properties of experienced objects are present, then I experience enjoyment. If these same properties are present, then value is ascribed. If I do not experience enjoyment, then those properties are not present."[31] The error in this reasoning is obvious. Fisher ends his paper with the statement that aesthetic enjoyment is not a formal requirement of aesthetic evaluation, nor is it a material condition of evaluation.

Like Fisher, Graff maintains that "many aesthetic situations are characterized by the lack of any links between evaluation and experience."[32] He distinguishes two basic types of situations in which a discrepancy between experience and evaluation appears. Besides the situation taken into account by Fisher, "I don't like this work of art, but I know that it has aesthetic value," Graff rightly notices the possibility of a reverse situation: "I like it, but I know it is a kitsch."[33] Graff does not question the fact that the recognition of the value of the work of art may be accompanied by a positive aesthetic experience, but he believes that it is not necessary for the recognition of value to occur. The recognition of value does not have to be emotional; it may proceed in a completely cool manner.

Fisher and Graff question the belief in the necessity of a close relationship between the aesthetic evaluation of the work of art and the aesthetic experience evoked by it. However, they do not generally negate the existence of the connection between aesthetic experience and evaluation. It could be expected that such theoreticians as George Dickie or Jerzy Kmita would be far more radical in this respect. Neither of these authors has devoted a study to this problem, but both have written a number of works about art, aesthetic objects, aesthetic evaluation, and value. They consistently avoid in their works concepts like "aesthetic experience" and "aesthetic attitude," replacing them with categories like "social practice," "social institution," "axiological preferences," "social hierarchy of values," "rules of cultural interpretation," "artistic conventions," and the like.[34]

Equally strongly, though for different reasons, the belief in the independence of aesthetic evaluation is expressed by Karl Aschenbrenner, who maintains that evaluation and evaluative concepts are not determined by aesthetic experience but, conversely, that the aesthetic responses of the perceiver are determined by the scope and character of the critical concepts that he commands.[35] I believe that there is rather a mutual conditioning. Aschenbrenner is right when he speaks of the conceptual determination of aesthetic expe-

rience, but he does not take into account the conditioning of critical concepts and utterances by aesthetic experience.

The latest tendencies in contemporary art seem to support the
views questioning the relationship between aesthetic evaluation
and aesthetic experience. Representatives of many of the most radical tendencies in contemporary art programmatically attempt to
break with the entire artistic tradition, and they are nearly always
successful. We should not be unduly troubled by the demands and
postulates of the most radical innovators with regard to the response to their works, the more so as some of them protest against
any evaluation of their works. But Fisher's and Graff's considerations deserve attention quite independently of the possible arguments in their defense emerging from the controversial phenomena
of contemporary art. If we abstain from extra-artistic (political, religious, ethical, etc.) evaluations of art and restrict ourselves to
forms in which art is evaluated for its own sake rather than as an
expression of something beyond it, it is difficult not to admit that
the actual use of this kind of evaluation supports to some extent the
considerations of the two authors. But is every evaluation of art
that takes into account its specificity and relative autonomy really
an aesthetic evaluation? A reply to this question was given by
Stanisław Ossowski.

Ossowski on Aesthetic and Artistic Evaluation

A few years before the publication of his *Foundations of Aesthetics*, in an essay called "On the Opposition between Nature and
Art in Aesthetics" (1928), Ossowski stated for the first time that
there are two different kinds of evaluations of aesthetic objects
and two "altogether different" conceptions of aesthetic value. "Objects that aesthetics deals with are in some cases evaluated with regard to the experiences involved in their perception, in others with
regard to the creative effort which gave birth to a given object." [36]
These two conceptions of value and evaluation are confused in actual practice, a confusion that, according to Ossowski, is only partly
justified.

Ossowski believes a certain duality is connected with the concept of value in general, not only in the realm of aesthetic values.
In economics, for example, alongside the concept of the value of
the product is the concept of utility value. The same object can be
evaluated from two points of view, and the results of these two types
of evaluation can be totally different. Likewise, in aesthetic evaluation the genetic aspect (creative effort) and the functional one (the

effect on the perceivers) can be distinguished. "We ascribe a value to objects, either in view of how they arose or in view of what they give us";[37] we evaluate them in the light of their causes (the creator's activity) or their effects (the perceiver's experiences). These "two methods of evaluation in aesthetics might be called, briefly, valuation with respect to beauty and valuation with respect to artistry."[38] Consequently, we must assume the existence of two basic varieties of what we call aesthetic value in the broad sense of the term: the value of the aesthetic object, whose measure is to be found in the aesthetic experiences of the perceiver (this value may characterize both natural phenomena and man-made objects) and the artistic value, measured by the creator's artistry (this value can characterize only man's activity). These two conceptions of value, however, are distinguished neither in popular evaluations nor in theoretical considerations. As a result, according to Ossowski, in contemporary European cultural milieux "aesthetic value" functions as "a collage of concepts," since important co-relations exist between them. The aesthetic experience of the "recipient" is often the test of the fruitfulness of creative effort, and the appreciation of the craftsmanship may enrich and intensify, and sometimes even stimulate, aesthetic experiences.

Thus, the realm of aesthetic values is neither uniform nor homogeneous. It is both possible and necessary to distinguish two different ways of valuing and two distinct types of values: (1) those connected only with art—artistic values; and (2) aesthetic values, proper to all objects, including works of art, evoking aesthetic attitudes and aesthetic experiences. The former are in fact objective in nature, since they are tested by such properties of the work of art as can be established objectively (e.g., originality of conception, degree of technical difficulty, perfection of performance, functionality, faithful reproduction of reality, etc.).[39] The valuation of the work of art with regard to its artistic value does not have to depend on aesthetic experience, though it requires competence and connoisseurship, which do not characterize every "recipient of art." Consequently, we can say, according to Ossowski, that artistic values are aristocratic. On the other hand, aesthetic values are democratic because their only test is aesthetic experience.[40] However, they are not objective but objective-subjective (relational) in nature. They can be reduced neither to the properties of the object nor to the experiences of the subject: they are a result of a definite correlation between certain properties of the object and the experience of the subject.

Ossowski's differentiation of aesthetic values differs from the analogous differentiation made by Ingarden. Ingarden regards aesthetic values as objective, absolute, and nonrelational, and artistic values as objective and relational (instrumental) at the same time. Ossowski, on the other hand, views aesthetic values as relative and relational, and artistic values as relative and objective. Both theoreticians share the conviction that the discovery of artistic values is a more difficult problem demanding high competence on the part of the valuing subject, and that this discovery does not have to be directly connected with aesthetic experience.

An analogous typology of aesthetic values and kinds of evaluation was proposed by Zdzisław Najder. He maintains that two types of values, artistic and experiential, are proper to art.[41] Artistic values are connected with aesthetic objects themselves; they refer to the internal structure of a given work and to its relations with other works representing the art of the past, present, and future. In our considerations of artistic values, we do not use the category of the perceiver at all, and we need no aesthetic experience to appraise this value. When evaluating the work of art we make use only of such categories as "perfection of execution," "technique of performance," "expressiveness of artistic devices," "attitude toward artistic tradition," "innovation," "originality," "forgery," "style," "artistic convention," and "poetics of the genre," judgments that pertain to the artistic values of the work. Experiential values, on the other hand, pertain to relations between the work and its perceivers. In appraising the experiential values of the work of art, aesthetic experience is the basic and necessary condition of all judgments. Here we take into account the richness and intensity of a given experience as a whole and the quality of its particular constitutive components: sensual impressions, emotional experiences (affections, moods, states of tension and consolation), the activity of imagination, and reflection. Najder, like Ossowski, is aware that "both kinds of value are closely interrelated. We apply the criteria of artistic value that we do because we assume that the results of the qualities so chosen will be experientially satisfactory; we evaluate works of art experientially using artistic categories of style, convention, trend, or motif."[42]

Thus, I do not mean to separate these two types of evaluation in the actual valuing of works of art, because to do so is both impossible and unnecessary. In the same way it is very difficult to separate the aesthetic evaluation (in the broad sense) of art from extraaesthetic forms of its evaluation in actual practice. I am concerned with the theoretical awareness of these two interrelated but different types of evaluations and the need to take them into account in theoretical considerations.

Conclusions

If the analysis proposed by Ossowski and Najder is accepted (the elements of this analysis can be found in the works of other authors),[43] then the problem in question will have the following solution. Aesthetic evaluation in the narrow sense proposed by Ossowski is inseparably connected with aesthetic experience, constituting its basis and starting point. Aesthetic evaluation in this sense is not, however, the only form of evaluation that takes account of the specificity of art as a form of creativity and the specificity of its immanent values. Artistic evaluation is of equal importance to art, and it is not alien to its nature. This kind of evaluation need not be connected, though in actual practice it often is, with any aesthetic experiences and may proceed in terms of a purely cognitive attitude. This solution withstands confrontation with actual evaluations of art.

If the aesthetic values of art are to constitute the same class of values as the aesthetic values of nonartistic phenomena (the beauty of nature, man's nonartistic products, and the human body), then we cannot eliminate aesthetic experiences from the process of aesthetic evaluation. Aesthetic experience is somehow *ex definitione* connected with the realm of aesthetic phenomena. Art has always been one of the most important sources of aesthetic experiences, and that is why it has been evaluated from the aesthetic point of view. Despite the significant changes that have occurred in the art of the twentieth century, art as a whole has not ceased to be the source of aesthetic satisfaction for its perceivers; thus, aesthetic evaluation in the narrow sense (in connection with aesthetic experience) continues to be justified. However, it is also true that some acknowledged works of contemporary art do not really provide any aesthetic gratification, or provide it only to very few perceivers, without losing their status as artistic works. That is why Fisher and Graff are not wrong when they maintain that we can and may evaluate the work of art as a work of art, making no reference to aesthetic experiences. It is, however, questionable whether they are right in giving this form of evaluation the name of aesthetic evaluation. I believe that we have only two possibilities here: we can expand our understanding of the concept of "aesthetic phenomena" and "aesthetic evaluation" so much that they will lose their original meaning and specificity, or we can accept the fact that aesthetic values (in the narrow sense proposed by Ossowski) are not the only essential and specific values of art. The acceptance of the latter solution and acknowledgment that the kind of evaluation that Ossowski and Najder call artistic is also possible and justified leads to the recognition that aesthetic evaluation (in the narrow sense) is not the only legitimate way of evaluating art as a specific and relatively autonomous form of creativity.

Notes

1. See David W. Prall, "A Study in the Theory of Value," *University of California Publication in Philosophy* 3 (1921): 217, and *Aesthetic Judgment* (New York, 1929), pp. vi, 5, and 326.

2. Prall was engaged in a controversy with Dewey, who regarded value judgments as value-constituting factors. See David W. Prall, "In Defence of a Worthless Theory of Value," *Journal of Philosophy* 20 (1923): 128–37.

3. Prall, *Aesthetic Judgment*, p. 320.

4. See Mieczysław Wallis, *Przeżycie i wartość* [Experience and Value], (Cracow, 1968), pp. 12–18, 31.

5. John Dewey, *Art as Experience* (New York, 1958); C. I. Lewis, *An Analysis of Knowledge and Valuation* (LaSalle, Ill., 1946), pp. 387 and 407; Stephen C. Pepper, "On the Relation of Philosophy to Art," *Revue Internationale de Philosophie* 18 (1964): 187–88; Thomas Munro, *Toward Science in Aesthetics* (New York, 1956), p. 249; David W. Gotshalk, *Art and the Social Order* (New York, 1962), pp. xiv, 158, 175–76.

6. Lewis, *An Analysis of Knowledge and Valuation*, p. 375; Stephen C. Pepper, "Values and Value Judgments," *Journal of Philosophy* 46 (1949): 429; Arnold Berleant, "The Experience and Judgment of Values," *Journal of Value Inquiry* 1 (1967): 25 and 31, and his *The Aesthetic Field* (Springfield, Ill., 1970), pp. 166–67.

7. John Dewey, "The Objects of Valuation," *Journal of Philosophy* 15 (1918): 256.

8. Dewey, *Art as Experience*, p. 365; see also pp. 145–46.

9. Monroe C. Beardsley, *Aesthetics: Problems in the Philosophy of Criticism* (New York, 1958), p. 531; see also his other works: "The Discrimination of Aesthetic Enjoyment," *British Journal of Aesthetics* 3 (1963): 297; "The Classification of Critical Reasons," *Journal of Aesthetic Education* 2, no. 3 (1968): 62; "Aesthetic Experience Regained," *Journal of Aesthetics and Art Criticism* 28 (1969): 3.

10. Monroe C. Beardsley, "The Aesthetic Point of View," *Metaphilosophy* 1 (1970): 51.

11. Beardsley, "The Aesthetic Point of View," 47; cf. his *The Possibility of Criticism* (Detroit, 1970), pp. 14–15.

12. Beardsley, *The Possibility of Criticism*, p. 80.

13. Ibid., p. 15.

14. Beardsley, "The Classification of Critical Reasons," p. 62.

15. See Roman Ingarden, "Artistic and Aesthetic Values," *British Journal of Aesthetics*, 4, no. 3 (1964): 198–213.

16. Ibid., p. 212; see also Roman Ingarden, "Zasady epistemologicznego rozważania doświadczenia estetycznego" [Principles of Epistemological Consideration of Aesthetic Experience], in *Studia z estetyki*, 3 (1970): 170.

17. Roman Ingarden, "O poznawaniu dzieła literackiego" [On the Cognition of the Literary Work of Art] in *Studia z estetyki*, 3 (1970): 240.

18. Ibid.

19. Roman Ingarden, *The Cognition of the Literary Work of Art* (Evanston, Ill., 1973), pp. 415–16.

20. Cf. pp. 378–81, ibid.; see also "Zasady epistemologicznego rozważania," p. 167.

21. Ingarden, *The Cognition of the Literary Work of Art*, p. 208.

22. Ibid., pp. 208–9.

23. Ingarden, "Uwagi o estetycznym sądzie wartościującym" [Remarks on Aesthetic Value Judgment] in *Studia z estetyki*, 3 : 164.

24. *The Cognition of the Literary Work of Art*, p. 416.

25. Ibid., p. 417.

26. See pp. 322, 378–82, ibid.

27. Cf. Ingarden, "Uwagi o estetycznym sądzie," pp. 155 and 157.

28. Ingarden, *The Cognition of the Literary Work of Art*, p. 378.

29. Ingarden, "Uwagi o estetycznym sądzie," p. 160.

30. John Fisher, "Evaluation without Enjoyment," *Journal of Aesthetics and Art Criticism* 27, no. 2 (1968): 135–39; Piotr Graff, "O rodzajach braku związku między przezyciem estetycznym a oceną estetyczną" [On the Kinds of Lack of Connection between Aesthetic Experience and Aesthetic Evaluation], in *Studia Estetyczne* 7 (1970): 45–54.

31. Fisher, "Evaluation without Enjoyment," p. 139.

32. Graff, "O rodzajach," p. 45.

33. See pp. 45–46, ibid.

34. See George Dickie, *Art and the Aesthetic: An Institutional Analysis* (Ithaca, 1974), in particular chaps. 1, 7, 8; Jerzy Kmita, ed., *Wartość, dzieło, sens: Szkice z filozofii kultury artystycznej* [Value, Work, Sense: Studies in the Philosophy of Artistic Culture] (Warsaw, 1975), pp. 17–36, 119–42, 177–95.

35. See Karl Aschenbrenner, "Conceptual Determination of Aesthetic Experience," *Dialectics and Humanism*, 3, (1976): 107–15.

36. Stanisław Ossowski, "O przeciwieństwie przyrody i sztuki w estetyce" [On the Opposition between Nature and Art in Aesthetics], in *Dzieła*, vol. 4 (Warsaw, 1970), p. 49.

37. Stanisław Ossowski, *The Foundations of Aesthetics* (Warsaw and Dordrecht, 1978), pp. 301–2.

38. Ibid., p. 303.

39. Ibid., pp. 322–23.

40. Ibid., p. 303.

41. Zdzisław Najder, *Value and Evaluations* (Oxford, 1975), pp. 142–43.

42. Ibid., p. 143.

43. I refer here to Joseph Margolis's differentiation between "aesthetic appreciation" and aesthetic evaluation, and the differentiation of two kinds of value judgments: appreciative judgments and evaluative judgments, which he also calls verdicts. In his considerations of aesthetic evaluation, Margolis consciously avoids using the concept of "aesthetic experience," even though it functions in the differentiation he makes. It turns out that in contradistinction to aesthetic evaluations made on the basis of some system of intersubjective criteria (professional critics employ them most often), aesthetic appreciation is inseparably connected with the personal taste and preferences of the perceiver of art and with the aesthetic enjoyment he experiences. See Joseph Margolis, *The Language of Art and Art Criticism* (Detroit, 1965), pp. 127–29, 139–41.

5

Kant on Experiencing Beauty

STEPHEN BARKER

Kant's *Critique of Judgment* is the third and final work of the triad that constitute the main pillars of his philosophical system. Less often read and studied than the *Critique of Pure Reason* or the *Critique of Practical Reason*, the *Critique of Judgment* is nevertheless the culminating work of these three, mediating between its two predecessors and moderating the starkness of the contrast they pose between the mechanistic world of our sensory knowledge and the suprasensible realm to which as free agents we must suppose that we belong. The *Critique of Judgment* also covers much new ground in a new way, dealing with human appreciation of the beautiful and the sublime in its first half ("the critique of taste") and in the second half dealing with what Kant takes to be our inevitable viewing of natural phenomena as purposive ("the critique of teleological judgment").

Even if the *Critique of Judgment* is generally not as well known or as well understood as are Kant's earlier *Critiques*, its suggestive richness and its historical importance have been recognized by attentive readers. Thus, for example, Monroe Beardsley, referring to the first half of the *Critique of Judgment*, speaks of it as containing an aesthetic theory "which, in its originality, subtlety, and comprehensiveness, would mark a turning point in this field."[1] In spite of the great philosophical interest of this work, however, there is much in it that is puzzling and cryptic and cries out for interpretive explanation. I believe this is especially true of the intriguing but elusive theory about the experiencing of beauty that Kant advocates as a basis for his answer to the problem of objectivity. In this paper I want to draw attention to the theory's need for interpretive explanation and, following out a suggestion of Beardsley's, to propose an account of what it means, which I hope may help toward filling this need. I shall not be trying to defend Kant's theory or to criticize it, but only to suggest a way of understanding what it is.

The Antinomy of Taste

Prominent among the philosophical problems with which Kant deals in the first half of the third *Critique* is the problem of objectivity: to what extent can judgments of taste be objectively valid for all persons? (For brevity, let us concentrate upon judgments concerning beauty, and neglect the sublime.) In Kant's exposition the question of objectivity is presented in the form of "the antinomy of taste,"[2] a seeming contradiction between two opposing opinions of ours (a "thesis" and an "antithesis") concerning the status of judgments of taste.

Kant's rather crabbed way of stating the thesis is: "The judgment of taste is not based upon concepts." What he is getting at, I think, is that judgments about what is and what is not beautiful cannot state known truths about matters of fact. And this seems to imply that there is no objective truth about what is beautiful; if one person regards an object as beautiful and another person regards it as not beautiful, it looks as though neither appraisal can be any more correct or more mistaken than the other. In support of this thesis, Kant insists that no judgment concerning beauty can ever be proven to be correct or incorrect ("There is no disputing about taste"). That is, no matter how much factual truth one accumulates concerning an object, nothing logically follows as to whether the object is beautiful or not.

On the other hand, as "antithesis" of the antinomy, Kant puts forward the opposing view that the judgment of taste *is* based on concepts. Here, what he is getting at, I believe, is that in making judgments about what is beautiful we do claim objectivity, and we think it legitimate to do so. We who make such judgments seriously cannot regard them as merely subjective and arbitrary. In support of the antithesis, Kant emphasizes the difference between "This is beautiful" (a judgment of taste) and "I happen to like this" (a judgment of inclination); in making the former judgment, but not the latter, one is affirming that others are somehow mistaken if they disagree with the appraisal being expressed.

This antinomy of Kant's embodies vividly one of the most vexed and controversial problems of philosophical aesthetics, a problem that has continued to be of very active concern for twentieth-century thinkers, as it was for philosophers of the past. In more recent times, lesser thinkers than Kant have usually taken a short cut through the antinomy by flatly denying one side or the other. Kant's philosophy of aesthetics gains much of its special interest, I think, from his unwillingness to dismiss either side. For him the antinomy is a serious one in which each side is to be taken seriously. Kant thinks that what is needed here (as with the Antinomies of Pure Reason) is a way of resolving the conflict that does justice to both sides. Each side must be seen as having a sound point to make, even if its way of making its point is one-sided and misleading.

In his resolution of the antinomy, Kant endorses the thesis to the extent of saying that judgments of taste are not based on any *definite* concepts, the way judgments in mathematics, natural science, and ethics are. In those areas, Kant holds that strict proof is possible and objectivity in a strong sense is available. At the same time, he endorses the antithesis to the extent of saying that judgments of taste can have a legitimate, though different, kind of objectivity. In his jargon, the judgment of taste *is* based on a concept, but on an *indefinite* concept (elsewhere, he speaks of an *inexponible* idea).[3]

What can this mean? Setting aside for the moment the jargon about concepts, we can explain the gist of Kant's answer as follows. Judgments about beauty are judgments that we humans make because of a special kind of functioning of two of our cognitive faculties, imagination and understanding, and these only. One is entitled to presume (though one cannot prove) that all human beings have the same kind of cognitive faculties. Therefore, it is legitimate to assume that all humans must in principle be able to reach agreement in their judgments concerning beauty. The agreement will not be achievable through proofs, logically compelling our assent as to what is beautiful and what is not. No proofs are possible. But we may presume that agreement is in principle achievable because all human beings have the same kind of cognitive faculties, and all of us should respond in the same way to any given work of art or natural phenomenon—provided each of us allows his imagination and understanding to function in this special way, undisturbed by other tendencies of the mind. That is, provided each of us attends to the object with a purely aesthetic attitude.

In calling something beautiful, one is claiming to be appraising it from the purely aesthetic attitude, but one can be mistaken about one's own attitude. According to Kant's doctrine, disagreements about beauty, where they arise, must always result from undetected (but detectable) impurity in our attitudes. For example, suppose that one person sees a snake and judges it to be ugly, while another person sees the snake and judges it to be beautiful. The explanation of the disagreement may well be that the first person has mistakenly allowed his aesthetic judgment to be contaminated by his fear of the snake, whereas the second person has adopted a purely aesthetic attitude in his contemplation of the complex, irridescent patterns of the reptile's skin—he has abstracted from all consideration of the harm or benefit associated with the object, and so has achieved a properly aesthetic appraisal of it.

The aesthetic attitude, according to Kant, is an attitude of *disinterested* contemplation of the patterns of our sense experience.[4] Here, disinterestedness involves setting aside all interests: everything that pertains to the volitional part of human nature, which Kant variously speaks of as appetite, inclination, or desire. We abstract from all our desires for or against the existence of the object, from all our concerns about how it can thwart or satisfy our desires. To *cultivate* one's taste is above all to learn to do this ("That taste always is barbaric which needs a mixture of *charms* and *emotions*," he says;[5] and he points out that art can present as beautiful even things that from a practical standpoint are displeasing or horrible).[6] In principle, we are able to learn to perform this abstraction. Therefore, it is proper to presume agreement in principle about beauty among all human observers, because the only faculties then operative in forming the appraisal of beauty will be cognitive faculties common to us all, which operate in the same way in all of us.

The Problem

This sketch of Kant's way of dealing with the question of objectivity leaves much unexplained. Above all, what is to be his theory of the special functioning of human cognitive faculties that supposedly occurs when we disinterestedly reflect upon beautiful things? In his account of the matter, what Kant tells us is that in experiencing beautiful objects, our cognitive powers are "in free play,"[7] which somehow is related to the "form" of the object rather than to its sensuous "content." This "free play" can lead to a "harmony" between the imagination and the understanding,[8] which provides "entertainment of the mental powers"[9] and yields disinterested pleasure.

These points are deeply suggestive, but they do not provide a clear description of what is supposed to be going on. What sort of "free play" is this? Surely not just any kind of day-dreaming or woolgathering will do. It must be a definite mental process, and we need more of a description of what it is. But how does calling it "play" help at all, when (as Beardsley has pointed out)[10] the experience of play does not seem essentially to involve the presence of unity, dominant pattern, and consummation—traits that are essential to aesthetic experience? Furthermore, why should this kind of imaginative activity, whatever it is, be more pleasurable than other uses of our cognitive faculties? The pleasure is supposed to result from "harmony" between the imagination and the understanding, but what can this mean? How can two different faculties harmonize or clash? It is not obvious how the notions of play, pleasure, and harmony are supposed to be interrelated. Each of the various things Kant says is suggestive in an impressive way, but he gives us too little help in understanding his points and in seeing how they are related to one another.

Here it would be helpful to our understanding and appreciation of Kant's position if we could have an interpretation of what he is trying to say. We need a plausible hypothesis about the meaning of his cryptic remarks, one that would spell out what is supposed to be going on when human beings experience beauty. It would be desirable here to have an interpretation that goes beyond Kant's own cryptic words and proposes a way of understanding his viewpoint so as to interrelate the various things he says.

Have commentators on Kant's philosophy already provided such an interpretation? A number of scholars have worked seriously on the *Critique of Judgment* and shed light on many aspects of it. In English alone there are books by H. W. Cassirer, Theodore Uehling, D. W. Crawford, Paul Guyer, and others.[11] These and other available treatments of Kant's aesthetic theory have much to tell us that is relevant and solidly helpful. I think, however, that they do not offer as much as one would like to have on the particular problem just referred to.

In this paper, I shall try to propose a solution to this problem by suggesting an interpretation of what may lie behind Kant's cryptic words. In developing this interpretation, I want to try to follow out a suggestion that I think is implicit in Beardsley's statement of the matter. Writing of Kant's account of the enjoyment of beauty, Beardsley refers to understanding and imagination as "idling, so to speak, not seriously directed to the pursuit of knowledge"; and he writes that "these faculties can play at knowledge, in a sense, enjoying the harmony between them without being tied down or biased by particular sense-intuitions or particular concepts." Under these circumstances, Beardsley writes, there arises pleasure in the harmony of these two cognitive faculties.[12] I believe that Beardsley's formulation that the faculties "play at knowledge" points in a helpful direction. His brief account can, I think, be expanded into a solution of our problem. In the later part of this paper I shall try to propose that solution. But first there is need for more discussion of the background of our problem in Kant's thought.

Determinant Judgment

In order to approach our problem, we need to consider Kant's views about the logical character of judgments. He introduces the term "determinant" to describe those judgments that are "based on definite concepts."[13] He seems to hold that in all those areas of human experience where knowledge is attainable, knowledge is formulated in "determinant" judgments. This includes theoretical knowledge (knowledge of what is the case), which belongs to mathematics and natural science; and it also includes practical knowledge (knowledge of what ought to be the case), which belongs to ethics. A determinant judgment, he says, is one in which a concept is antecedently available and a particular is subsumed under it. This way of putting the matter is stiff and awkward, but leaving out some of the complications (and skirting the controversies that can quickly arise), I think it can be interpreted along the following lines.

It is in the simplest type of a determinant judgment that a particular phenomenon is subsumed under a general concept. Thus, for example, when I judge that something before me is a circle and that something else is a dog, what I am doing is subsuming the phenomena under the concepts of the circle and the canine, respectively. Other, more complex kinds of judgments would have to be explained in relation to this simple paradigm.

But what is it to subsume a particular phenomenon under a concept? Kant seems to hold that to have a concept is to know a definition (we might also say a general rule, or criterion) establishing the necessary and sufficient conditions for a thing to be of the given kind. My concept of the circle is perhaps that of a closed plane figure, all points of which are equidistant from some one point in the plane. Here the definition provides a general rule for identifying circles when one encounters them. When I grasp that this rule applies to the shape before me, I am subsuming the phenomenon under the concept of the circle. Or, again, my concept of the canine perhaps is that of a four-legged, barking animal. Here too I have a definitional rule for identifying instances. If I experience the phenomenon before me as an animal, as four-legged, and as barking, then I shall judge that it fits my criterion; that is, I subsume it under the concept of the canine.

If having a concept is understood as the possession of a definitional rule of this kind, then Kant seems to be supposing that it will
always be possible in principle to give a proof that a particular thing
is of the given kind. To prove that the shape before me is a circle, I
need only verify that it fully satisfies the rule. Here the proof can be
codified in deductive form: "All and only those closed plane figures,
every point of which is equidistant from a given point in the plane,
are circles; this is a closed plane figure, every point of which is equidistant from a given point in the plane; therefore, this is a circle."
In this way, I think, Kant's notion of what it is to have a definite
concept is connected with his deductivistic notion of provability.
What is deductively provable can genuinely be known, he seems
to suppose.

However, for Kant the understanding is the faculty that deals
with concepts, considered as abstract rules. The minor premise of
the above syllogism cannot be verified merely by the understanding;
something more is needed. For a concept to be employable in human knowing, the conditions stipulated in the definitional rule must
be ones that connect with our sense experience ("Thoughts without
content are empty, intuitions without concepts are blind").[14] Here is
where the faculty of imagination comes in. Imagination is the faculty that is supposed to mediate between understanding and sensibility by organizing sensory material and connecting it with concepts. The point is that one must have a regular way of imagining
(sensuously representing—visually or otherwise) points and same-
ness of length if one is to be able to apply that definition of the
circle. The rule by which the imagination operates, Kant calls a
"schema" of the imagination ("This representation of a universal
procedure of imagination in providing an image for a concept, I
entitle the schema of this concept").[15] The schema that goes with
the concept of the circle is comparatively straightforward, but the
schema for the concept of dog would be more complex, for it must
include, among other components, a regular way of imagining
barking and legs. These leave leeway for the imagination, since barking can be loud or soft, high- or low-pitched, and so on; legs can be
short or long, fat or thin. The schema has to be a complex rule for the
imagination, prescribing just how much leeway is allowed.[16]

The faculty of imagination is at work when the mind sets itself
to imagine an instance of a concept (e.g., when one imagines a circle); here the imagination synthesizes a mental image in which sensory qualities are combined in a form conforming with the definitional rule of the concept. The imagination is also at work in
the recognition of phenomena encountered in experience; here

the imagination presumably must run through the schema to tell whether the form of the encountered phenomenon measures up to the definitional requirement. Moreover, our sensations of a concrete thing are typically very incomplete (e.g., one visually senses only part of the outer surface of the dog), and imagination, working in a largely unconscious manner, must synthesize further images to augment these (so that one's experience becomes that of perceiving a solid creature that has a far side and insides). In this activity, the imagination is guided throughout by definite rules of schematism, laid down ahead of time; these rules strictly limit how much leeway, if any, the imagination is to be permitted in its operations of synthesizing images.

Reflective Judgment

In the *Critique of Judgment*, Kant reveals a doctrine that he had not hinted at in his earlier works: not all judgment is determinate; there is another type of judgment, "reflective" judgment.[17] In reflective judgment, one does not have a definite concept under which one decisively subsumes particular phenomena. Instead, one encounters particular phenomena and tentatively *seeks* a concept (a rule, a regularity) under which to subsume them.

Kant never explicitly connects his contrast between determinant and reflective judgment with the distinction between deductive reasoning and inductive reasoning (his philosophy of logic discourages this, by viewing all reasoning as deductive). Yet his characterizations of the two forms of judgment do present them as very like deduction and induction, respectively. With determinant judgment, one has a definitional schema for a concept, one finds phenomena conforming to the schema, and so one judges (or deductively infers) that the phenomena fall under the concept. With reflective judgment, one encounters phenomena, one imaginatively constructs some rule to which they conform, and one judges (or inductively infers) that this may perhaps be the rule really governing them.

Some additional indication of Kant's view of reflective judgment is provided by his account of how thinking proceeds in the empirical part of natural science (we might call such thinking inductive reasoning, though Kant, for his own reasons, does not call it that). With regard to theoretical knowledge, Kant holds that our minds impose upon nature certain laws (of mathematics and of the metaphysics of nature), and these we can know *a priori* because their origin lies in ourselves. But the rest of our knowledge of nature pertains to aspects of it that are not up to us, and we have to arrive empirically at knowledge of these aspects. Kant holds that reasoning in the empirical part of natural science has to employ the notions of parsimony, continuity, and simplicity.[18] In his search for empirical laws, the natural scientist has to proceed *as if* nature tended to be simple, continuous, and parsimonious in its workings. Only by doing so will he have guidelines to direct his choice among competing hypotheses. In scientific investigation, the data collected up to any given moment are always logically consistent with many conflicting hypotheses; scientific thinking would be paralyzed if it had no guidelines for choosing among all these hypotheses. And Kant thinks that to regard the natural world as tending toward simplicity is to regard it as designed by a supernatural being who planned and created it.

When something is in every respect under the control of an intelligent creator, what character will he impose upon it? Kant holds that an intelligent creator, if his creative power is absolute, must be expected to produce an *organic whole* as his creation—a whole, every element of which mirrors the structure of the rest, combining simplicity with diversity in a pattern of maximum coherent articulation (this idea of the character of an organic whole probably comes to Kant from Leibniz).[19] Parsimony and continuity will be aspects of this sort of organic whole.

The upshot is that the natural scientist must regard nature as if it were an organic whole, created by an all-powerful Intelligence. The empirical patterns of laws of nature must be seen as manifesting the purposes of the Being; only in this way can scientific thinking proceed in the empirical realm. This way of thinking involves reflective judgment. Reflective judgment is the mental activity of conjecturing general rules to fit particular phenomena one observes, and these conjectures are framed through regarding the phenomena as if they belonged to an organic system, intelligently designed.

Now, in our viewing of nature, we find some phenomena that we can know to be purposive (e.g., clocks, which we discover are always made by clockmakers for the purpose of telling time); but with the vast majority of phenomena (e.g., the motions of the planets, the eruptions of volcanoes, the growth of a blade of grass), we cannot verify that they are designed by any intelligence, nor can we know what purposes they serve, if they are designed by anyone. Yet we must regard them *as if* they were designed, through and through, even though we cannot know that this is so. Hence, reflective judgment involves what Kant calls "purposiveness without a purpose": purposiveness, in that phenomena are to be viewed as thoroughly organized by intelligent design; but without a purpose, in that we cannot know what purposes, if any, they really do serve.[20]

From the standpoint of scientific investigation, all of nature has to be viewed as if purposive; but in the natural world some particular phenomena more urgently demand to be viewed in this way than others do. This is because some phenomena display especially strongly the character of *self-contained* organic wholes. This purposiveness is a sort of *Gestalt* quality that we find in the structure of these phenomena: they are wholes whose elements fit together in an inexhaustibly rich pattern of unity in diversity. One group of such phenomena are living organisms (plants, animals). In them, all the parts have to be regarded as serving the needs of the whole organism. In a plant, for instance, the roots must be viewed as there in order to gather moisture and nourishment, the leaves in order to collect sunshine, and so on. The second group of self-contained organic phenomena that we encounter are works of art and beauties of nature. Works of art and beauties of nature display the thorough-going interrelationship of elements that is characteristic of organic wholes, each part having to be regarded as being the way it is in order to contribute to the whole effect. With a fine work of art, the organized structure outruns anything the human artist was consciously aware of as he created it: he was inspired by genius, "an innate mental disposition, through which nature gives the rule to art."[21]

Notice that these two classes of phenomena overlap: some organisms are beauties of nature. In these cases, one and the same phenomenon can be regarded teleologically (from a scientific standpoint) or aesthetically (from the standpoint of taste). Kant's example is a flower.[22] The botanist must regard the parts of the flower as functioning as (i.e., having been intelligently designed as) organs of reproduction; he makes teleological judgments about the flower, and does not get aesthetic pleasure from doing so.[23] An observer appreciating the beauty of the flower regards its shape and its pattern of color as exhibiting systematic interrelationships that must be regarded as having functions (i.e., as intelligently designed), but to which he cannot assign any definite functions—yet contemplating them pleases him.

In his resolution of the antinomy of taste, Kant holds that judgments of taste are reflective judgments. Unlike determinant judgments, they do not subsume particular cases under definite concepts, but they do, so to speak, subsume them under an "indefinite" concept, that of purposiveness without a purpose. This is a concept lacking any definite schema to govern the imagination.

Clues to an Interpretation

In pursing an interpretation of Kant's theory of the functioning of imagination and understanding in the appreciation of beauty, we must go beyond the background considerations discussed so far. There are four further clues, attention to which may be helpful.

1. When Kant talks about what goes on in the appreciation of beauty, his words indicate that he thinks it is some kind of on-going *process*. It seems to be more of a process than ordinary examples of determinant judgment are. Ordinary examples of determinant judgment usually seem to occur in a flash: experiencing a phenomenon, one instantly judges it to be a circle or a dog. The mental process of running through the schema and checking that the phenomenon at hand fully conforms to it occupies very little time. In contrast, in the experiencing of a beautiful object, Kant seems to think that the mind dwells on it in a prolonged process of reflection, tracing more and more of the formal aspects of the object. "We *linger*," he says, "over the contemplation of the beautiful because this contemplation strengthens and reproduces itself."[24]

2. Kant describes the experiencing of beauty as involving the *play* of the imagination in relation to the understanding. Somehow he wishes to contrast the experiencing of beauty with the workaday employment of the mind in determinant judgment. There is something playful, spontaneous, and free in the former, in contrast with the sober, earnest rigidity of the latter. However, not all free play of the imagination leads to the experience of beauty. Kant mentions a fire on the hearth and a rippling brook as phenomena that the imagination may take as starting points for its reverie.[25] Such phenomena have charm for the imagination but need not be beautiful. Therefore, we must suppose that beauty involves some special kind of play of the imagination. To speak of play here suggests that there is some kind of game that the mind engages in. Now, the better sort of games are activities governed by rules of play but allowing the players scope for ingenuity and self-expression in their pursuit of the goal of the game. In appreciating beauty, the mind seems to be engaging in some rather special and quite excellent kind of game.

3. Kant states that *pleasure* is essentially involved in the experiencing of beauty. But because the pleasure of contemplating beautiful things is disinterested, it cannot result from the satisfaction of any of our desires: neither our subjective appetites (hunger, thirst, etc.) nor our rational desire for moral betterment. The disinterested aesthetic attitude involves abstracting from all that. So how does it arise?

It might be suggested that Kant regards this pleasure as simply arising from the exercise of our cognitive faculties, especially the imagination. Here the idea would be that using one's faculties is, per se, pleasurable. No doubt there is something in this idea, but it is quite inadequate as an explanation of the pleasure we take in beauty, for Kant certainly does not think that use of the cognitive faculties in general gives the special joy that comes from the contemplation of beautiful things. It is clear that he does not believe that we derive this special joy from making determinant judgments or teleological judgments. Why then should arriving at judgments of taste be pleasurable in a special way?

A deeper suggestion might be that beautiful objects seem to have been designed expressly to mesh with our cognitive faculties, and this gives us pleasure because it suggests to us that mankind is not alone in the universe. The suggestion would be that we take comfort in encountering hints of the presence of an Intelligence who controls the universe and heeds our needs. Perhaps the source of the pleasure would be the hinted confirmation of the moral postulate of the existence of God. Or perhaps the pleasure comes in a more generalized way from the satisfyingness of friendly encounter, as "spirit greets spirit,"[26] counteracting the metaphysical homelessness that we might otherwise feel. However, this suggestion will not do either as an explanation of the pleasure associated with beauty. Teleological judgment (e.g., viewing the flower as an organ of reproduction) gives us as strong a hint as beauty does that we are in some kind of touch with an Intelligence who designs things for the best. Yet teleological judgment lacks the special pleasure associated with beauty.

Here the answer would seem to be that pleasure will arise from a cognitive activity when a difficult challenge has been posed, voluntarily accepted, and successfully met. The challenge must be of a sort that one does not always succeed in meeting. The achievement, then, comes as something of a happy surprise. Intellectual puzzle games have this character of voluntarily accepted challenge—provided they are difficult enough so one is aware ahead of time that one may fail to find the solution. I believe Kant supposes that determinant judgment and teleological judgment do not pose challenges for us; they are more cut-and-dried cognitive activities, whose challenge the mind does not voluntarily accept and in which success is reliably assured, with no surprises in store. But in our reflection upon beautiful things, the pleasure we feel must result from our having succeeded, somewhat contrary to expectation, in achieving the special goals set by the game of aesthetic reflection in which we have voluntarily become involved.

4. Some works of art Kant dismisses as lacking in "spirit."[27] These have little beauty; that is, they cannot be aesthetically contemplated with much pleasure. What is it about some objects that leads Kant to stigmatize them in this way? Chiefly, I think, they are insipid because they are too *regular* in their form; their structure too much follows rules of a simple kind. Kant says that "all stiff regularity is repugnant to taste."[28] And elsewhere he says that fine art "must seem to be as free from all constraint of arbitrary rules as if it were a product of mere nature."[29] Works of art lacking in spirit have structure that too much follows rules that are easy for the observer to detect. They contain no surprises. With such an object, a little reflection enables the observer to detect reliably how the structure is going to unfold, and this somehow destroys aesthetic satisfaction.

"Free Play" as a Game of Inductive Projection

Assembling these clues, and remembering Beardsley's suggestion about the cognitive faculties' "playing at knowledge," I think we can press on to formulate an interpretation of Kant's theory about the experiencing of beauty.

When one is confronted with a phenomenon, one's cognitive faculties naturally will tend to do cognitive things. They strive to find order in the phenomenon. They will subsume it under a definite concept or general law, if they can. But suppose that the phenomenon is a sunset or a symphony, and one has voluntarily chosen to view it disinterestedly (abstracting from all desires) and to contemplate its sensory aspect (setting aside scientific inquiries about its physical causes). One inspects the pattern of colors or sounds, seeking to grasp its structure. Then one quickly finds that one possesses no definite concept that can provide, in the way that is wanted, a rule for grasping the structure in the elements of the phenomenon. To be sure, one has the concept of the sunset, and the concept of the symphony, and the phenomena do conform to the respective schemata for these concepts (to judge that this is a sunset or that a symphony is to make a determinant judgment). But the concept in no way provides any rule telling why this particularly superb sunset has just this distinctive pattern of color harmonies; nor does the concept of the symphony tell us why Beethoven's Fifth sounds exactly as it does—and that is what one is reflecting about, at this point. Kant's position is that with organized phenomena such as beauties of nature or high-quality works of art, determinant judgment is swiftly and conclusively defeated in its attempt to cognize the "why" of the detailed interrelations of the elements.[30]

What, then, can one's cognitive faculties do when definite concepts fail? Even though the mind cannot spell out any definite law or rule to cover the interrelationships of the elements of the sunset, the imagination is not defeated. It goes ahead without the guidance of any definite concept of the understanding. What it does is to try to build up, step by step, an *indefinite* (or "inexponible") concept of the structure of the phenomenon. That is, it tries to develop a "feel" for how this organized phenomenon is put together, even though this feel cannot be conceptually articulated.

As we noted earlier, Kant supposes that when one experiences a concrete object, one's imagination is continually forming images of portions or aspects of the object that one has not yet inspected. Similarly, when one reflects upon a natural beauty or a work of art, one's imagination must be framing images of aspects as yet unscrutinized (there is always more to such an object than one can exhaustively sense at one time). In imagining the as yet unsensed, or as yet insufficiently sensed, portions of the object and how they are related to what has been sensed so far, the imagination has no firm guidance; there is no definite schema that it must obey; it is on its own. It must frame images, hoping that they will turn out to be correct ones. The game it has to play is a game of inductive projection in dealing with the sequence of awarenesses: guessing, from the character of what has been sensed, the character of that which has not yet been sensed. It is a cognitive game, played inarticulately and largely at an unconscious level.

As one's disinterested reflective contemplation of the organized object proceeds, one tests step by step whether one's developing feel for how it is put together is working out correctly. Do the similarities and differences that one has imagined to exist among the elements of the whole actually turn out to be there? In framing its conjectures, the imagination is guided by the indefinite conception of the purposiveness of an organic whole: unity in diversity, and so on. This guideline gives the imagination leeway, not just within definitely prescribed limits, but without any rigid limits whatever.

Both natural and artificial phenomena, and both living and nonliving phenomena, can be suitable objects for this contemplative game. But of course some phenomena turn out to be more rewarding than others. Some phenomena have too boring a structure; one quickly gets the feel of how they are put together, and it then becomes uninteresting to continue with further reflection because there is too little cognitive challenge. Some other phenomena are too intricate in their structure; viewers cannot make head or tail of them—that is, can make little headway toward getting the feel of their formal structure. Such things are not aesthetically satisfactory either. Still other phenomena exhibit a negative kind of purposiveness in their form: through gross disproportions or clashing tonal contrasts, they appear as if designed to defeat the mind's contemplative expectations when it surveys them in step-by-step fashion. These we deem ugly.

The best and most aesthetically satisfying objects will be those in the contemplation of which the human observer[31] can make considerable headway toward getting the feel of how they are put together, although his efforts never totally succeed. An object of great beauty will pose an inexhaustible cognitive challenge—an eternal puzzle—to the imagination; but it will be a challenge that the human imagination is capable of making great progress toward solving. Yet as one solves the initial stages of the puzzle, getting much of the feel of the object, additional puzzling aspects emerge to challenge one further.

Here, then, I think, is what Kant may have meant by his talk of "harmony" between the faculties. Awareness of harmony arises when the imagination's projections are subsequently confirmed by further scrutiny of the object, such scrutiny being conducted under the aegis of the understanding. Thus, for example, after hearing a slow movement of music, the imagination may expect to hear a brisk one; when the *presto* comes, understanding verifies (by a determinant judgment) that this is indeed a fast movement. The understanding's determinant judgments as to what the objective facts are about the music thus harmonize with (that is, confirm) what the imagination had projected ahead of time. This gives pleasure because it indicates that the mind is succeeding, to this extent, in its self-imposed and voluntarily undertaken cognitive game of trying to get the feel of the phenomenon.

Notes

1. Monroe C. Beardsley, *Aesthetics from Classical Greece to the Present: A Short History* (New York, 1966), p. 210.

2. *Critique of Judgment* (hereafter *CJ*), section 56. In J. H. Bernard's translation (New York, 1951), this is on pp. 183–84.

3. *CJ*, section 57, Remark 1; Bernard, p. 187. Kant's account of the resolution of the antinomy must be read in light of his "Transcendental Deduction of Judgments of Taste," *CJ*, section 38; Bernard, p. 132.

4. CJ, section 2; Bernard, pp. 38–39.

5. CJ, section 13; Bernard, p. 58.

6. CJ, section 48; Bernard, p. 155.

7. CJ, section 9; Bernard, p. 52.

8. CJ, section 35; Bernard, p. 129.

9. CJ, section 22; Bernard, p. 79.

10. Monroe C. Beardsley, *Aesthetics: Problems in the Philosophy of Criticism* (New York, 1958), p. 530.

11. H. W. Cassirer, *A Commentary on Kant's Critique of Judgment* (London, 1938); Theodore E. Uehling, Jr., *The Notion of Form in Kant's Critique of Aesthetic Judgment* (The Hague, 1971); Donald W. Crawford, *Kant's Aesthetic Theory* (Madison, 1974); Paul Guyer, *Kant and the Claims of Taste* (Cambridge, Mass., 1979).

12. Beardsley, *Aesthetics from Classical Greece to the Present*, p. 216.

13. CJ, Introduction, section IV; Bernard, p. 15. In this passage, Kant seems to say that determinant judgment only subsumes under universal transcendental laws, but I think it makes better sense to disregard this wording in favor of the view that there can also be empirical determinant judgments in which particulars are subsumed under empirical concepts or laws.

14. *Critique of Pure Reason*, A 51 (= B 75). The translation is that of Norman Kemp Smith (New York, 1929).

15. *Critique of Pure Reason*, A 140 (= B 179). A helpful discussion of Kant's doctrine of schematism is found in Robert Paul Wolff's *Kant's Theory of Mental Activity* (Cambridge, Mass., 1963), pp. 206–23.

16. The notion that all or most ordinary concepts are "open" concepts, so important to Wittgenstein's later thought, certainly did not occur to Kant. Kant, I believe, regards ordinary schematized concepts as always completely definite.

17. CJ, Introduction, section IV; Bernard, p. 16. One might well question the defensibility of Kant's distinction between the two types of judgment, as Frederick P. van de Pitte does in his "Is Kant's Distinction between Reflective and Determinant Judgment Valid?" in Gerhard Funke, ed., *Acten des 4. Internationalen Kant-Kongresses* (Berlin, 1974).

18. CJ, Introduction, section V; Bernard, p. 18. Compare *Critique of Pure Reason*, A 650–63 (= B 678–91).

19. A good discussion of this is found in Lewis White Beck's *Early German Philosophy* (Cambridge, Mass., 1969), pp. 226–27.

20. Beardsley formulates this as "purposeless purposiveness" in his *Aesthetics from Classical Greece to the Present*, p. 216. But that, I think, makes Kant's phrase too nearly self-contradictory. There is lack of purpose only in the sense that we cannot know the purpose; we are not to suppose that there is none, let alone that we know there is none.

21. CJ, section 46; Bernard, p. 150.

22. CJ, section 16; Bernard, p. 65.

23. CJ, Introduction, section VI; Bernard, p. 29.

24. CJ, section 12; Bernard, p. 58.

25. CJ, section 22, General Remark; Bernard, p. 81.

26. If we permit ourselves this Hegelian formulation, it must be with the reservation that in Kant's view we cannot verify, and so cannot know, whether we are really greeting Spirit.

27. CJ, section 49; Bernard, p. 157.

28. CJ, section 22, General Remark; Bernard, p. 80.

29. CJ, section 45. Bernard, p. 149.

30. Kant is, of course, committed to denying in principle that there could ever be any complete reductive explanation of organic structures in terms of mechanical ones. Neither judgments of taste nor teleological judgments could be analyzed into mechanistic judgments.

31. Note that, for Kant, pure intelligences (e.g., God) cannot be expected to agree with us about what is beautiful, as their mental faculties would be unlike ours. God lacks imagination and does not find anything beautiful. See CJ, section 29, General Remark; Bernard, p. 111.

6

Beardsley on Aesthetic Experience

JOHN FISHER

What a wise man says is not likely to be nonsense.
Plato, *Theaetetus*

Some time ago, in the midst of one of those now all too rare quintessential collegial exchanges, I said to Monroe Beardsley, "I have often wondered why you haven't written more on aesthetic experience." His reply was, "I have written a good deal about aesthetic experience. You know how central it is to my aesthetics." But we were not disputing. I was wishing that he had elaborated more on some of the puzzles generated by his writing about aesthetic experience. He was citing the surely certifiable fact that he had written a great deal about aesthetic experience, a concept indeed central to his aesthetics. His essay "Aesthetic Experience Regained" is a classic response to criticism.[1] The term "aesthetic experience" appears repeatedly in most of his works. One cannot claim to have understood his aesthetics without coming to grips with aesthetic experience. I am neither Beardsley's disciple nor his detractor on this issue, but one who, like him, against the stream, believes in the usefulness of the maligned concept of experience in aesthetic theory, in spite of its evasiveness to easy analyses. If, as Whitehead once remarked, "experience" is the most deceitful word in philosophy, how much more so when used in aesthetics.

In "Aesthetic Experience Regained" Beardsley hoped to rehabilitate a concept that had lost its respectability in sophisticated circles. If he failed there, there is little chance that my remarks here will return the accused to a useful place in the society of respectable ideas. What I hope for in this essay, which honors a man in the only way a scholar can really be honored, by the open consideration and critical assessment of his ideas, is for us to take an unbiased look at the concept of aesthetic experience, and neither prematurely run it up the flagpole and salute it nor, to mix the metaphors, try to nail down the coffin lid.

There is a famous fresco of Saint Augustine by Botticelli in Florence. It contains, among other things, the representation of a book. From a distance, and from below, the ordinary observer perceives that the book contains words. It certainly looks that way. Observers knowledgeable in the techniques of painting and those who take a closer look perceive that they are not words, but squiggles to convey the illusion of words. Those who take an even closer look are sometimes startled to discover a few words, a partial sentence, among the squiggles (it says something like "and when you go outside the Porta al Prato . . ."). It is an embarrassingly crude analogy, but I sense that students and first readers take Beardsley's notion of aesthetic experience for what it claims to be: a clear contribution to the understanding and evaluation of aesthetic objects. Through the years the scrutinizing skeptics have unrelentingly argued that when you look at it closely, it does not make sense. I propose to look again, more closely, and see whether the critics' position is really that secure—whether perhaps the squiggles will yield something positive and declarative. I shall not dispute for a moment, however, that, come what may, some squiggles remain.

The incentive for considering a category of experience that singles out a special response to artworks is understandable. If I say that the performance was outrageously bad because I was looking at the violinist's unshined shoes, you will rightly call my attention to what I should have been perceptively tuned to. If I "ooh!" and "ah!" over a nondescript painting because it has just knocked down two million dollars at the auction, you tell me that my appreciation is economic, not aesthetic. If I have chills and thrills listening to a performance of Buxtehude on the old organ of St. Johanniskirche in Lüneburg because I am thinking that those sounds (with the exception of those from the Rückwerke) are the same sounds that J. S. Bach produced on that very instrument when he was a student, you say my response is historical or sentimental and my experience not aesthetic. Some people who would never attend an opera in New York, people who switch stations when an operatic aria is heard on their favorite radio station, travel thousands of miles at great expense to rural Sussex to see Verdi or Rossini performed in an uncomfortable little theater and marvel at the performances' incredible aesthetic qualities, a marvel that, I suspect, has more to do with salmon mousse and chardonnay on the grass by the lake between the acts than with music or theater. Cathedrals and oratorios bear timeless testimony to how close religious experience and aesthetic experience can be, and the slightest consideration of the audience at a contemporary performance of Verdi's *Requiem* will show

how far apart. Aesthetic purists always distinguish. Relativists do not care. Most of us are quite familiar with the constant skirmishes between the chosen people and the philistines on this issue—proof that there is something important at stake.

Etymological considerations are not at all to the point here. It makes no difference whether Aristotle or John Dewey or anyone else first used the expression "aesthetic experience." It is Beardsley's use of the term that interests us, and it is clear that he wants to use it simply as the experience characteristic of our intercourse with aesthetic objects.[2] It has to do with response, with what reading a poem or listening to a sonata or looking at a still life does to us and for us. Of course that is not a definition. I do not believe that Beardsley anywhere has given us a definition of aesthetic experience. Kennick thinks he gives one in "Aesthetic Experience Regained" because of his use of the connective "if and only if."[3] Beardsley says "a person is having an aesthetic experience during a particular stretch of time if and only if the greater part of his mental activity during that time is united and made pleasurable by being tied to the form and qualities of a sensuously presented or imaginatively intended object on which his primary attention is centered."[4] I do not read that as a definition. There are many ways in which "if and only if" can be used without meaning "is defined by." (The sentence "There is a current flowing in this loop if and only if switches A and B are closed" defines nothing.) Dickie calls Beardsley's treatment a set of directions for locating aesthetic experiences. That is probably pretty accurate. He gives us sets of criteria that can distinguish aesthetic experiences from all other kinds of experiences. That is, of course, a task that philosophers have taken seriously since people began musing theoretically about the arts. Is there a unique response to aesthetic objects? Can this be isolated in practice? Conceptually? One has only to think of *Republic* or *Phaedrus* to acknowledge how ancient is the problem, and to think of the quarrels among American philosophers in the last decades to acknowledge how current.

Beardsley's generalizations about aesthetic experience, first laid out in his *Aesthetics* in 1958, and never really deserted, are familiar: an aesthetic experience is an experience of some intensity in which attention is firmly fixed upon certain components of a phenomenally objective field. It is an experience of some intensity. It is coherent to an unusually high degree, and it is usually complete in itself. These components, of course, can be found individually in other experiences, but not in these specific relationships. Aesthetic experience is a *kind* of experience, not a specific experience, and the objects that produce such kinds of experience are called aesthetic objects, whether they are artworks or objects of another kind. Producing aesthetic experiences is one thing that these objects do, and what they do best. It is what they are good for.

The question of whether we can isolate a special aesthetic character of experience was again addressed in Beardsley's presidential address to the American Philosophical Association in 1978.[5] Skeptics have gleefully pointed out that if such a character existed, surely someone long ago would have succeeded in articulating it in a satisfactory manner. Beardsley agrees that the complexity of the task (it does call for a more subtle phenomenological investigation than has ever appeared in current literature) puts the requisite analysis out of reach, but he offers a set of five properties, which he modestly labels "symptoms" of aesthetic experience. With a formality perhaps inappropriate to the obvious introspectiveness of the analysis, he insists that the first is necessary and at least three of the remaining four must obtain. They are: object directedness, a felt sense of freedom, a sense of detached affect, a sense of active discovery, and a sense of personal integration, of wholeness. The vagueness of these symptoms is obvious, and Beardsley thinks—indeed says—that it is essential, although the concept of essential vagueness is one that only a famous philosopher can embrace. I do not recommend it for beginners. I am not objecting to the characterization of these symptoms. Intuitively I agree with these observations. I do think, however, that whether it is I or Monroe Beardsley who is accepting them, they are the result of hunches hardening into characters. (And I suppose we could call the technique from which they result the method of hardening hunches.) If the pudding won't set you can always put it in the freezer, but then don't let it stand too long at room temperature later.

In spite of the informality of the symptomatic approach, no one should think that Beardsley's interest in aesthetic experience is casual. The analysis is undertaken for a specific purpose; to allow for a theory of aesthetic value. If aesthetic objects are specific generators of aesthetic experience, then the aesthetic value of an object is to be discovered in the magnitude of the aesthetic experience produced. It is a functional theory, and the adjunctive use of "good" as applied to an aesthetic object is a functional definition. He first advances the following equivalence: "'X is a good aesthetic object' means 'X is capable of producing good aesthetic experiences,'"[6] but that is obviously riddled with circularity. To circumvent this, he observes that good aesthetic experiences are aesthetic experiences of a fairly great magnitude, which yields the generalization: "'X has aesthetic value' means 'X has the capacity to produce an aesthetic experience of a fairly great magnitude.'" Now that has the advantage of obscuring the circularity by couching it in the vagueness of "magnitude," about which all we really know is that the greater the magnitude the more of an aesthetic experience it is, and that magnitude is a function of the variables unity, intensity, and complexity. Now that knowledge may be considerable, after all, and perhaps should not be despised, but it has always seemed to me that it never terminated the dependence upon the prior value assumptions which characterize functional theories in general. Much more recently, in his presidential address to the American Philosophical Association, Beardsley argues—with, it seems to me, something less than complete persuasiveness—that the alleged circularity (of which he seems now aware) can be avoided by distinguishing kinds of values, by observing that "value" is not defined by means of "a value." That is, when we speak of *a* value (and this should not be confused with a valuable *thing*), we are referring to value-kinds, and this is only legitimate when the kind has been articulated, when distinctions have been made explicit.[7]

Thus, we have a *picture* of aesthetic experience—not an account, not a theory, but a description. It is not a psychological account, nor should we fault Beardsley for not giving us what he never promises or considers vital. It is not a full philosophical account and, despite what both his defenders and detractors say, not a theory. I think that we do have grounds for some complaint about that, but I also believe that there are reasons why the rounded theory does not materialize. (I must add at this point that no one is asking Beardsley to produce a theory in the strict, scientific sense of a deductive system, but only in the softer sense of a conceptual scheme that relates facts and principles in ways that yield the kinds of generalizations that help us to understand. Definitions, generalizations, and applications are the hallmarks, not necessarily predictability and those other marks of hard theories.)

I want to suggest first that an early commitment to the thesis of the works called "The Intentional Fallacy" and "The Affective Fallacy,"[8] and the derivative consequences of that commitment raised serious problems concerning the possibility of developing a full-blown theory of aesthetic experience, ever. The affective fallacy was the name given to the confusion of what a work *is* and what it *does*. One thing that it does is engender experiences: experiences of awe, of appreciation, of disgust, and so on (in perception, in interpretation, in criticism).

The affective fallacy begins when one attempts to derive standards of criticism from the emotional, affective, psychological effects of an artwork and ends in extreme relativism, subjectivism, and impressionism. The more that reader-oriented or reader-response critics insisted that the work cannot be understood apart from its effects, the more their focus centered upon the New Critics. The disciplining autonomy of the New Critics ruled out discussion of feeling in order to achieve rigor like that found in the sciences: objectivity. Views other than theirs, they thought, totally precluded objectivity. Of course subjectivity was neither the goal nor the achievement of these theories. It was not subjectivity, as Jane Tomkins rightly maintains in *Reader-Response Criticism*,[9] but a way of conceiving a text that reorganizes the relationship between the text and the reader. Even the dualistic view of Roman Ingarden, in which the work can be construed as consisting of a text created by the author and a realization created by the reader, seems too close to fallacious affectiveness for Beardsley. Ingarden believed that it made sense to talk about aesthetic experience, so long as one did not attempt to simplify a very complicated process, for indeed that is what he conceived aesthetic experience to be, a process in which we give ourselves up to the charm of the aesthetic object. For him the aesthetic experience begins (at least most often) in perception, which grasps the harmony of qualities of which the text is composed. So far no conflicts. But Ingarden saw the process as much deeper, more profound. We, the observers or readers, act within the process. There is a creative aspect to aesthetic experience that goes quite counter to the notion that the work is the thing. What this active part of the response entails is never totally clear. Perhaps a feel for it can be gotten from Virginia Woolf's comment on Jane Austen: "She stimulates us to supply what is not there. What she offers is, apparently, a trifle, yet is composed of something that expands in the reader's mind and endows with the most powerful form of life scenes which are outwardly trivial." To be sure, the affective fallacy must be interpreted only in the restricted way in which it was intended, but its hardnosed putting down of emotive factors in interpretation and criticism aligned its originators consciously or unconsciously against the theorists of experience, even though it turns out that aesthetic experience is an inescapable element in this theory of criticism.

Stanley Fish and his ilk, for instance, boldly embrace the alleged fallacy and in so doing become the radicals of literary theory. The poem is what it does. Fish muses that he himself at first saw readers' experiences as responses to authorial intentions in the formal features of a text, but later on the specifiable features disappear, and as a result the pre-existing text to which the reader responds is denied. The experience of the reader becomes so important that it is the reader himself who writes the text. Textual meaning is independent of the work. Experience is so important that the data about the "work" are denied objective status and are seen as products of interpretation. Response theorists are willing to share their critical authority with even the most untutored reader. They allow what the New Critics would not: reports of individual readers about their experiences in reading.

Of course the variability of readers, the private aspects of experience, and the old trap of the inescapable subjectivity of response are often seen as deadly threats to reader-centered or experience-based criticism. Wolfgang Iser counters this threat by denying the variability. David Bleisch calls response a pre-emptory perceptual act that translates a sensory experience into consciousness, and counters the variability by embracing it, and making it a principle of value. Fish counters this unchecked relativism by postulating a community of readers, an interpretative community, that generates meanings. But these are readers, observers, responders, experiencers. It is extremely difficult, even if one is under the spell of John Dewey and considers the Work the basic, neutral, formal, and immutable element in aesthetics, to make the moves necessary for a full theory of aesthetic experience. The dramatic announcement of the young Beardsley was a commitment to do so, and it is a commitment from which he has never seriously wavered.

A second reason why no adequate theory of aesthetic experience is forthcoming is the recurrence of an old problem in aesthetics. However you name it, it is the attribution of the same property to aesthetic objects and to the experience of the beholder. The property so important to Beardsley is unity. Even if you agree, he admits in "Aesthetic Experience Regained," that an artwork (as experienced) may be more or less unified, you may very well have difficulty with the second assumption, that we can also apply "unified" to the experience of the artwork. That is, not only is *Medea* unified, but my experience of *Medea* is unified also. Experiences as well as artifacts have aesthetic qualities, and the presence of these qualities in experience is due to (determined by) the presence of that quality in the work of art. In "The Metaphysical Poets" Eliot distinguished the chaotic, irregular, fragmentary experience of the ordinary man from the poet's mind, which is "constantly amalgamating disparate experience."[10] The unity and the wholeness, however, come from the poem, which contains "the objective correlative of the poet's experience" (no one-to-one correspondence, however). My point is not that the constant critics, like Dickie, for instance, who argue that the term "unified" cannot intelligibly be applied to experiences, are necessarily correct, but only that Beardsley's insistence that such terms *are* applicable makes the development of a full theory of aesthetic experience extremely difficult. Beardsley, incidentally, is not oblivious to the objections of critics who point to what seems to be an almost intuitive move from object to subject. In the "Postscript," the introduction to the new edition of *Aesthetics*,[11] he notes their objections, but simply reasserts that unity is a merit in artworks, and hence a positive criterion of criticism because it enables the artwork to afford a unified *experience*, and thus to have aesthetic value. What makes it difficult to penetrate the concept of aesthetic experience is that we are constantly pushed back into the object. It is not that the unity of my experience is *like* the unity of the work, that it is a metaphor or another linguistic device to suggest similitude. It seems as if the unity is the same unity in each case. My experience is unified in the same way that the work of art is unified, and indeed derives from that unity. That assertion does not preclude a theory of aesthetic experience, but it may account for some of the difficulties in reaching a full theory.

A third reason why the theory is never adequately completed has been the absence of a theory of art in Beardsley's aesthetics. From the earliest years it was the aesthetic object that generated experience. He did not close in on the artwork, for he was skeptical of the then current attempts at successfully managing a definition of art, and, like most of us, he was overimpressed by the arguments that no real definition of art (i.e., one giving necessary and sufficient conditions) could possibly be defended. Now he admits that that omission was probably contumacious and that he probably overstated the disadvantages of using as a general concept one that had to be defined intentionalistically. From the start, however, Beardsley's relentless attack upon intention should have been seen— as it was not always seen—as directed against arguments in the area of criticism, and criticism alone. Unfortunately it was read by many to indicate a general rejection of human intentions as being relevant in any area of art or the aesthetic. Whenever writers found a shard of intention in Beardsley's diggings into the creative process, for instance, they would whisper "veiled intentionalism" and call him an intentionalist in spite of himself. Nowhere has Beardsley rejected intentions out of hand. It was only in the area of value that he proscribed intentions so vigorously; yet in the literature intention becomes distorted, like a pitcher's elbow, from unnatural use. In his "Postscript" he muses, "I have found it impossible (though not for want of trying) to find a way of avoiding commitment to a concept of aesthetic value. . . . I find myself always driven back to the idea that in calling an artwork a good one . . . we must be ascribing some form of (nonmoral) value to it."[12] It is in this area alone that Beardsley's hostility to intentional theory belongs. If he had been compelled in the 1950s and 1960s, rather than merely goaded, to define art, he would undoubtedly have done so in much the way he now penitently proceeds. In "Postscript" he confesses, "It was no doubt perverse of me, in the first edition of [*Aesthetics*], to carry on about artworks at such length while omitting to provide a definition of art. . . . I did not want to become enmeshed at length in a question that however popular at the time . . . did not then convince me of its importance or promise any very satisfactory and agreeable resolution." In the essay "Redefining Art" in *The Aesthetic Point of View* he finally defines art: "an artwork is either an arrangement of conditions intended to be capable of affording an experience with marked aesthetic character or (incidentally) an arrangement belonging to a class or type of arrangements that are typically intended to have this capacity."[13]

Now that definition is of great interest. I think it is one of the more important sentences to emerge from his recent speculations in aesthetics. It is not a solution to our problem. It is an entry into theorizing that could well promise at last the successful handling of aesthetic experience, and it is important, among other reasons, because of what it excludes. It does not cite, nor does it give any indication of being designed to generate, a consideration of value. Whatever aesthetic experience is (and "aesthetic character" remains undefined), it is handled outside the context of value, whereas previously value and experience were constantly linked; indeed, the only reason for investigating experience was that it might yield a theory of value. Dewey is still there, but the view is more Panofskian. Panofsky's position was "a work of art always has aesthetic significance (not to be confused with aesthetic value): whether or not it serves some practical purpose, and whether it is good or bad, it demands to be experienced aesthetically."[14]

I think that this marks a distinct change in direction. It is consistent with Beardsley's second thoughts about aesthetic experience's being the basis upon which a theory of aesthetic value can be built. He now admits that that basis is too narrow to accomplish the task. Yet in that admission we may have the opening of new avenues toward a deeper understanding of aesthetic experience.

From the beginning Beardsley has had the goal of distinguishing an aesthetic experience from a nonaesthetic experience in terms of its internal properties. I have suggested some reasons why I think a satisfactory theory has not yet been forthcoming. A satisfactory theory would have to deal with the differences between listening to music, reading a poem, and looking at a painting. (Beardsley admits this on p. 527 of *Aesthetics*.) A satisfactory theory would have to provide definitions, spell out the features of aesthetic characters, establish causal relationships, and provide generalizations and some degree of explanation. These are not, I think, expectations in excess of what we have a right to demand. Yet we should not lose sight of the fact that contrary to the unfortunate models of most believers in aesthetic experience, Beardsley has not been content with merely the recognition of the affective. He has done as much as anyone to call attention to the importance of thinking about experience and to insist that impressionistic commitments alone will not do. For all of these grumblings that he has not wrapped up the package, he has probably come as close to developing a theory of aesthetic experience as anyone. Because of his trenchant treatment of so many problems in aesthetics, we come to demand more of Monroe Beardsley than we do of others. We expect completeness of him, where we are satisfied with only encouraging insights from others. We expect from him not only intensity and complexity, but unity as well. And that is surely a tribute not only to his skill and style, but to his ideas in aesthetics, a quarter of a century of ideas that, whether one agrees with them or not, must be taken seriously by anyone who takes aesthetics seriously.

Notes

1. "Aesthetic Experience Regained," *Journal of Aesthetics and Art Criticism*, 28 (1969): 3–12.

2. *Aesthetics: Problems in the Philosophy of Criticism*, 2d ed. (Indianapolis, 1981), p. 527.

3. W. E. Kennick, *Art and Philosophy*, 2d ed. (New York, 1979), p. 397.

4. Beardsley, "Aesthetic Experience Regained," 5.

5. "In Defense of Aesthetic Value," *Proceedings and Addresses of the American Philosophical Association* (1979): 723–49.

6. Beardsley, *Aesthetics*, p. 530.

7. Beardsley, "In Defense of Aesthetic Value," p. 738.

8. William K. Wimsatt, Jr., and Monroe C. Beardsley, "The Intentional Fallacy," *Sewanee Review*, 54 (1946): 468–88, and "The Affective Fallacy," *Sewanee Review* 57 (1949); 3–27.

9. Jane P. Tomkins, *Reader-Response Criticism: From Formalism to Post-Structuralism* (Baltimore, 1981).

10. T. S. Eliot, "The Metaphysical Poets," in *Selected Essays* (New York, 1932), p. 247.

11. Beardsley, *Aesthetics*, p. lxi.

12. Ibid., p. lix.

13. Monroe C. Beardsley, *The Aesthetic Point of View*, ed. Michael Wreen and Donald Callen (Ithaca, N.Y., forthcoming).

14. Erwin Panofsky, *Meaning in the Visual Arts* (New York, 1955), p. 11.

Art and
Society

7

Art and the Romantic Artist

GEORGE DICKIE

I shall honor Monroe Beardsley in the way he will appreciate best, by criticizing one of his philosophical views. I shall try to counter the incisive attack Beardsley makes on the institutional theory of art.[1] Beardsley proposes as a contrast with the institutional conception of art and artist what he calls the "Romantic" conception—an artist working and producing art in isolation from any institutions. Of course he does not think that all artists work in such isolation, but if even one could, Beardsley thinks that the institutional conception of art must be false. Beardsley characterizes the Romantic artist as follows:

> Withdrawn into his ivory tower, shunning all contact with the business, government, educational, and other institutions of his society . . . he works away on his canvas, carves his stone, polishes the rhymes and meters of his precious lyric. . . . Of course, we cannot deny that the Romantic artist may be supplied electricity by an institution, that his paper or canvas has to be manufactured, that his very thoughts will be . . . to some extent "moulded" by his acquired language and previous acculturation. But that is all beside the point, which is (on this account) that he can make a work of art, and validate it as such, by his own free originative power. And it is this claim that has in recent years been explicitly challenged by those who hold that art is . . . essentially institutional.[2]

In a way, what I shall want to argue against Beardsley is that although an artist can withdraw *from contact* with various of the institutions of society, he cannot withdraw *from* the institution of art, because he carries it with him as Robinson Crusoe carried his Englishness with him throughout his stay on the island.

Beardsley does not argue in favor of the Romantic conception of art; rather, he argues against several particular versions of the institutional view, finding them all inadequate. Consequently, everything Beardsley says may be true and the Romantic view false if an as yet unformulated version of the institutional theory or some other non-Romantic view is true.

Beardsley begins his attack on institutional theories by formulating two principles, either of which, he claims, states a sufficient condition for art's being essentially institutional.

> 1.1 If the existence of some institution is included among the truth-conditions of "A is an artwork" then artworks are essentially institutional objects.
>
> 1.2 If the existence of some institution is included among the truth-conditions of "this artwork has property P," where P is a normal property of artworks, then artworks are essentially institutional objects.[3]

Beardsley takes the second principle to apply to views such as the following: works of art belong to genres, and belonging to a genre is an institutional property; hence, works of art are institutional. I shall ignore this principle and the claims associated with it.

Beardsley takes the first principle to be the principle of an institutional theory such as mine. There are several problems with Beardsley's claim. First, the name "A" in the antecedent of the first principle is ambiguous; it could refer to some particular object or to all the members of the class of artworks. It must be understood in the latter way; otherwise it lacks the generality to support the consequent, which has the form of a universal generalization. I assume that Beardsley wishes "A" to be understood in this general way. Second, he has formulated the first principle in terms of a *sufficient* condition only, but my theory claims that institutionality is both necessary and sufficient. He states the first principle in this weaker form, presumably, because he wants to formulate two principles, each of which is sufficient, and because if institutionality could be shown not to be a sufficient, this would show it not to be necessary *and* sufficient. But even if Beardsley were to show that the first principle is false, he would not have shown that institutionality is not a necessary condition of art. And, of course, he would have to show that institutionality is not necessary in order to show that the Romantic view is true. As noted earlier, Beardsley does not argue in a positive way for the Romantic view. Furthermore, he does not attempt to show that institutionality as such is not sufficient, but that particular theoretical accounts of institutionality have not been shown to be sufficient. Consequently, even if everything Beardsley says is true, he will not have shown that institutionality in some form is not sufficient.

In what follows I shall first note and accept some of the criticisms Beardsley makes of my theory, thus amending my conception of the institutional nature of art. Second, I shall focus on Beardsley's conception of the Romantic artist in order to use it as a foil in developing an account of the institutional nature of art.

Before beginning a discussion of the notion of the Romantic artist, it will be useful to consider a very important point that Beardsley makes. He distinguishes between what he calls "institution-types" and "institution-tokens." By "institution-type" he means a practice such as tool making, storytelling, or marriage. By "institution-token" he means an organization such as General Motors, Columbia Pictures, or the Roman Catholic Church.[4] Institution-tokens execute the kind of activities specified under institution-types. Of course some institution-types (practices) can exist without institution-tokens (organizations).

Beardsley uses the distinction between institution-type and institution-token to criticize an aspect of my theory. He cites the definition of "work of art" from *Art and the Aesthetic*: "A work of art in the classificatory sense is (1) an artifact (2) a set of the aspects of which has had conferred upon it the status of candidate for appreciation by some person or persons acting on behalf of a certain social institution (the artworld)."[5] Beardsley raises a number of questions about various elements of the definition, but at the moment I am concerned with only one. He notes that I characterize the institution of the artworld as an "established practice," which in his terminology makes it an institution-type. He points out that the definition contains expressions such as "conferred," "status," and "acting on behalf of," which typically have application within institution-tokens (the University of Illinois, the United States government, and the like). The difficulty, as Beardsley sees it, is that the artworld as I have conceived it is not an institution-token but a practice. "Does it make sense," Beardsley queries, "to speak of acting on behalf of a *practice*? Status-awarding authority can center in an institution-token, but practices, as such, seem to lack the requisite source of authority. Perhaps the artworld, as Dickie conceives it, could not confer status."[6]

Beardsley is, I think, completely right on this point. The formulation of the institutional theory that I have given is not coherent. The expressions in question are much too formal and appropriate only for groups of the kind Beardsley calls institution-tokens. These expressions led me to give inaccurate descriptions of the artworld and some of its functions. For example, I attempted to give

accounts of how the conferring of the status of candidate for appreciation occurs in the artworld. It now seems clear that the activity
of creating art does not involve conferring. If, however, the institutional theory as I formulated it earlier is not correct, it does not
follow that no correct institutional theory can be formulated; nor
does it follow that the Romantic view of art is true. Stated very generally and without elaboration, what I now mean by the institutional approach is the view that a work of art is art because of the
position it occupies within a cultural practice, which is, of course,
in Beardsley's terminology an institution-type.

Jeffrey Wieand has refined and extended Beardsley's remarks
on institutions by distinguishing between Action-institutions and
Person-institutions.[7] Action-institutions are types of acts, such as
promising and the like. Actions of this kind are governed by rules
that those who participate in the activity understand. The tokens
of an Action-institution are the particular performances of that
type of action. Person-institutions are organizations that behave as
quasi persons or agents, as, for example, the Catholic Church and
General Motors do. Typically, selected members of the organization
act on behalf of it. Person-institutions can participate in Action-
institutions, as when an organization promises to do something.
Given Wieand's refinements, I now want to say that artmaking is an
Action-institution and does not involve any Person-institution in
any essential way. Of course, many Person-institutions—museums,
foundations, churches, and the like—have relations with artmaking, but no particular Person-institution is essential to artmaking.

Now that Beardsley's and Wieand's criticism has been accepted, let me return to Beardsley's Romantic conception of art and
artist, which he takes to be the antithesis of the institutional view.
A discussion of the Romantic view will be useful in stating the institutional view in more detail and making it plausible. Of course,
Beardsley's description of the Romantic artist was stated with my
earlier formulation of the institutional theory in mind, but this fact
does not affect the conflict between the Romantic conception and
the general institutional point of view. But what exactly do the two
points of view disagree about? Beardsley is quite right that the fact
that society supplies an artist with electricity, canvas, paper, or the
like is irrelevant to whether his art is Romantic or institutional in
nature. But Beardsley also lumps in with these irrelevancies the fact
that an artist's "very thoughts will be . . . to some extent 'moulded'
by his acquired language and previous acculturation." In this quickly
passed-over idea about the molding of thoughts lies buried the issue
that divides the Romantic and institutional theories. Being sup-

plied with some kinds of thoughts by one's society can be like being supplied with electricity or canvas, but being supplied with other kinds of thoughts is very different. The similarities and differences bear looking into.

If Beardsley is talking about the molding by the cultural environment of thoughts about, say, social justice, racial attitudes, sexual mores, governmental actions, human affection, and the like (the sorts of things that can be the subject matter of art), then the fact that an artist has such culturally derived thoughts when he creates art is irrelevant to whether his art is essentially institutional. And I do not think that anyone would have supposed that these kinds of thoughts are relevant. If, however, the culturally derived thoughts that an artist has are not merely thoughts about the subject matter of art but thoughts about *art itself*, then things are different and there is good reason to think that the art he creates is essentially institutional. Of course, not every thought about something that is a work of art is relevant here. For example, I am *not* talking here about thoughts of objects that, although they are in fact works of art, are not known to the thinker to be works of art. A person's remembering or reflecting on an ancient artifact that he does not realize is a work of art is a case of a thought about art in one sense, but it is not a relevant case. A person's seeing and then thinking about *Fountain* in any way without knowing that it is a work of art is another example of a thought about art that is not a relevant case. Relevant thoughts about art are thoughts about objects that the thinker knows to be art, thoughts about the activity of producing art, and the like. In short, relevant thoughts are thoughts that involve an understanding in some degree of the concept of art; they are, as noted just above, thoughts about *art itself*. If an artist creates works of art at least in part because of the thoughts of the relevant kind that he has derived from his language and acculturation, then a possibility is opened up that the existence of something that might be called the institution of art is a conditon for his work's being a work of art.

Two questions now naturally arise: (1) how do the relevant thoughts about art function in an artist's experience; and (2) what does it mean to say that these thoughts about art involve something that might be called the institution of art? In answering the first question, it must be said that thoughts about art function in two ways. At one end of the range, they might take the form of *conscious* thoughts about art itself, as is no doubt frequently the case when dadaists, creators of happenings, and the like do their work. At this same end of the range are those who create art of a traditional kind and who at some time during the creative process consciously view their work as falling under the category of art. At the other end of the range, thoughts about art are never consciously in mind at any time during the creative process, but the artists create what they do as a result of their previous exposure to examples of art, training in artistic techniques, or general background knowledge of art. The first question has now been answered; thoughts about art may function consciously or unconsciously, just as thoughts do in countless other domains. In answer to the second question, it may be said that thoughts about art involve something that might be called the institution of art because the artists described employ those thoughts consciously or unconsciously as a framework within which they work.

Can art be created outside the kind of framework I have suggested? I believe that Beardsley thinks it can be and that this is the point of his notion of the Romantic artist. His description of the Romantic artist, however, is not an effective contrast to the institutional view, because it is not clear what Beardsley means by saying that an artist's very thoughts will be to some extent molded by his acquired language and previous acculturation. Drawing now on what was just said about thoughts about art, one can make his notion of the Romantic artist an effective contrast by understanding the Romantic artist's "free originative power" to create works of art as an ability to create works of art independently of the framework within which artists work, the framework that is typically acquired by having experienced examples of art, having had training in artistic techniques, having been given a background knowledge of art, and the like. Having sharpened up the conception of the Romantic artist, one finds it very difficult to imagine such a being existing in the world today. How could anyone over the age of two or three years escape knowledge of the basic elements of the framework? Grandma Moses and such primitive painters do not qualify as Romantic artists: they are not people totally ignorant of art; they are people who have a basic understanding of art, although they may be ignorant of many art techniques and the latest doings in advanced art circles. Thus, at the very least the occurrence of a Romantic artist seems highly implausible. Even so, despite the implausibility of such an event, it may seem logically possible that a Romantic artist could spring up. One *can* imagine a member of a primitive tribe that has no conception of art or a member of our own society who is so culturally isolated as to be completely ignorant of art. One can conceive of either of these individuals suddenly having and employing the kind of framework I have been discussing and as a result making a work of art with whatever materials are at hand. This thought experiment, however, obviously does not show that a work of art can be created independently of the framework being sketched, for it pictures art being created within the context of an art-specific framework. What this thought experiment *does show* is that it is logically possible for art together with its framework to have a Romantic occurrence.

I have now distinguished between two things, both of which Beardsley's view supports: (1) the occurrence of a Romantic artist, and (2) the Romantic occurrence of the institution of art. That something of the magnitude of a full-blown institution will occur spontaneously is quite implausible. The present concern, however, is not with whether it is logically possible for the whole institution of art to spring into existence; it is the question whether art can be created independently of a framework—that is, whether there can be an occurrence of a Romantic artist. The question is whether one can create a work of art simply by the exercise of one's, to use Beardsley's phrase, "own free originative power." Beardsley's notion of a Romantic artist, as I have interpreted it, holds open the possibility that artmaking in at least some cases could be totally a product of individual initiative, a process that could occur in a cultural vacuum.

Suppose that a person totally ignorant of the concept of art (the member of a primitive tribe or the culturally isolated individual mentioned above, for example) and unacquainted with any representations were to fashion a representation of something out of clay. Without trying to diminish the significance of the creation of an unprecedented representation, such a creation would not be a work of art. While the creator of the representation would certainly recognize the object as a representation, he would not have any cognitive structures into which he could fit it so as to understand it as art. Someone might make the mistake of identifying art with representation (a deeply ingrained identification) and thereby conclude that the representation is art. Once this temptation is put aside, we can see that the creator of the representation cannot recognize his creation as art and that, therefore, it cannot be art. This case should not be confused with the case discussed earlier of the artist who creates art without consciously having a thought that he is creating art, for such a person could have the relevant thought. In the case in question, the person who creates the representation could not have the relevant thought or thoughts because he lacks the relevant cognitive structures. Art cannot exist in the contextless vacuum that Beardsley's view requires; it must exist in a cultural matrix, as the product of someone fulfilling a cultural role.

It seems inconceivable, then, that there could ever have been a Romantic artist or that there could ever be one in the future. Now, although a Romantic artist—that is, someone creating art without a framework—seems inconceivable, someone might still think that the institution of art itself must have had a "Romantic" beginning, for otherwise it could never have gotten started. The implausibility of this idea—the institution of art springing into existence with its inventor functioning as a Promethean art-giver (with framework thrown in)—is something of an embarrassment to the Romantic explanation of art and its origins. Moreover, it is perfectly reasonable to suppose that art did not have the instantaneous beginning that the Romantic-origin thesis requires. Art may have emerged (and no doubt did emerge) in an evolutionary way out of the techniques originally associated with religious, magical, or other activities. In the beginning these techniques would have been no doubt minimal, and their products (diagrams, chants, and the like) crude and in themselves uninteresting. With the passage of time, the techniques would have become more polished; specialists would have emerged, and their products would have acquired characteristics of some interest (to their creators and others) over and above the interest they had as elements in the religious ritual or whatever other kind of activity they were embedded in. At about this point it becomes meaningful to say that primitive art had begun to exist, although the people who had the art might not yet have had a word for it.

To give a possible account of the beginnings of art that does not have a role for a Romantic origin does not, of course, show that there was in fact no Romantic origin, but the suggestion that some untutored person suddenly had and employed the kind of framework I have been discussing and thereby created the institution of art at a single stroke just seems like too much to swallow. I want to emphasize again that the question of the Romantic origin of the institution of art is not the main issue that divides Beardsley and me. The fundamental issue is whether there could be a Romantic artist, a person who creates art independently of a framework.

There is, however, something about Beardsley's notion of the Romantic origin of the institution of art that should be taken account of. The Romantic originator as I have depicted him is a rather complex individual, and it is this complexity that makes his existence implausible. It is more plausible to think of what might be called Romantic protoartists: that is, persons whose actions initiate practices that over a period of time develop into something recognizable as an institution of art. I have in mind such actions as the use of a pigment to color a traditional object or a traditional representation, an action that enhances the object or representation. The actions I am envisaging can be identified with the polishing of techniques and the development of specialists that I spoke of earlier. The cumulative effect of such acts of individual initiative in certain circumstances might ultimately be the creation of an institution of art. The kernel of truth in Beardsley's conception of a Romantic originator can thus be incorporated into the institutional view without swallowing the whole conception.

It is possible, perhaps even probable, that Beardsley really intends "Romantic artist" to refer to the kind of individual I have just called "Romantic protoartist." Understood in this way, a Romantic artist would be an individual who contrives an object because he likes one or more of its characteristics (representative, expressive, aesthetic, for example); according to Beardsley, the object so created would be a work of art. Beardsley's view would be, on this interpretation, that the first artifact that initiated the particular chain of events that resulted in an artworld system is itself a work of art. Now, I said earlier that the action of such an individual as Beardsley here conceives no doubt lies at the beginning of the development that resulted in a system within which works of art are created. The institutional view, however, is that it is only further along in the chain of events envisaged that it becomes reasonable to say that there are works of art—namely, at a time when roles have become established with regard to the creation and "consumption" of such artifacts.

Notes

1. Monroe C. Beardsley, "Is Art Essentially Institutional?" in *Culture and Art*, ed. Lars Aagaard-Mogensen (Atlantic Highlands, N.J., 1976), pp. 194–209. My essay is excerpted from a chapter of a forthcoming book.

2. Ibid., p. 196.

3. Ibid., p. 197.

4. In giving these examples of types and tokens, I am not attempting to correlate the particular types and tokens in the two lists of examples. I am not, for example, saying that General Motors is the token of which tool making is the type.

5. George Dickie, *Art and the Aesthetic* (Ithaca, N.Y., 1974) p. 34.
6. Beardsley, p. 202.
7. Jeffrey Wieand, "Can There Be an Institutional Theory of Art?" *Journal of Aesthetics and Art Criticism* 39 (1981): 409–17.

8

The Praxis of Art and the Liberal Dream

CHARLES DYKE

I

I want to discuss a question in social philosophy: whether it is possible to integrate art fully into a society, and, if so, what the nature of this integration might be. The immediate background of the question at the present time is the emargination of art in most contemporary societies.

The emargination of art is the brutest of facts. Imagine Frank Sinatra's current yearly earnings at the disposal of the Metropolitan Opera Company.[1] Imagine Sylvia Plath having sold as well as Jacqueline Susann. Imagine as many people attending the legitimate theater in a year as now go to the movies. Fantasies, all fantasies; and the fantasy proves the point. For the society at large, the arts are utterly marginal. A tiny percentage of the population supports the arts with the aid of what they can extract from the public purse on grounds of nostalgia, guilty conscience, and snobbery. The overwhelming majority has no contact with, or interest in, the arts.

This lament is often countered by the observation that it has never been true that a majority in any society has had any intrinsic connection with the arts. In addition to being false, and based on a cultural and historical myopia, this claim runs counter to any claim that human life is becoming more civilized, more humanized, more cultured. To say that art is no more emarginated in our society than in any other is to give up to an inevitable elitism.

The second piece of evidence for the emargination of art in our time is that every movement in the arts in this century, every "ism," has involved itself with the problematic relationship between the artist and his public or between art and society. The richest literature comes from the period of Expressionism, Dada, the Bauhaus, Futurism, and movements contemporary with them, but the issue is still raised in our own day. Now, some of these movements have concluded that the issue ought ultimately to be ignored and the autonomy of art preserved even in the face of threatened isolation. Others have sought to bend the arts toward broad accessibility. Others still have ended in a critique of society aimed at bending it to the arts. But whatever the conclusions, the point is that they proceed from a common premise: that the emargination is a genuine phenomenon.

II

The world in which our problem arises is a Liberal world. I would argue—and others have argued—that this is true even for the part of the world that considers itself socialist. The Liberal world organizes social space and assigns meaning to the human phenomena within that organized space. We need to find out where art fits within Liberal social space.

It shouldn't be necessary after all this time to defend a global use of the word "Liberal" or the reference to Liberal society as a particular, ideologically informed historical moment. The self-deception required to speak otherwise is, in any case, well beyond my capacity.

A convenient way to proceed will be to re-examine a fundamental tension within Liberalism—a tension institutionalized in many ways within Liberal societies. Then we can examine two responses to this tension and, through these responses, find something of an answer to the question at issue.

I have argued elsewhere[2] that Liberalism is stretched between two attractive poles: the authority of the individual conscience and the belief in objective right and wrong. In the political or philosophical context, it is easy to trace out the consequences of the tension between these two ultimately antithetical poles. There is, for example, the doctrine of the separation of legislative and judicial powers. In economics the two poles are found as consumer sovereignty on one side and the belief that economic life ought to work out for the best for all on the other. The economic dimension will figure significantly in what follows.

In direct reference to the arts, the two poles are epitomized by Hume's phrase "the standard of taste." "Taste" pins the question of the value of art directly to the authority of individual conscience (here individual judgment). "Standard" embodies the obligatory reference to the other pole. The two poles determine the shape of all Liberal theories of the value of art, which begin with individual subjectivity and then subject this subjectivity to critical criteria. By the way, it is far from inevitable that the problem of the value of art should be set in these terms. To think that it must involves an exercise in historical myopia and cultural chauvinism.

But what of Liberal social space? Here the tension between the two poles has been broken to a great extent. In terms of the organization of the life of the average person, consumer sovereignty has won out. It may, as Karl Polanyi has argued,[3] have taken until the middle of the nineteenth century for market society to become fully installed. And it may be that the critique of this society in terms of objective right and wrong has never ceased—even among Liberals. But the fact remains that market society and its managed counterfeits give shape to life. It is solidly entrenched and becomes ever more impervious to moral criticism.

With individual conscience (consumer sovereignty) as the organizer of social space, the place of art within this space is clear. The space as a whole is defined by the market, and any art within it must be a commodity—or propaganda in the service of influencing market decisions.[4] So artworks, whatever form they take, are items to be bought, sold, and traded. Now, this is not to say that there are not other things to be done with works of art. Who could deny of fine wine that it can be appreciated even though it's bought and sold? The issue of reduction (of art to commodity) has to be thought of from the right direction. Market society already does the job of reduction for us, and whatever else we want to say about art has to be said in the face of the *de facto* reduction. From the point of view of the market, art is essentially commodity, and only accidentally whatever else we may please. The reasons we might have for consuming art are irrelevant to the market except insofar as they indicate how the art market may be manipulated.

The further consequences of this placement of art within the organization of society are fairly obvious. The artist is primarily a producer. The fact that we think of his production as a creative act is as irrelevant to the market as the boredom of an assembly line worker—except insofar as the marketability of the product is affected. The person who looks at, listens to, or reads art is a consumer. Any esoteric pretensions the consumer might have while looking, listening, or reading are simply data for market researchers. We come to the gallery operator, publisher, and impresario. There is no need to belabor their role as entrepreneurs. This is well understood and generally conceded. I wonder if anyone ever asked Moe Septee about his aesthetic theory.

The role of the critic deserves special mention. He has an obvious affinity for the other Liberal pole, objective standards, and he might well try to find and apply such standards conscientiously. Whether or not he does so, his major function is that of taste-maker. His influence over the marketability of art products can be enormous. With respect to theater, where his role is traditionally strong, he can be decisive. Young composers have the same night-mares about music critics that young painters have about gallery owners. The critic can't avoid being a shill, no matter what his in-tegrity may be. As long as art is a commodity, anything he says about it that affects its consumption one way or another takes the form of advertisement. There is not a thing he can do about it.

The next consequence of art's being a commodity is the plight of the artist. I will have a good deal to say of this in a later section. The choice of art as a career is a special one. More than any other, this choice must be made in full awareness of the possession of spe-cial skill. Furthermore, there is no way one can become an artist without a consciousness of being in a tradition of artists—a tradi-tion that may be dealt with in a variety of ways, but must be dealt with. Part of the artistic tradition is faithfulness to art. This com-bination of circumstances makes the artist's place in market society marginal, to the point where it's romanticized as such, and has been ever since market society came to maturity. It also puts constant pressure on the artist, who is, after all, always pulled between two worlds. While this is familiar to the point of triteness, and while artists at all times may have had some difficulties in making a living, it must be pointed out that their plight is a by-product of market society.

The final consequence to be sketched is that art as commodity competes in the market with every other commodity. This has to be seen clearly, for it accounts, in the final analysis, for all other conse-quences we could mention. We imagine everyone with a budget. Budget resources in hand, the individual faces an environment of things to buy, trade for, or otherwise acquire through the expendi-ture of held resources. The commitment to consumer sovereignty requires that the environment of commodities be undifferentiated, so that the consumer's choices are based on the pairwise comparison of items, whatever these items might be. It might be objected that various *sorts* of commodities fill different roles in consumers' lives, and thus the commodity environment is differentiated. But the re-ply is that this is no business of the market. Commodities compete for budget resources on equal terms. Of course the general propen-sity to choose certain commodities will vary with variance in bud-get and price, but once the necessities of life are taken care of, these differentiations will be of concern only with respect to marketing.

So, for the populace as a whole, art competes with all other consumer goods.

It is sometimes said that art has always competed with everything else available in the environment (which is simply historically false), and even that this competition is inevitable. It is easy to say that the time "spent" on art is time not "spent" on something else, and from this it then follows that art necessarily "competes" with everything else. And why not? This is just to say that art is one thing that can be chosen for mortal beings: choices made entail alternatives rejected. It is sometimes thought that the fact that, for mortal beings, choices made entail choices rejected is enough to show that art is, like everything else, a commodity. But of course this would only be so as long as people organized their choices on a market basis: that is, as long as their operative values and rationality were those on the basis of which you could generate a price system. There are innumerable other systems of value and rationality in terms of which choices can be organized—all perfectly consistent with the fact that if you are engaged in artistic activity there are lots of other things you cannot be doing at the same time.

It's clear how this organization of social life fits with a subjective individualism with respect to the value of art and the manipulation of taste. What is to happen to critical standards of taste? Well, these seem to be the province of critics, teachers of literature, and aestheticians. They are the bearers of the other pole of Liberalism.

Critics have by far the greatest impact. Their association with the mass media virtually guarantees this. In an earlier time, when critics tended to be accomplished practitioners of the art they were criticizing, a better case could be made for the critic as the standard-bearer of objective excellence in the arts than can be made now. The occasional artist-critic still exists—Virgil Thomson and Robert Penn Warren obviously need to be mentioned—but their impact relative to that of less distinguished critics simply reinforces suspicions about the emargination of art and its confinement to an elite minority.

Oddly central to this emargination are the teachers of literature. As bearers of standards, they introduce these standards in some degree or other to an overwhelming majority in present-day society. High school education, while not universal, is nearly so, and enormous numbers of people still manage to find their way into colleges and universities. Teachers of literature provide the experience of reading literature as art to vast numbers of people. In most cases, it seems to me, they provide the *only* occasion for such reading. I do not necessarily mean this in terms of what's read (classics, etc.) but in terms of how it's read. Now, these teachers of literature continually lament the difficulty (even impossibility) of giving their students any real sense that reading literature in the light of responsible critical standards is worth doing. This lament is no mere fashionable academic gripe. The situation they lament is real and, among other things, threatens the teachers' livelihood. But we have to say to the teachers of literature: "Listen. You people have been teaching literature to generations of students for as long as we need remember. Yet the public at large has no abiding respect for that literature. The citizens who now don't want to pay your salary are your former students. You people are obviously failures of long standing and, by this time, have no one but yourselves to blame for your current problems." But then the teachers are tied to the pole of artistic standards, and the students, with few exceptions, are tied to the pole of consumer sovereignty.

III

We can now move to the response of aestheticians to this assemblage of social facts. Among Liberal theoreticians two obvious reactions are possible: cast your lot with consumer sovereignty and the market that goes with it, or pursue the search for standards.

The first group comprises those who argued that the definition of art and the establishment of artistic standards are the province of the "artworld."[5] The artworld is the ensemble of those engaged in the production, criticism, dissemination, and enjoyment of art. There are several encouraging aspects to this view. First, it concedes that the important questions of art are to be answered by means of the dialectical interchange of those primarily concerned with art. Second, it involves a surprising concession to present-day reality. For no observer of the arts in this century could deny that in terms of material, form, sound, and style, the artworld has led us to a conception of art in our artworld's own terms. This is especially obvious because the terms have changed so frequently.

The institutional theory of art, then, presents a picture of a live, evolving social dynamic within which art is made, appraised, and appreciated. This dynamic seems to offer a possible way to reconcile the two poles of Liberalism: the authority of individual judgment, and the establishment of objective standards. Each participant in the artworld makes his/her own contribution to our overall understanding of the nature of art and of the worth of any particular artwork. Every act of participation in the artworld is an expression of individual judgment. Critical standards are arrived at as the consequence of the interpersonal give and take of artworld members. The social dynamic itself is the reconciler of individual judgment and objective standards.

This is an attractive picture—especially at this level of vagueness. When historical concreteness is demanded of the picture, it tells a different story. For the structure of the artworld at a given time is all-important in determining the possibilities for art at that time. The institutionalists have to realize that what is institutionalized in *today's* artworld is the activity of buying and selling art. The market organizes the artworld; hence, any dialectic of individual judgment and critical standards must take place through the mediation of the market structure. The members of the artworld enter that world in their roles of producer, consumer, and so on: the roles I sketched earlier. Individual judgment is the judgment of the bearers of these roles, and critical standards are those that emerge in the market. Furthermore, art can never protect its autonomy in this artworld, because the market within which art trades has no boundaries of its own at the boundary between art and nonart. As we saw earlier, with respect to the market, art and nonart are undifferentiated, or differentiated only accidentally in the demand schedules of some consumers.

In the artworld organized by the market, you would expect prices to emerge as the measure of the value of art. And so they do. Any other concept of value that emerges is peripheral and, as I have said, irrelevant except insofar as it is useful in manipulating demand schedules. Thus the dialectic of value in the artworld as market.[6]

The concept of artworld and the institutional theory of art in general can be applied to other institutionalizations of art at other times and in other climes. It is interesting to think of the artworld of the Medici and the Piccolomini. It certainly was not an artworld organized by the market. It was organized in terms of power, prestige, and the display of culture. None of these was brokered in a market. J. P. Morgan was a banker, and so was Lorenzo il Magnifico, but that ought not to delude us into thinking that the artworlds in which they participated were at all the same. What was the artworld that saw the writing of Greek tragedy?

Well, if institutional theories of art wish to command credence (and they have much of interest to say), they might wish to explore historical differences between artworlds. The important point is that while such theories are capable of dealing with art in many various settings, they are *not* capable of abstracting from those settings to an overarching concept of artworld ("the form of

artworldliness") that will allow an ahistorical analysis. Different
ways of life are institutionalized at different times, and art fits into
these ways of life in very different ways. Indeed, since one of the
functions of the artworld is to answer the question "What is art?"
there is no reason to expect that the answers to this question in two
different periods will be the same, though historical threads are obviously going to be traceable from period to period. Most important, there's no reason to expect that the value of art as it's understood by one artworld will be that understood by another artworld.
There's no reason to expect an overarching ahistorical theory of the
value of art to emerge from any comparison of the many different
institutionalizations of art.

What is certain, though, is that if "artworld" is to be a persuasive and useful concept, it must be part of "realworld"; and the realworld of art is, in ourworld, the institutionalization of the art market. Consequently it must make do with price as the standard of
taste, thus reconciling the two poles of Liberalism at the auction
block.

IV

The other (and more numerous) group of Liberal aestheticians
is devoutly ahistorical. They too want to reconcile the two poles of
Liberalism, but their primary allegiance is clearly to objective standards. I'll conduct this discussion entirely in terms of the theories of
Monroe Beardsley. In choosing to do so, I am exercising my sovereign judgment that his theory is the best of its kind on any standard. Furthermore, its sophistication, humanity, and sensitivity
make it especially useful for my purposes.

In an early work Beardsley explicitly bifurcated the theory of
aesthetic value in terms of roles.[7] He discussed the value of art first
in terms of the artist, then, separately, in terms of the consumer—
identified as such. I do not want to go into the earlier view in detail
except to emphasize that Beardsley accepted the market's distinction between producer and consumer at that time, and accepted it
to the extent that he could not discuss the value of art univocally.
The later theory is contained in Beardsley's presidential address to
the American Philosophical Society.[8] It is a very beautiful theory. I
think that its very beauty betrays it.

The first thing to notice about the later theory is that the artist does not figure in the theory in any intrinsic way and the consumer no longer appears at all. The latter omission can be accounted for, I think, in the light of what happened to the notion of

"consumer" in the twenty years between the early theory and the later one. Consumerism became a social issue. The life of consumption was subjected to question and attack. It seemed better to avoid the picture of the consumer that would inevitably come to mind in, say, a 1980 reading of the theory. This isn't to say, obviously, that the social world of 1979 wasn't organized by the market, with the consumer having a central role; it's just to say that by 1979 Beardsley found reason to distance himself from the real social world and produce a theory that floats free from that world. In place of the artist and the consumer, we are offered the otherwise unspecified contemplator of the aesthetic. The objective standards of aesthetic value are defined in terms of the values of contemplation to the contemplator. Let's look at the contemplator as Beardsley presents him/her to us. We assume that the contemplator is contemplating something of high aesthetic value, and contemplating it properly according to Beardsley's view. Then many, though perhaps not all, of the following conditions must obtain.

The contemplation is directed *by* the aesthetic object *to* the aesthetic object. The contemplator's attention is attracted to the aesthetic object by that object itself. The contemplator feels free. In particular he/she is freed from concerns of past and future and, as it were, feels that he/she is giving him/herself up freely to contemplation. The contemplator is, in some sense, emotionally detached from the object of contemplation: for example, if the depiction of the frightening is being contemplated, the contemplator has enough emotional distance not to be frightened. He/she has the appropriate aesthetic distance.

The contemplator has a sense of active discovery. He/she engages in the task of discovering coherent meaning and rises to the challenge of discovering the intelligibility of the work with exhilaration. And, finally, the contemplator feels the following (and here I quote rather than paraphrase). Beardsley must (on grammatical grounds) have the contemplator in mind here, rather than "the aesthetic experience" that he claims to be describing. The contemplator must experience "a sense of integration as a person, of being restored to wholeness from distracting and disruptive impulses (but by inclusive synthesis as well as by exclusion), and a corresponding contentment, even through disturbing feelings, that involves self-acceptance and self-expansion. For short: *a sense of wholeness.*"[9]

The appearance of the aesthetic contemplator makes an ahistorical theory possible (even inevitable), and it makes it possible to appeal (if tacitly) to an aesthetic tradition that long antedates the appearance of market society. The contemplator—*qua* contemplator—is independent of social system and social role. The values of his/her contemplation are, presumably, the same no matter where the contemplator is located historically. In other words, the appearance of the contemplator signalizes the appearance of "man"—now "person"—who transcends time and place.

It needs to be noted that the two most important earlier appearances of the transcendent person, fulfilled by the contemplation of art, occurred at times when the underlying social system identified roles (even classes) that could legitimately be assigned the contemplation of art as part of the legitimate and primary function of their role. These two appearances were in classical Greece and in the Renaissance. Present-day society identifies no such role. In fact, the principle of consumer sovereignty prohibits the specification of such roles, since if they exist as defined roles people won't come equal to the market.

Now, it's my claim that this portrait of the aesthetic contemplator stands to the sovereign consumer as standards of right and wrong stand to private conscience or private judgment. Liberalism must try to weave together both strands. The possibility of doing so depends upon finding free individual choice in conformity to the objective standards. In the religious (moral) context where this has its roots, individual conscience must conform to God's will. Politically, the Rousseauean formulation is probably paradigmatic: the individual will and the general will must coincide. And now here, in the appreciation of art, the consumer must become the contemplator.

Whenever we're offered an ideal or set of standards embodied in a hero or holy person—as we are here offered the aesthetic contemplator—we are ourselves invited to contemplate the ideal. My contemplation of Beardsley's ideal provokes worry, for I find that I'm either confronting a hopelessly utopian fantasy (the Liberal dream) or I'm being invited to accept the emargination of art.

First, the emargination: I ask whether we can go out into the world and find the contemplator as a real person. The immediate answer is that we might be able to catch him/her in the act in the museum or the concert hall. If so, the question of emargination then becomes one of statistics. How many people are ever found in museums and concert halls, and how frequently are they found there? Not many, and not very often, is the only honest answer. If we went on to ask how many of even these few actually measure up as Beardsleyan contemplators, then the statistics take another turn downward. It's certainly far from Beardsley's intent to circumscribe an aesthetic elite. But once the consumers of art are held to his standards—in order to reconcile the two Liberal poles—then elitism is *de facto* inevitable. The poles are reconciled but rarely, and in the lives of but a few. How could we expect consumer society to consent to anything else? The investment of time and money required to become a Beardsleyan contemplator is too costly for all but a few intellectuals and the very rich.

The deeper problem though, is the hopelessness of the Liberal dream. I chose Beardsley's theory precisely because it's the most poignantly hopeless. The vision of the aesthetic contemplator he provides is the most deeply human in the Liberal literature. It's unexcelled as a statement of the significance that aesthetic experience can have in a life. But that life is disembodied. When we juxtapose the image of the contemplator to any normal life in market society, we create immediate dissonance. The key to seeing this is the most ennobling of Beardsley's conditions, the one quoted above. The contemplator seeks wholeness and fulfillment. But wholeness as what? As an insurance salesman planted in front of a string quartet for a few hours? Giving himself over to aesthetic experience can't make him whole. It's a guarantee and an affirmation of his fragmentation. Success in contemplation requires a total compartmentalization. To achieve it he must block out the rest of his life. Aesthetic contemplation, even with all its potentially enriching demands, and, in fact, precisely because of them, becomes a particularly esoteric form of escape. The real whole of life, that whole defined by market society and enforced by the rules for making a life in such a society, has to be left behind. A radical discontinuity has to be crossed. If the good bourgeois gets a "sense of wholeness" from his night at the opera, what in the world is the whole that he gets a sense of? Beardsley demands that it be his own wholeness, but that's utterly impossible. The ideal of the aesthetic contemplator is directly counter to the ideal member of market society.

Now, there are two possible replies to this point. The first is that it is unreasonable to demand the integration of everyday life and aesthetic experience. Art, for instance, should be a release from the cares of life into another realm of experience. The only thing required in order to reconcile our consumer sovereignty to our aesthetic standards is for us to organize our consumption patterns and our budgeting of time in such a way that aesthetic contemplation becomes one of our many avocations. To demand otherwise would be to say that no one could legitimately enjoy sport unless he/she gave his/her life over to it. But the reply to this is that it assumes a confined realm of aesthetic experience that is itself unreasonable. If Beardsley is right about the aesthetic experience, then it ought to be a possible component of any human activity, including sport. Further, we may be trapped in the radical split between creating and contemplating that Beardsley has had to assume at the start. Only this split allows us to think of aesthetic contemplation as a specialized kind of doing—something to be picked up and set down as opportunity dictates.

Second, if it's true that the normal member of market society cannot find himself or herself whole in aesthetic contemplation, perhaps we ought to excise that condition from the characterization of aesthetic experience. But why should we truncate our demands simply on the basis of their incompatibility with a particular form of social organization? It would be a shame to give up the demand for a sense of wholeness. Indeed, it has been suggested that the major object of our aesthetic attention ought to be our own life. If we find that our lives are not a satisfactory source of aesthetic experience for us, are we to say, "Oh well, we'll just have to look elsewhere. And furthermore, why should we expect to get a sense of wholeness from our own lives—or seek that sense of wholeness in the beautiful things available to our senses?" Before we give that up, especially now that Beardsley has given it to us, we ought to examine alternatives.

V

Criticizing a theory consists in producing dissatisfaction with it. In the occasional case this can be done by showing that the theory isn't true. I wouldn't know how to begin to do that in the present case. On other favorable occasions you can produce dissatisfaction with a theory by showing that it's formally contradictory. I doubt that Beardsley's theory is. It sometimes is possible to produce dissatisfaction with a theory by showing that it leads to evil or distasteful consequences. In itself Beardsley's theory leads us to aesthetic experience of the most fulfilling, ennobling sort. But while the theory isn't formally contradictory, and while, by itself, it doesn't have evil consequences, it involves contradictions and leads us astray. The way to produce dissatisfaction with Beardsley's theory is to show that it only makes sense within a single way of life, built on a single model, with a single dominant set of roles defined in it; that the theory is necessary in order to avert the banalization of something conceded by all parties to the controversy to be too important to be left to that fate; and that the world envisioned, taken together with the theory, does produce contradictions—in short, to show that no reconciliation between the society and the theory can be found.

This is why I've proceeded by the route I have. Unless we can take an honest look at the people around us and an honest look at the Beardsleyan contemplator, and try to find a real place in our world for the latter, we won't see what's wrong with the full picture. In this full picture, the Beardsleyan contemplator stands as the accuser. The world won't accommodate many of his sort, and it won't accommodate him at all on a full-time basis. His chosen pastime isn't recognized as inherently valuable but has only secondary value as a species of consumption. On the other side, the world accuses the contemplator. As contemplator, he's unproductive, sponging up beauty in a private experience that he might well enjoy in isolation. Furthermore, his contribution to the round of production and consumption is likely to be minimal, unless a way can be found to make him pay for the beauty he consumes. He contributes but little on the demand side, nothing at all on the supply side: hence, the emargination of art and the overwhelming pressure to direct people's aesthetic interests toward more productively consumable objects. If the Met goes under and the discos thrive, this is no more than the triumph of consumer sovereignty, and, from the point of view of market society, so be it—for now.

VI

The argument needs two more steps to reach a satisfactory stopping point. For if it ended here it would consist merely in unproductive carping. First I have to deal with the device most commonly suggested by Liberals for closing the gap between the two poles. Then I have to try to sketch the outlines of an alternative way of looking at the whole situation—not to close the gap, but to prevent it from opening.

Almost all Liberals dream of democratic government among an enlightened populace, where the enlightenment is meant to promote the conformity of individual judgment to objective standards. In other words, education is the device meant to bring the two poles of Liberalism together. There's no need to provide references for this view, except to mention Rousseau and Mill, in whose work the device is fundamental. The view is ubiquitous in the Liberal democracies over the last three centuries. Nearly as ubiquitous is the notion of the cultivation of taste, a notion put into practice in ways as different as the Grand Tour and singing in kindergarten, with virtually every species of education in the arts having been explored at one time or another.

In each of these cases—moral-political education and aesthetic education—a certain number of assumptions have to be made if there is to be hope that the educational task will have a successful outcome. The main assumption is that the moral, political, or aesthetic standards taught (or, rather, adopted after some suitable educational experience) can somehow be made attractive enough to be widely accepted. It's at this point that otherwise empirically inclined thinkers become rationalists. The rightness of the principles espoused must somehow shine through in a superior appeal to the rationality being nurtured in the educational process. Historically, of course, divine revelation fulfilled this function, and some replacement has been sought by Liberals ever since. It's no surprise that all solidly empiricist theories have ended at the consumer sovereignty pole, so that some sort of rationalism has seemed the only live alternative. The fact of the matter is that no satisfactory theory has ever come forth. The education of *homo economicus* thus seems a good deal simpler than that of *homo aestheticus*.

It's worth noting that as *homo aestheticus* is defined by Beardsley, programs of Skinnerian reinforcement are ruled out for all practical purposes. The complexity of the "reinforcers" seems to take care of this. Theoretically, though, interesting questions are raised. Suppose that after a relatively simplistic program of reinforcement (along, say, hedonistic lines), a subject showed a marked increase in the frequency with which he reported "felt freedom," "detached affect," "active discovery," and "a sense of wholeness" when his attention was directed to just those objects that we normally consider great art. Would *homo aestheticus* have been successfully trained? I imagine that few aestheticians would say so, and I imagine that Beardsley would want the aesthetic experience itself to take over as the reinforcer. Whatever the outcome of this training, we'd still be left with the problem of telling the true aesthetic experience from its counterfeit. Beardsley's conditions 2 through 5 are all subjective, and this is disastrous for any theory of aesthetic education, since we could never be confident that any educational program had succeeded. Increasing the attendance at concerts, gallery openings, and the like wouldn't necessarily be a mark of success. The point to notice here is that this problem is a natural consequence of the structure of the problem of aesthetic standards imposed by Liberalism. Both poles must be respected, and the "individual conscience" or "consumer sovereignty" side immediately demands the choice between subjectivism and behaviorism. Then, when the attempt is made to bring objective standards into the picture, they eventually end in subjective indeterminacy (as Beardsley's do), or they reduce standards to concatenations of behavior (as the institutionalist theories do). In either case the education of *homo aestheticus* becomes problematic.

Aesthetic education is also put into jeopardy by the radical separation of the artist and *homo aestheticus* the contemplator. We're familiar with the double curriculum of every music and art department in the contemporary university: [10] the courses where an art is taught and the courses where the appreciation of art is taught, the Lit courses and the writing courses. The effect of·this system is to convince most students that art is something that someone else does and that they then look at. Furthermore, we're currently struggling against the extension of this view to the written word, which a few produce and the rest consume. Of course, overall, this is an accurate picture of our society. The example of writing is a crucial one, for it shows most clearly how far the arts have gotten away from us. If we've come to the point of having no respect for or interest in writing as a skill, when it's potentially an everyday activity, then what hope is there for more esoteric skills to be of interest? The awakening of interest is centrally, rather than peripherally, relevant to aesthetic education precisely because of the nature of the objective standards. Their link to either behavior or subjective preference *must* involve the awakening of interest and appreciation. But as long as the artist and the contemplator are separate, the teaching of contemplation is the teaching of a certain kind of consumption. There is no connection between that consumption as an activity and the activity on which it depends: the production of art. Since contemplation is simply a species of consumption, the standards of excellence associated with it are ranked alongside standards of excellence for any other species of consumption and can claim no superiority over them.

Here, of course, is the classic problem of defending poetry over pushpin. In the market, poetry always loses. It can't be otherwise, for the activities of poetry contemplation and penny pitching are not, as such, given a primary role in the market. The activity of consuming is. Consequently the standards of consumption have priority, and any other proposed standards must give way to them. This situation gives rise immediately to a Gresham's law of standards: the standards of those activities that give the most impetus to economic activity are to be adopted at the expense of the standards of any "less economically fruitful" activity. While pushpin doesn't fare too much better than poetry on these grounds, snowmobiling, amusement parks, and commercial television do just fine. What meaning has aesthetic education under these conditions?

The other side of the coin is the education of the artist. The production of art has to compete with other occupations as a way of making a living. Again we might think of the poles: individual choice and standards. Here the standards consist of the reasons why one might pursue artistic activity: "calling," the development of natural abilities, or a host of other desiderata. To use another of Beardsley's notions, something has value if it has warranted eligibility. So the value of being an artist would depend on the reasons adduced as warrant for electing to pursue an artistic career. But the individual choice is primarily constrained not by reasons intrinsic to artistic production, but by the reasons intrinsic to the labor market. Above all, the question for the budding artist is "Can I make a living at it?" The answer to that question, for all but the lucky few, again depends upon the ability to achieve commercial success and to let the day-to-day pursuit of artistic activity be governed by the dictates of the market.

Of course we're really talking about two markets: the artworld market discussed by the institutional theorists, and the so-called world of commercial art, which consists almost entirely of advertising art but includes certain other sorts of illustration and design. There is, in addition, the possibility, however slight, of satisfying artistic talent in the mass media and in commercial music. In any case, for the artist there are perforce four terms to the problem: the need to make a living, personal aspirations, public taste, and prevailing aesthetic standards. It's no surprise that if you pluck the representative art student out of class and ask her about her career and her views on art, you get the following. She's going to go into television or advertising, with the hope that she can "raise the standards." But when asked about her own artistic standards, she'll say that art is a matter of personal expression, and that neither public nor academic critics can be trusted to understand—let alone fairly evaluate—her serious artistic production. Schizophrenic as this might be, it's not far from the only sensible position for the budding (mediocre) artist to take. The compensation is a few years of the romantic, self-righteous life of neo-Bohemia.

The problem of the resolution of the artist's individual choice with objective standards is even more difficult than the resolution of the tastes of the average person with those of *homo aestheticus*. In the first place, the burden of creativity is placed on the artist and with it the *prima facie* assumption that it's the task of the artist to break through the crust of accepted standards. How is this taught? And what status do objective standards have if the artist's job is to struggle against them? Another tradition might talk of a dialectic, but the Liberal tradition has no place for this, especially when it seeks timeless standards.

Can the artist's choice be made to conform to objective standards through the teaching of technique? This might vary from art to art, but the dominant view seems to be that mere technique produces academic exercises, not great art. Thus, the standards of *homo aestheticus* need not, and probably will not, be approached by academic training in technique. On the other hand, this simply points out once again the separation of the artist, for in the mastery of his craft and in the pursuit of the resources needed as a foundation for any approach to greatness, the artist needs precisely that technique taught in the academy. But once that technique is isolated and taught for its own sake, it becomes available for exploitation on the basis of any standards of consumption—those of *homo economicus* as well as those of *homo aestheticus*.

The praxis of the market prevails over the praxis of art. Producing and consuming are the primary organizers of life. The primary values elected are market values, and other values are pursued, if at all, in marginal, dispensable activities. Art, stored up by tradition, survives, but as an ill-assimilated artifact. The response to all this might seem to be that it was ever thus, and the praxis of art necessarily survives marginally. There are always more important concerns (of economics, politics, etc.), which structure life at the expense of any centrality of artistic praxis.

That view may be short-sighted for a number of reasons, and I'm not about to hazard a prognostication about the future of art. But to complete the argument of this paper, and to provide a necessary contrast, I'd like to look more closely at the praxis of art.

VII

To begin with I have to clarify my understanding of praxis, a much vexed concept. It seems to me that there are two important features of a praxis. First, it's a knowing doing, where the knowing isn't separated from the doing. Second, a praxis is a fundamental organizer of life. People who have been attracted to the concept of praxis have usually been trying to distinguish those activities that are native to a people, understood at a gut level and second nature, from those activities that are alien, imported, and laboriously learned.[11] We need to apply the concept to the two activities in question here: consumption and art.

While it's perfectly understandable how the word "consumption" has come to mean what it does today, still, reflections on earlier root meanings of the word provide us with some useful inanities. To start with, savor the experience of consuming a Calder mobile—say the big one hanging in the new building of the National Gallery. Munch, munch. Hard on the teeth. So "consuming" can't mean "eating." Similarly, it can't in general mean "using up." For, again, art isn't used up in its use. Just like everything else, it's subject to the thermodynamic ravages of time, but the use made of it doesn't consume it. More generally, if you look at all those things now called "consumer goods," you'll find that a large proportion of them are not, or need not be, "consumed" in any but the present-day sense. And what is this present-day sense? Well, says L. W., "To imagine a language is to imagine a way of life." So to imagine "consuming" we have to imagine the way of life in which the term could have been expanded so broadly. This way of life, of course, is the one organized and structured by the market. Only within such a structure could the term have been expanded so broadly. But as expanded, what does it mean? Is there a human activity called consumption that can be recognized as such and is defined by the market? I think eventually we'd have to say that there isn't, and that there's a basic incoherence in the concept. But for the present suppose that we can get close enough by saying that the activity of consuming is the activity of shopping and buying. This may seem strange because we tend to think of shopping and buying as *preceding* consumption rather than *being* consumption. But this is simply one of the nostalgic throwbacks to a prior language (hence prior way of life) that we'll have to shed if we want to talk of "consuming" in the market sense. No other activity could be defined as consumption by the market. No other activities are common to consumption so defined.

Good. Now we can ask whether the activity of consumption is, or could be, a praxis—a knowing doing. First, it would have to be a knowing doing in its own terms: no fair talking about what you'd do with the things you shop for and buy. To retreat to that level would be to make consumption secondary to other activities and other purposes—that is, a mere instrumentality of another praxis. The market can't tolerate that, nor can the concept of consumption. So shopping and buying have to be knowing doings in their own terms. If, for example, we want to talk about being good at them (being good consumers), we have to refer to getting a good bargain, taking advantage of sales, and so on. Keeping a good budget and managing household accounts will pretty surely be facets of the knowing doing. Like all praxis, consuming would require that the knowing and the doing weren't separate; that the activity be performed skillfully by the person performing it; that the *areté* or *virtù* associated with it be located in the doer. You could *learn* to do it well, but you couldn't hire someone else to do it for you or to manage it for you—that is, provide standards for your consumption. As soon as a gap opened up between your own judgment and a set of external objective standards, you'd know that the activity was becoming alienated from you: not *your* praxis, though perhaps someone else's.

These might seem to be high standards to place on consuming as a praxis, but we have to reflect that many people strive to fulfill just these standards, and that we are constantly urged to do so. The rigor of the standards is supplied by market society, not by me. Furthermore, books, syndicated columns, extension courses, and television programs all pitch in to help us achieve success in this activity. The opportunities to exercise our skills are ubiquitous and can easily come to organize and structure our lives.

I've already said quite enough about how art fits in with consuming: marginally, and for but a few. If Beardsley's standards are accepted, consuming as a praxis and the appreciation of art are split even farther apart.

Now, what would it be like for art to be a praxis? The first point to look at is the relationship between knowing and doing. For, as we've seen in the discussion of Beardsley's separation of the artist and *homo aestheticus*, there is a strong possibility that the knower and the doer will be separate people. Remember the roles that exist for critic, aesthetician, and *homo aestheticus* as public. All of them, at one time or another, make claims to be expert, not only with respect to their own roles, but also with respect to the role of the artist. Performers, conductors, composers, sculptors, and indeed all artists, are subject to their discursive scrutiny. In short, they all claim to be knowers of the artist's doings—without being doers themselves. We can compare this with older times, when the church dictated content, the church walls dictated medium, and iconography dictated style. The knower and the doer were well separated (thank heaven for Saint Sebastian). Alternatively, we can make an even better comparison and remember the radical separation—by caste—of the artist and the contemplator during ancient times. The point is that the separation of knower and doer makes art the praxis of no one. From this point of view, the current state of education in the arts is simply a consequence of the failure of art to be a praxis. Both educated parties, educated in their separate ways, are alienated from the praxis. More important, though, they're alienated from each other and meet only in uneasy circumstances: the market. It's in a somewhat futile attempt to recapture knowing and doing in their own hands that artists retreat to a very private, subjective theory of artistic expression. This simply widens the gulf between themselves and any potentially appreciating public.

We're thus brought to what I think is the central part of any

attempt to see how art could be a praxis. To be a knowing doing
that structures life, art would have to regain its ability to communicate—that is, its ability to be socially meaningful. It would have to
be impossible for the artist to crawl into his subjectivist hole to
create and for *homo aestheticus* to crawl into subjectivist contemplation potentially (always) and actually (most of the time) in no relation at all to the artist. The sharing of both the knowing and the
doing of art must become the central concern of all those engaged
in art as a praxis. Buying a piece of art isn't at all intrinsically a
communicative process involving the artist as knower-doer. It surely
isn't intrinsically an instance of the praxis of art on the part of the
buyer. The mode in which it occurs is that a sound or image understood in some way by the artist is cast into the market; then this
sound or image, understood in some way or other by a buyer, is drawn
from the market. The same sound or image is sold and bought. The
meaning to the artist and the buyer need not have any relationship.
This will be true as long as the potential communication between
artist and public is mediated by the market. For the meaning of an
item in the market is irrelevant to the market. (This remains true
even in the pseudomarket of the new industrial state.)

Inevitably this failure of shared meaning is reinforced by Liberal aesthetic theory. This theory must proceed in terms of the two
poles. The pole of private judgment ensures that each artist and
each contemplator has the right to reject shared meaning in favor of
subjective meaning. Then, when we come to objective standards,
we find that they have to be formulated in a way that will allow the
private subjectivity of an isolated contemplator to be legitimized
and communication with the artist to be unnecessary.

Furthermore, the work of art can't claim to produce a feeling
of wholeness in the face of its mediation by the market. For the
presence of the market is a constant reminder that the structure of
our social whole is not a structure in art's own terms. Nowhere is
the atomism of Liberalism more devastating than in relation to art.
Any whole that art might establish is immediately fragmented in
the awareness of the role of the market. Our art life is an adjunct to,
or an escape from our "whole" life: a "hobby" rather than an organizer and meaning-giver. In Liberal society art is not a creator of a
whole life, but rather the accusing demonstration of the fragmentation of life.

Art is no necessity in our lives. It's brought in from afar as a
diversion. Hence, art can be no praxis for us; and this is as true for
the artist as for the contemplator: when, occasionally, we manage
to become part of a whole in which art threatens to become a

praxis, and in which art is at last what forms, binds, and gives meaning to a small community, then we begin to see how art could be a praxis, a knowing-doing organizer of life. Any dealings with the market then recede to items of housekeeping. The concept of consumption becomes bizarre.

For us, though, these opportunities are ephemeral and limited. They always feel stolen and, to those of us with Puritan backbones, almost furtive. They eventually produce a feeling of fragmentation rather than wholeness. The real world of business, making a living, leading a solid bourgeois existence, is always waiting for us to return to it in abandonment of our art. Ironically, the Liberal theorists most assiduous in arguing that aesthetic value and economic value are mutually exclusive end up as the champions of fragmentation and thwarters of wholeness. Isn't the feeling of freedom the contemporary concert-goer gets while contemplating a Mozart symphony just the feeling of relief at having escaped for a while?

What I've said here may well be common knowledge, banal, platitudinous, truistic, redundant. But it's true; and since true, it argues the hopelessness of the Liberal dream. The Liberal dream is an idle one when confronted with present-day reality. Liberal defenders of art are reduced to dispensing miserable antiquarian advice: store art away in museums in wait for a better world; keep the love of art alive among a small group of faithful who will protect its memory, write about it in esoteric and learned publications, and, in short, guarantee its emargination.

No one with a sense of art as a fundamental human praxis can sit still and tolerate that emargination. But then, the task is not to find a place for art in society, but to find a society that has a place for art.

Notes

1. On the very day when I *concimare* this paper with footnotes, the Met has announced the cancellation of its 1980–81 season due to failure to come to contract agreement with its musicians.

2. Charles Dyke, "Collective Decision-Making in Rousseau, Kant, Hegel, and Mill," *Ethics* (1969): 21–37.

3. Karl Polanyi, *The Great Transformation* (Boston, 1970).

4. See John Willet, *Art and Politics in the Weimar Period* (New York, 1978), p. 137.

5. The term "artworld" may be associated, in some minds, with the work of Arthur Danto, "The Artworld," *Journal of Philosophy* 61 (1964); and George Dickie, *Aesthetics: An Introduction* (Indianapolis, 1971). As the argument progresses, it will be seen that this is the wrong association.

Danto and Dickie present us with an art fantasy rather than an artworld. For a more realistic appraisal of artworlds, see Marx Wartofsky, "Art, Artworlds, and Ideology," *Journal of Aesthetics and Art Criticism* 38 (1980): 237–47.

6. See Calvin Tomkins, "Profiles: A Good Eye and a Good Ear," *New Yorker* (26 May 1980); and Pauline Kael, "The Current Cinema: Why are Movies so Bad? or The Numbers," *New Yorker* (23 June 1980).

7. Monroe C. Beardsley, *Aesthetics: Problems in the Philosophy of Criticism* (New York, 1958), pp. 571ff.

8. Monroe Beardsley, "In Defense of Aesthetic Value," *Proceedings and Addresses of the American Philosophical Association* (1979): 723–49.

9. Ibid., pp. 741–42.

10. The following discussion owes much to the essays in Luciano Anceschi, ed., *Perche continuamo a fare e a insegnare arte?* (Bologna, 1979), especially Umberto Eco, "I Due Lati della Barricata."

11. I am indebted to the study of "praxis" and "Habitus" in Pierre Bourdieu, *Outline of a Theory of Praxis* (Cambridge, 1977).

9

Preservation, Projection, and Presence
Preliminaries to a Consideration of Pictorial Representation

FRANCIS SPARSHOTT

This essay proposes six theses. First, pictorial representation is to be considered as a practice, so that the conditions of representation are in the first instance conditions of recognizability, not of formal similarity. Second, the primacy of the condition of recognizability is a biological absolute, and alternative claims to epistemic primacy are baseless. Third, in understanding overheard discourse, we do not postulate referents for descriptions we hear, but assemble descriptions on the assumption that discourse is referential, so that the basis of our understanding is the world the discourse projects; and a like presumption of reference probably plays an analogous part in picturing. Fourth, a unified theory of picturing might construe pictures as projecting samples of possible worlds. Fifth, a recent proposal to revise the theory of propositional attitudes would modify that unified theory of picturing in a way consonant and some recent theories about the art of painting. Sixth, the theory of picturing as thus modified looks like a theory of the imagination.

The train of thought linking the six theses is consecutive, though winding. Whether it leads anywhere worth going remains unclear.

Recognition

To say that a picture represents something by looking like it seems neither controversial nor much in need of explanation. But it has been doubted. Resemblance can be neither a necessary nor a sufficient condition of representation, because a cartoon of Churchill as a bulldog looks less like the politician it represents than like the dog, and an identical twin is not a representation of his twin.[1] The force of the first of these examples may be counteracted by pointing out that those who cite it do so in a way that betrays knowledge of the fact that it is a deviant case just because there is no likeness; that of the second, by arguing that the fact that we are dealing with pictures shows that only certain kinds of likeness are relevant; but we then meet the objection that it is still impossible to specify in a precise and noncircular way what characteristics a representation must share with what it represents.

Like its counterparts in real life, the argument in the preceding paragraph is strange. The initial contention speaks of one thing's "looking like" another, but the objections are couched in terms of a "resemblance," which in turn is construed in terms of shared characteristics. And one reason for saying that one cannot specify *a priori* what characteristics must be shared is that it is presumed that *a priori* specification must use formal criteria, formality being equated with what can be specified in terms of formal logic. No argument is ever adduced to show that "sharing characteristics" is a more appropriate notion than "looking like," or to suggest that the latter notion should be expected to be reducible to the former, especially when the characteristics in question have to be formally specifiable.

The apparent relegation of recognizability to the periphery of representation is, in any event, deceptive. If we do not identify a picture as representing a horse because something in it looks like a horse, it can only be because the picture is *recognizably* a picture of a horse—a horse-picture. But what do horse-pictures have in common? They may be in any style or technique, of any kind of horse, in any conditions, from any angle; all they can have in common is that horses can be recognized in them by anyone who knows what a horse looks like and can use that kind of picture pictorially. The ability to recognize horse-pictures is parasitic on the ability to recognize horses. And the same holds for pictures of dragons or unicorns: the ability to recognize unicorn-pictures depends on the general skill of recognizing kinds of animals. Those who say that being of-a-unicorn is an "unbreakable, one-place predicate" of pictures may be right if they mean no more than that speaking of pictures of unicorns does not commit one to admitting unicorns into one's ontology, but not if they mean that the predicate can be correctly applied otherwise than on the basis of the skill of recognizing unicorns in pictures, a skill that is parasitic on the skill one would use in recognizing unicorns if there were any.

The Primacy of Recognition

Nelson Goodman's elegant treatment of what he calls "representation" has earned its influence and deserved its reputation. It is, however, an essay in formal logic; its claims to relevance to the practice of making and using pictures are not substantiated. How logic is related to epistemology, and how epistemology is related to the psychology of perception, are not questions that can be allowed to go by default.

The importance of distinguishing the formal characteristics of the symbolization that pictorial representation employs from the nature and conditions of the practice of representing becomes evident when we ask ourselves the intractable but inescapable question: what is the survival value of consciousness? The question is intractable both because it has no clear meaning, it being notoriously impossible to define consciousness acceptably, and because even to the extent that it is meaningful, one cannot see how any hypothetical answer might be verified or falsified. But never mind. What I mean by "consciousness" will be sufficiently apparent from what follows, and the difficulty about verification is inherent in historical and evolutionary speculation. At whatever risk of absurdity, we cannot refrain from exercising our minds in these areas, because to ignore them distorts our thinking into yet greater absurdity.

Two likely advantages of consciousness spring to mind. One is flexibility. An animal guided by feelings and anticipations of pleasure and pain differs from one that responds automatically to inputs in proportion to their strength, however modified by conditioning, in that the conversion of modifiers into things to be taken more or less urgently into account makes strategies possible. The key to strategies is the rearrangement of priorities. An animal's (especially a predator's) chances of survival must be enhanced by every increase in the complexity of the strategies open to it—in the cunning with which it can hunt, lurk, hide, dodge; and this complexity measures the range of its consciousness. To put it another way: the applicability of successively wider ranges of predicates specific to conscious behavior answers to corresponding increases in flexibility and organizing power. These increases must have great survival value. If consciousness can develop, then, it will develop; if it can increase it will increase. No doubt every item of conscious behavior answers to a process in the cerebral cortex, but that is neither here nor there. In the first place, changes in the cerebral cortex are behaviorally induced. In the second place, most significantly for our present purposes, the vocabulary of sentience is the only language we have for describing what it applies to, and we have no grounds for thinking that it could be translated into a language of which the conceptual apparatus would be differently organized. And in the third place, to suppose that the phenomena of consciousness are epiphenomenal or conceptually eliminable is to suppose that consciousness has been biologically selected although it confers no advantage and therefore could not have been selected. That is nonsense, and it is not made less nonsensical by the number of people who seem to believe it.

The second advantage of consciousness is that it makes possible a transformation of responses. What an animal perceives and thus can respond to answers to its needs as an organism, not to anything that can be independently characterized in physical or chemical terms. Perceived similarities in color and flavor, magnitudes of perceived differences, the difference between perceptible and imperceptible radiations and vibrations, could not have been predicted in advance of experience. Kant's split between the known world and the postulated things-in-themselves is echoed by a difference between the world directly available to perception and the world discoverable by instrumental investigation. And this difference must be biologically conditioned. What a species can notice must be just what its members are advantaged by noticing.

The advantage that consciousness bestows in making available systems of classification and discrimination based on the needs of the organism is continuous with that conferred by the facilitation of a system of recognitive structures directly related to those needs. The fact that we as organisms exist requires that what we in the first instance recognize as "the same" is not the same-shape patch projected on the retina or the same-wavelength light impinging, but the same *thing* and the same *kind of thing* in endlessly varying circumstances. To survive, a predator must recognize its prey in all surroundings, in all lights, from all angles, and must be able to do so in unprecedented situations and disguises. Any increase in this very specific skill, however small, must convey a striking genetic advantage. Craftiness and versatility in recognition, and not something in any way different from or simpler than that, is what will be directly selected. In any practical context (including that of a practice of pictorial representation), nothing can count as likeness that will not serve to underpin necessary recognitions. Epistemological reductions that neglect this rule are merely sentimental or fanciful, unless they are devised for some specific analytic purpose that defines the limits of their relevance. The onus is on those who would replace recognizable likeness by a concept of "similarity" proportional to the number of shared "characteristics," a shared characteristic being then (inevitably) equated with common membership of any class whatever, to explain the epistemic relevance of this concept. This cannot be done by appealing to formal logic, because logical considerations derive from the mere fact that formal logic is formal. And logic is epistemologically and metaphysically neutral. To be a premise is not to be a privileged kind of truth, but to occupy for the nonce a certain place in an argument; to be the value of a variable is not to enjoy a metaphysical dignity, but to be assigned for the nonce a certain place in a formula.

The standard reply to the point just made is that only what can be reduced to the strictly formal analysis of symbol systems is philosophy; the considerations for which primacy is claimed here are mere anthropology. And it is true that the separation of formal from material considerations embraces some of the great intellectual achievements of the last century. But the considerations urged here are not contingent facts of natural history. The argument is that a sort of epistemic primacy must be conceded to whatever is shown to be the necessary basis for the activity of any sentient being, and *a fortiori* for that of any rational animal. Excluding such considerations from philosophy does not discredit them; it is a mere matter of classification. And, on the other side, formal analysis should not be allowed material significance. Our minds can conceive of worlds organized on alternative bases, permitted by physics or by set theory, but to conceive of such "worlds" we must continue to live in the world, the accessible organization of which depends on the system of recognitions our bodies depend on. The ability to transcend this system in thought does not make us free to cancel or ignore it. Biological priorities are the only real absolutes we have. Just what those priorities are, and hence how consciousness is best described, has yet to be determined, a task to which the vague generalities here do not substantially contribute. What seems beyond dispute is that the phenomena of consciousness exist and are irreducible, that they could not exist if they did not have survival value, and that what has that value is the organization of the life-world that consciousness alone makes possible. But if that is true, the likenesses through which we recognize individuals and species are *in principle* irreducible.

A skill so necessary and so necessarily extensible in indefinite ways as that of recognizing individuals and kinds in the most various conditions—a skill, moreover, in which the least increase must give its possessor a genetic advantage—might be expected to extend to what is pictorially represented. The ability to see things in hiding and in camouflage should extend to enable us to see "them" in pictures—though not, of course, to make us mistake their pictured versions for themselves. The viability of a picturing convention would then depend on its affording a basis for a new range of recognitions on the basis of the ranges of recognitions we can already make. We would expect this, not because the ability to recognize things (let alone mythical beasts) in pictures has any survival value, but because the associated extensibility of the skill must have: the possession of surplus recognitive capacity. In addition, the ability to use symbol systems of the most diverse sorts has its own, very obvious and obviously great, survival value, in which again any advance must confer an advantage; and this has been widely recognized. What has not been seen is that the advantage of versatility in recognitive skill is quite different from that, and is equally certain. The fundamental peculiarity of Nelson Goodman's discussion of representation is the unspoken assumption that versatile skill in the use of symbol systems and versatile skill in recognitions cannot coexist, so that to make room for one requires that the other be explained away or reduced to its supposed rival.

Recognitive skill is not inerrant. Mistakes are possible in life as in art: wasps sting nails to death; hunters shoot cows. Identifications are best bets. But evolutionary success is entirely a matter of best bets: of strategies of individuals, or strategylike aspects of the production of progeny, that give the best chance of survival overall. Theoretical discussions of pictorial representation are plagued, as epistemology once was, by the demand for certainty. But actual discussions of what particular pictures show are content with probabilities, and (since there is usually no payoff) work with an elaborate system of assumptions that can be summed up by saying that the best bet is presumed to win. Identifications that are *prima facie* less likely are presumed wrong: in real life they would arise from the correction of errors, and since in picturing we do not suppose there to be a way of discovering error, the possibility of error is discounted. So, the best bet wins.[2] If no bet is clearly best, the uncertainty is assigned to the representation as a built-in ambiguity—a status that is often retrospectively conferred as old certainties fade.

Projection

A person who doodles may draw a horse, or a centaur, or an unnamed and hitherto unimagined and unpictured beast. It makes no difference. In each case, what he seeks to do is to make the beast appear on the page: appear to himself, and incidentally to others. He may depend on some beast or picture he has seen as a model or merely rely in a diffused way on his visual experience of beasts and pictures and his practical experience of depicting. But reference back to an original need play no part in what he is doing; no one watching him would suppose that the horse he drew must refer back to a real horse or horses, any more than a centaur would. What makes the doodle a drawing of a (real-life or imaginary) beast is that it is organized as a beast-appearance; that is, it trades on our skills of beast-recognition. The reason for not making being-a-beast-picture an unbreakable, one-place predicate of pictures rather than a quasi reference, a projection of what it would denote if it denoted anything, is that it is certainly a normal and probably a necessary condition of communication that references are grasped ahead of referents. We do not first see an organized pattern and then wonder what, if anything, it is based on; we initially construe the pattern on the basis of our recognition of what is projected, and there is no way of construing the picture or other communication otherwise than on the basis of that recognition. Defects in the skills of visual recognition are defects in the ability to read pictures.

The point that is to be made here may be more easily grasped if we consider conversation, in which references typically take the form not of isolated characterizations, but of a dispersedly allusive referential discourse in which the hearer must make out the allusions by relying on his knowledge of what it is to characterize and be characterized. In what follows, overheard discourse is proposed as a partial analogue for pictorial reference because a picture once painted is cut loose from its originating context. The painter goes away, and the spectator who comes along afterward exposes himself to a communication that does not engage him in colloquy.

One comes to understand overheard discourse by picking up items of information and provisionally assigning them to objects of which one begins to form an idea. Such an idea is formed on the basis of one's general knowledge of the world, of what characteristics tend to go together, and of specific historical realities; and also on the basis of one's knowledge of the methods and limitations of reference, of lying, error, exaggeration, meiosis, metaphor, allusion, periphrasis, aposiopesis, and so forth. One does not wait to be provided with a set of mutually exclusive and internally consistent descriptions, each explicitly assigned to an entity tagged with a single name, and then postulate the existence of the entity corresponding to each such name-and-description pair. On the contrary. One begins by assuming that the conversation is about a finite number of real things and people, and one makes this defeasible presumption a principal tool in provisionally grouping together the partial characterizations and veiled references, reshuffling one's groupings and reconstructions as additional information makes new linkages and extrapolations probable. If one did not thus actively employ the assumption that the bulk of what one overheard referred to a limited number of entities with whose probable variations one's antecedent knowledge of the world had made one reliably familiar, one could make nothing of what one heard.

What overheard discourse comes to do for the auditor, then, is to project a set of multiply related things and persons about whom and which it is; and to understand the discourse is principally to identify the projected relations and relata correctly. The objects of the discourse are not internal to it: they function as what it is about, not as its content, and this is their function even if "they" are fictive entities. Besides, the descriptions that carry the reference are likely to be full of contradictions, since we cannot expect that all who take part in a conversation will be truthful or infallible. Nor, on the other hand, is the unity of reference in such a self-contradictory body of information dependent on the reality that is its target: there need be nothing in a body of discourse to show whether its object is real or fictive, and, if fictive, whether it is culturally established or invented for the nonce, just as no feature internal to any utterance or set of utterances distinguishes it as essentially veridical or lying. Intelligibility cannot wait on verification. But if the relations and relata that the discourse projects cannot be merely internal to the discourse (since that may be self-contradictory) and cannot depend on the real world (since its object may be invented), they cannot be reduced to personal conceptions of the auditor either, because he may either understand or fail to understand what is being said; that is, he may either grasp or fail to grasp the world that is being projected. As we usually put it, he may or may not know what these people are talking about.

The notion of projection and presumptive reference introduced here has close affinities with Kaplan's concept of vividness in names.[3] He equates vividness with whatever brings something named or pictured forcibly to mind; it is this forcefulness (which may be a function of the hearer's arbitrary interest), rather than any independently identifiable property of the name, that carries a presumption of reference and makes the name a candidate for exportation beyond its original epistemic context. The force of the believer's conviction enables him and others to refer confidently to the thing or person evoked by the name, although nothing can be attributed to that thing or person beyond what the name itself encapsulates, except the facts of its being believed in and thought about.

What projection as here conceived has in common with the generation of vivid names is that both have to do with a body of discourse bringing someone who appropriately understands it to a point where he recognizes a reference as being to "the same thing they were talking about before." But there are at least three important differences. First, the limitation on extrapolation that is essential to Kaplan's context is incompatible with projection as here conceived, since conjectural extrapolation is a prime tool of understanding. Second, Kaplan speaks of isolated items that accidentally achieve psychological prominence in a sea of indifferent discourse—or at least in the context of discourse of which the character need not be considered. But in projection as here conceived, the presumption of reference is neither exceptional nor accidental: a quite general presumption of reference, antecedent to the arousal of any specific interest, is supposed necessary to comprehension, identification being the proper outcome of a continuous working toward a system of identifications that is initially presumed possible. And third, and most important, Kaplan is concerned with the warranted assertability of propositions and the legitimation of inferences, whereas the context of this discussion of projection is understanding rather than belief.

In establishing the referentiality of a body of discourse, there are three operations. One is the generation of descriptions, the construction of likenesses; another is the construction and reconstruction of that which the descriptions and likenesses project; the third is the establishing of actual historical reference beyond the body of discourse, the discovery of who or what the subjects of discussion really are or were. Contrary to what is generally implied, the first of these operations presupposes the second. Our successive efforts to construct possible subjects for patches of discourse to be about control what we accept from continued discourse as constituting a single description. Talk is allusive, and allusions can be construed only by understanding how allusions may be made and what they might be made to. The point is not that an overhearer tends to believe that people talking in a certain fashion are talking about real people; he may be skeptical or not concerned either to believe or to disbelieve. The point is that the presumption of reference is cognitively functional, providing, as it were, a set of armatures on which the most disparate discourse may be hung. People-talk has the same form whether real or imaginary people are being talked about; beast-talk has the same form for real as for mythic beasts; machine-talk has the same form for actual, possible, and impossible machines. And, in general, talk about the real world has the same form as talk about imaginary words. In each case, what gives the talk its form is the kind of reality that the talk would refer to if it referred to anything, and the kinds of questions that one expects to be asked about that kind of reality.

The presumption of reference, with its associated armory of expectations, has to precede the construction of descriptions because the latter must be allowed to be fragmentary, often erroneous, and sometimes contradictory (and is not consistency the mark of a good liar?), and still refer to something: we construct the best consensus we can. It is because in all discourse, whether its primary target is the real world or not, errors and lies make projection indeterminate and understanding conjectural that self-contradictory characterizations of fictional characters give so little trouble to readers. Notoriously, Conan Doyle's Dr. Watson had a wound that was definitely in his shoulder and equally definitely in his leg. This does not worry us, because what we know of real people, not only those we read about in books but those we know personally and quite well, often harbors contradictions of the same order. There are things one cannot ask people about unless one is really intimate with them, and sometimes not even then, so that one is resigned to going through life with such information as that the younger son of so-and-so, who has only one son, is in trouble. The demand that all such contradictions be resolved plays no part in the thinking of even the most avid gossip. They are, of course, resolvable "in principle," but so is the question about Dr. Watson's wound; to say that something can be done in principle is to say that it cannot be done but the impossibility does not worry us, and that is just what is being argued here.[4]

We have been considering the condition of someone overhearing and partly understanding a conversation, an extended and continuous but limited body of discourse. It has been argued that his understanding proceeds by knowledgeable conjecture, continuously revised, as to what individuals and kinds those referred to must be; he understands the discourse, as opposed to misunderstanding or failing to understand it or day-dreaming about it, insofar as he recognizes that which it projects for his recognition. But the preceding paragraph invites us to go a step further. If we consider not one conversation, but all the discourse a person is exposed to lifelong, we may reflect that the world as each of us knows it is a projected world, occasionally supported by experience: it is what we extrapolate from what we have encountered, heard, and read. John F. Kennedy, George Washington, Alexander of Macedon, and George of Cappadocia figure in this world in essentially the same way. Nor can we suppose that our own participation in the conversation of mankind proceeds otherwise than on the principles we bring to understanding what others say. We rather seldom know if what we say about people is true or not, and sometimes we do not know if they existed or not. A teacher of philosophy who sometimes expounds Nelson Goodman and sometimes Herakleitos will be reluctant to build too intimately into his theory of symbol use a distinction between the fictional and the veridical.

The analogy between the skill of assigning purported references, however fragmentary and distorted, to their appropriate objects, and that other skill of recognizing persons, things, and places seen fleetingly or from unfamiliar angles, under changed aspects, under varied lights, or through obstructions, is very incomplete and rather faint, but it is clear enough. It becomes rather clearer and stronger when it is extended to what has been here argued to be a natural extension of that skill, the recognition of representations. In both cases, what governs the process is an overwhelming presumption that things are recognizable and to be recognized.

Pictures and Propositions

What, in general, are representational pictures pictures of? The drift of our previous discussion has suggested some such answer as "things and people in relation" but has offered no supporting argument. The question seems rather absurd. "Of anything" seems the most suitable answer; or at least, of anything picturable. Of anything visible, at least, and probably of anything namable or describable, since for any x taken at random, some responses to an invitation to depict x will be better than others, and only a very unresourceful person would be unable to respond at all. However, the answer our previous discussion most directly invites is "anything recognizable." Be that as it may, one might consider the advantages of some such formally unified account of the picturable as logicians have essayed for the believable, the fearable, and so on. They have found it convenient, in the interests of disambiguation and methodical consistency, to represent all objects of all such "propositional attitudes" as propositions: one who wants x wants it to be the case *that* he has x; one who fears y fears *that* y will happen or will harm him; one who believes p believes *that* p is true. But what are propositions? For practical purposes, states of affairs; and a state of affairs is a part of a world. A proposition thus turns out to be a set of possible worlds, those in which the state of affairs would obtain—a "region of logical space," as one favored metaphor has it; and a possible world can be construed as the counterpart of the set of all the sentences that would be true in that world.

What, then, is a picture of? We usually respond with a noun or a noun phrase: Caesar, or Caesar Crossing the Rubicon. But we do not, and should not, answer with a sentence or a set of sentences specifying a fact or a set of facts. There is no way that a picture of Caesar crossing the Rubicon can be a picture of *the fact that* he crossed it, rather than *the fact that* he was nervous when he crossed it, or *the fact that* the Rubicon is a fordable stream. Elliott Sober has equated "pictorial competence" in a given style with the ability to come up, for a given picture, with all and only those sentences whose truth is warranted by the picture's veridicality.[5] To do so, as we saw, would be to specify the highest common factor of the possible worlds to which the picture belonged. There would, however, be indefinitely many such sentences: speaking of "all" of them invokes a spurious totality. Not only is pictorial representation, on the face of it, analog rather than digital; more important, what sentences one can utter about the content of a picture depends on what questions one can think of to ask about it, and there is no way of foretelling what questions are yet to be asked. A picture is as semantically inexhaustible as the world, so that the test of pictorial competence should rather have been made the ability always to give true answers to questions about what is in the picture. The difference is fundamental: it is that between a repertory and a skill.

A picture is most readily spoken about as being of an object or a set of objects related in certain ways. But it is more correct to speak of it as presenting a sample of a world, within which objects may be identified as inexhaustibly characterized and interrelated: a region not of logical space, but of pictorial space, which is seen and in which things and people can be seen. Like a proposition, a picture is to be taken as a set of possible worlds, the worlds in this case being construed not as sets of compatible sentences but as possible ways of continuing, visible universes compatible with having the picture as a sample.

That every work of art is construed as belonging to a world, the world that would be constituted by consistent continuations of the same picture beyond its frame (and in corresponding ways in other arts), is a thesis developed in the context of phenomenology by Mikel Dufrenne.[6] But Dufrenne argues that a given work generates a single world. It seems better to say that a work generates a set of possible worlds, because a picture could be thus extended in indefinitely many ways, all of them consistent with the picture on various understandings of how the picture is constructed and what it shows. In fact, just how one understands a picture is precisely shown by what one would accept as a consistent continuation of it. (Continuity is irrelevant: in the limiting case in which a picture is understood as essentially bounded, as when the shape of the support is integral to the design, the relevant continuations would correspond to other pictures similarly bounded; the world of such a picture would be one of discrete particulars.)

The worlds most relevant to the present discussion are represented worlds, of which the picture shows ("projects") a sample. But the notion applies, and Dufrenne applies it, equally to nonrepresentational works and to the formal aspects of representational works, in which the system of relationships construed in a given way will sustain as consistent some kinds of possible continuations and repetitions and not others. And it applies on as many levels of analysis as we care to encompass, severally or together. As elsewhere, enumeration and systematization of the classes of possible worlds of which a given picture could be taken to be a sample maps the structure of one's understanding of the picture.[7]

The metaphor of "possible worlds" must play a very different part when embedded in the formalities of modal logic from any that it can play as a device for articulating the internal logic of pictures and what they project. But it is not easy to be precise about what the difference is, because even in modal logic it is not clear how much work the metaphor is doing in organizing the formalities. For the moment, having noted that the metaphor seems to open up analogous semantic strategies in both domains, we may leave the analogy to be explored or exploited by whoever will.

Pictures are not propositions, but we have been thinking of them as in some ways propositionlike. To the extent that they are so, one point remains to be made. Propositions got into our argument as objects of attitudes: what utterers say, what hopers hope, is that some proposition is true. But in the domain of picturing, while allowance was made for variety of *prima facie* objects, none was made for anything that would correspond to the multiplicity of attitudes. That was no accident. Pictures are all, as it were, in indirect speech from the start. A painter paints that-*p* and goes away, leaving that-*p*. A spectator comes along and sees that-*p*. A painter does not even *affirm* his painting within the domain of painting itself; for him to affirm it, there would have to be ways for him to have questioned it, commanded it, and so on, and there are none. As a talker he can make statements and ask questions about his painting, but as a painter he just paints it: the "proposition" is, as it were, entertained, and that is all. If we think we find an attitude, such as hope or irony, expressed in the picture, it is because we judge the proposition entertained to be inherently hopeful or ironic and suppose that it takes a hopeful painter to paint a hopeful painting; and that, as many have pointed out, is a shaky inference.

Propositions and Presence

We have been toying with the possibility of exploiting the possible-worlds metaphor as a way of coming to terms with some aspects of pictorial representation. But that metaphor itself has recently been subverted. We are now advised to think of the objects of attitudes not as propositions, but as properties. A proposition is a set of possible worlds, and "To any set of worlds whatever, there corresponds the property of inhabiting some world in that set. In other words, to any proposition there corresponds the property of inhabiting some world where that proposition holds."[8] To believe something is to ascribe to oneself the property of inhabiting one of the worlds that, on the older analysis, constitute the proposition one believes; to hope for something is to hope one will have such a property. The reason for the revision is plain. When I hope for something, what I hope is that *my* world will be one of those in which that thing is present. There could be a world indistinguishable from that world but containing, instead of me, a being exactly like me and having my identical history, but not me. I do not care what happens in that world; what I care about is what happens to the world in which *I* am present. And the only way to distinguish between the two worlds and thus preserve the link between my present self and my future aspirations is to ascribe the hoped-for world to myself as a property of mine.

Applying this transformation of the possible-worlds trope to picturing promises no immediate advantage, but let us see how it might work. What a picturer in picturing and a viewer in viewing ascribe to themselves must be presence to some of the possible worlds of which the picture represents (projects) a segment. But presence in what mode? Since the picture is indefeasibly in indirect speech, entertained rather than affirmed or anything like that, the pictured world can only be (in Aristotelian language) a pure potential presence that picturer and viewer actualize in their different ways. It is because the business of picturing as such admits no determinate attitude that what is self-attributed is not the property of inhabiting one of the possible worlds, but that of presence. We would also have to say that what is made present is not some one of the possible worlds, but all of those that are effectively projected;

but that is an issue that calls for elaborate treatment, for which there is no room here.

That a viewer actualizes the potential presence of a picture, in a way very like that envisaged here, was made criterial for painting as a serious art in a seminal article by Michael Fried.[9] This is disconcerting at first because the category of art has played no part in our argument. But what Fried is contrasting the art of painting with is not inartistic or merely functional picturing, but the "theatrical" quasi art in which the spectator and the occasion of his aesthetic experience are compresent in a scene that it was the artist's endeavor to contrive, and such phenomena are excluded from our scope no less than from his.

Presence and Imagination

To observe and understand a picture, it now seems, is to actualize the presence of its world or worlds, constituting it or them as present to oneself, but not as a real presence. To the real world, as exemplified by whatever part of it one is for the time being experiencing, one does not ascribe presence to oneself: one simply finds it there and finds oneself in it. The presence of the picture and its world(s) is thus affirmed in a mode that denies it in the act of affirming because the necessity of the affirmation testifies to the factitiousness of the presence. Similarly, we recognize what the picture projects—we see the unicorn in the picture—but neither mistake it for a unicorn nor take it as warranting any assertion about any actual entities it might stand for. The link with reality, as we saw at the outset, is that we recognize the unicorn in the picture only because we are engaged in extending our normal system of recognitions to picturing generally, to this style of picturing specifically, and to this picture individually. The unicorn and its world are denied reality in the very act of recognition that actualizes their presence.

The language of the last few sentences, which seems imposed on us by the way our argument has gone, is akin to that used by Sartre to characterize imaginative consciousness—a rubric that covers, among other things, all those states of mind in which we have to do with works of art as such.[10] Nor is the convergence of Sartre and Lewis a result of mere free association on our part: when Sartre came to develop his theory of imagination into a full-scale "phenomenological ontology," the attribution of the world to oneself conceived as pure presence was the essential move.[11]

To bring these meditations round full circle, all that is needed is a consideration of the survival value of imagination. But that work was started by Aristotle, who already regarded imagination, the envisaging of an object of which the actual presence is denied or prescinded from, as the precondition of action.

Notes

1. For this and other matters relating to the obliqueness of the contribution similarity makes to representation, see Nelson Goodman, *Languages of Art* (Indianapolis, 1968), and "Seven Strictures on Similarity," in his *Problems and Projects* (Indianapolis, 1972).

2. The system of presumptions in identification is discussed by Monroe C. Beardsley, "The Limits of Interpretation," in *Art and Philosophy*, ed. Sidney Hook (New York, 1966), pp. 61–87.

3. David Kaplan, "Quantifying In," in *Reference and Modality*, ed. Leonard Linsky (New York, 1971), pp. 134–37.

4. To say that something is possible in principle is to assert that one holds a theory according to which the thing in question would come about in certain circumstances that cannot in fact be brought about. Since the theory is not stated, it could be anything whatever; the effect of the assertion is therefore no more than what the text says.

5. Elliott Sober, "Mental Representations," *Synthèse* 33 (1976): 101–48.

6. Mikel Dufrenne, *Phénoménologie de l'expérience esthétique* (Paris, 1953), translated by Edward S. Casey et al. *The Phenomenology of Aesthetic Experience* (Evanston, 1973).

7. For the mapping function of a possible-worlds analysis, see David K. Lewis, *Counterfactuals: A Philosophical Study* (Cambridge, Mass., 1969).

8. David Lewis, "Attitudes De Dicto and De Se," *Philosophical Review* 88 (1979): 516. It is easy to see how Lewis's new position could be reached. Possible-worlds analysis harks back to Clarence Irving Lewis's *Analysis of Knowledge and Valuation* (La Salle, Ill., 1946), pp. 50 ff., according to which a proposition stands as predicate to the world as subject: to say that Mary has a little lamb is to assign to the real world the property of being qualified by Mary's possession of a little lamb. But the only difference between the real world and other possible worlds is my presence in the former. Thus, to believe a proposition *p* is to locate myself in a *p*-world.

9. Michael Fried, "Art and Objecthood," in *Aesthetics: A Critical Anthology*, ed. George Dickie and R. J. Sclafani (New York, 1977), pp. 438–60.

10. Jean-Paul Sartre, *L'Imaginaire* (Paris, 1940); translated by Bernard Frechtman as *The Psychology of the Imagination* (New York, 1947).

11. Jean-Paul Sartre, *L'Etre et le néant* (Paris, 1943); translated by Hazel Barnes as *Being and Nothingness* (New York, 1956).

Narrative in
Literature

10

Narrative and Hermeneutics

PAUL RICOEUR

Three assumptions govern the inquiry to which this paper is devoted. First, I assume that in spite of the apparent heterogeneity of the works that are usually dealt with under the loose heading of "narrative," it is still possible to ascribe a reliable identity to the activity of storytelling. The concept of plot—or rather of emplotment, as we shall say later—will be held as the structural principle underlying the family resemblances that obtain, say, between fictional and historical narratives as well as between epos, drama, and novel among the fictional kinds.

The first assumption raises no specific hermeneutical claim to the extent that its validity falls under the control of a mere structural analysis. But as it provides the necessary background for the second and more typically hermeneutic assumption, it has to be included within the broader scope of an hermeneutic of narrative. My second contention is the following: I assume that it is the task of an hermeneutic to disentangle from the referential claims of any literary work the kind of world that the work displays. In Monroe Beardsley's terms, such a world can be rightly called the "world of the work" under consideration.[1] In my own words, "what is to be interpreted in a text is a proposed world, a world that I might inhabit and wherein I might project my own most possibilities."[2]

My third assumption is built on the previous one. It says that the temporal character of human experience is the specific stake of the referential claims of narrative work. The work-world of narratives is always a temporal world. In other words, time becomes human time to the extent that it is articulated in a narrative way, and narratives make sense to the extent that they become conditions of temporal existence.

The vindication of this third assumption entails in fact that of the two previous ones, inasmuch as the assumed identity of the activity of storytelling relies on its ability to project narrative worlds and as this ability in turn is grounded in the deep-rooted correlation between narrativity as such and temporality as such. The assertion of this correlation constitutes the hermeneutical thesis of this paper.

In a sense, the thesis displays some kind of circularity, as all hermeneutical statements do. But the whole thrust of the paper is to show that the thesis is not merely analytic—that is, tautological—because we have a distinct access to the form of temporal experience, on the one hand, and to the structure of storytelling, on the other hand. In that way, what is at stake is not only the correlation between narrativity and temporality but the kind of circularity that it entails as an hermeneutical statement.

The Paradoxes of Time Experience

I suggest that we start from the paradoxes of time experience in order to show how they call for narrative activity if they are not to fall into sheer meaninglessness. By starting from the "worldly" side of our problem, we emphasize at the same time the ontological scope of the basic thesis.

Time has nothing paradoxical about it as long as it is described in terms of mere succession between abstract "nows" and as long as the mere quantitative character of intervals between distinct events is taken exclusively into account. The paradoxes that plague our human experience of time occur beyond the merely linear and chronological—or rather chronometric—character of time. They come with the attempt to make sense of the first dialectical relationship between past, present, and future and the second dialectical relationship between temporal parts and wholes.

Augustine will help us to elaborate the paradoxes pertaining to the more than linear and chronometric aspects of human time. Augustine's central paradox concerning time may be read in the eleventh book of the *Confessions*. The paradox proceeds from the solution or dissolution of two previous paradoxes received from the tradition. The first one reads: Time has no being, since the future is not yet, the past is no more, and the present passes away. Nevertheless, we say something positive about time, since we say that the future will be, the past has been, the present is there. The solution of this paradox is as follows: the past is in a sense present to the soul through the images of past events that we call memories; the future too is present to the soul thanks to some other pictures that we call expectations; memories and expectations, in turn, are related to the present, understood as attention or attentive intuition. But the solution of the paradox is itself a paradox, since we have to speak of three kinds of present, "a present time of past things, a present time of present things, and a present time of future things."

The paradoxical character of this threefold present comes to the forefront when we attempt to give an account of the fact that we speak in a meaningful way of time as long or short, as we do in the part of rhetoric devoted to metrics when we describe syllables as long or short. How is that possible, since the present has no extension? It is at this point that Augustine introduces the daring paradox that underlines the paradoxicality inherent in the notion of a threefold present. We must assume, Augustine claims, that short of being extended as a physical body, the soul is "distended" in a way that applies only to souls. The soul, he says, stretches out in length in a way that makes possible the comparison between different spans of time. Augustine exclaims: "'Tis in thee, o my mind, that I measure my times."[4] To make sense of this *distentio animi*, let us take Augustine's example of the recitation of a poem or a psalm. (As I shall say later, this example puts us on the way that leads from a consideration of time to a consideration of narratives.) When I start reciting, the whole poem is in the mode of expectation. But while I am reciting it, the expected future decreases, whereas the past increases, so to speak, at the expense of the future. There is therefore a movement coming from the future toward the past through the present, which is traversed by this experience of a decreasing future and an increasing past. But the initial paradox of the threefold present is enhanced rather than resolved, because the soul is distracted and distended to the extent that it is also attracted and intended toward the poem as a whole, as it is anticipated at the beginning of the experience. The dialectics of remembrance, expectation, an attention within the threefold present are accordingly duplicated by the dialectics between intention and distention, which make the present human, too human, in comparison with the eternal present of God, the absolute *Now* of *simul tota*, of the all-at-once.

These paradoxes are so compelling and so perplexing that Augustine may complain: What is time? I know when nobody asks me. But when asked to explain it, I no longer know.

Nevertheless, Augustine's analysis, by his very choice of the example of reciting a poem, paves the way toward a consideration of narrative activity as a "poetic" solution of the speculative paradox. The example both introduces the paradox and makes it meaningful and, so to speak, productive in the activity of discourse. The recitation both reveals and overcomes the paradox to the extent that it displays both intention and distention. Augustine himself gives a hint as to the way this path could be followed when he describes the recited psalm or poem as the miniature of broader and broader kinds of recitation that would encompass larger stretches of action, then a whole life, and finally the whole history of mankind.

Narrative and Plot

Our next task will be to show how narrative activity—storytelling as well as history writing—responds and corresponds to these basic paradoxes of time. In the same way that I have focused on one nuclear paradox in time experience, the paradox of distention and intention, I shall focus on one correlative structure of narrativity, that is, the structure that Aristotle delineates in his *Poetics* as the *mythos* of the epic or the tragic poem. The Greek word has been translated as either "fable" or "plot." The context shows that both senses must be preserved in our modern rendering of the term. What is at stake is the union of fiction and order within one and the same operation. More precisely, the *Poetics* being about the *poiesis* of the poem—that is, its structuration rather than its structure— we do justice to Aristotle's intention by using "emplotment" or "emplotting" to designate the making of the fable as both fictional and ordered. The choice of this literary category has the obvious advantage of underscoring the mediating function of the plot. A plot mediates between individual events or incidents and a story as a whole. This mediating role may be read in both ways: a story is *made out* of events to the extent that plot *makes* events *into* a story. An event, consequently, must be more than a singular occurrence, a unique happening. It receives its definition from its contribution to the development of a plot. A story, on the other hand, must be more than an enumeration of events in a serial order; it must make an intelligible whole of the incidents, in such a way that we must always be able to ask what is the point of the story, its "theme," to translate Aristotle's concept of *dianoia*.

Now, this mediating function of the plot between event and story results from the very complex operation that is the *poiesis* of the poem. It is this operation that both reflects and resolves the paradox of time—in a poetical manner.

It reflects it to the extent that the act of emplotment combines in various proportions two temporal dimensions, one chronological and the other nonchronological. The first may be called the episodic dimension. It characterizes the story as made out of events. The second is the configurational dimension, thanks to which the plot construes significant wholes out of scattered events. Here I am borrowing from Lewis O. Mink the notion of a configurational act, which he describes as a "grasping together." As such, it displays a significant kinship with the "reflective judgment" in Kant's *Critique of Judgment*, which operates in the aesthetic judgment of taste and in the teleological judgment applied to organic wholes. The act of the plot has a similar function: eliciting a pattern from a succession.

But the *poiesis* of the poem does more than reflect the paradox of temporality. By mediating between the two poles of event and story, it provides the paradox with a solution, which is the poetic act itself. This act, just alluded to as the act of eliciting a pattern from a succession, escapes description if it is approached from the side of the storyteller. It is less intractable if it is considered from the side of the one who follows the story. In that sense, the intelligibility of the story as a whole is its "followability."

To follow a story is to proceed forward in the midst of contingencies and peripeties, under the thrust of an expectation that finds its fulfillment in the "conclusion" of the story. But this conclusion is not the logical implication of some previous premises. It is the "ending" that provides the vantage point from which the story may be seen as a whole. To understand the story is to understand how and why the successive episodes lead to this conclusion, which, even if it is not predictable, must be finally acceptable as fitting in with the episodes gathered by the story.

It is the *followability* of the story that constitutes the poetical solution of the paradox of distention-intention. The followability of the story converts the paradox into a living dialectic. On the one hand the episodic dimension of the narrative draws narrative time toward the linear representation of time in many ways. First, the "then" and "and then" structure that provides an answer to the question "What next?" suggests a relation of exteriority between the phases of the action. Besides this, the episodes constitute an open-ended series of events that allow one to add to the "then" and "and then" and "and so on." Finally, the episodes follow one another in accordance with the irreversible order of time common to human and physical events.

The configurational dimension in turn displays temporal features that proceed from the transfiguration or the metamorphosis of the succession into a configuration. First, the configurational arrangement makes the succession of events into significant wholes that are the correlate of the act of grouping together and constitute the followability of the story. Thanks to this reflective act, the whole plot may be translated into one "thought," which is what we called earlier the "point" or the "theme" of the plot. But it would be a complete mistake to consider such a "thought" atemporal. The time of fable-and-theme is the narrative time that mediates between the episodic and the configurational.

Second, the plot's configuration superimposes "the sense of an ending"—to use Kermode's expression—on the open-endedness of mere succession. I have already spoken of the "ending" as the vantage point from which the story is seen as a whole. We may now add that it is more in the act of retelling than in that of telling that this structural function of the ending may be acknowledged. As soon as a story is well known—and such is the case with most traditional and popular narratives, as well as with the national chronicles of the founding events of a given community—to follow the story is less to encompass the surprises of discoveries within the recognition of the meaning of the story as a whole than to apprehend the well-known end as implied in the beginning and the well-known episodes as leading to this end. A new quality of time emerges from this understanding.

Finally, the recollection of the story governed as a whole by its way of ending constitutes an alternative to the representation of time as flowing from the past forward into the future, according to the well-known metaphor of the "arrow of time." It is as though recollection inverted the so-called natural order of time. By reading the end in the beginning and the beginning in the end, we learn also to read time itself backward, as the recapitulation of the initial conditions of a course of action in its terminal consequences.

In short, storytelling, as reflected in story-following, makes productive the central paradoxes that perplexed Augustine to near silence.

The Hermeneutical Circle of Storytelling and Time Experience

I should like now to come to grips with the epistemological difficulties arising from the circular connection that obtains between storytelling and our nearly mute experience of time. We may be seduced by two mutually exclusive accounts of this connection.

Under the influence of the first account, we may be tempted to say, on the one hand, that narratives bring "consonance" where there is only "dissonance." In that way narratives give shape to what is shapeless. But then the forming function of narrative may be suspected of cheating. At best they provide the "as though" of fictions that we know are only fictions, that is, literary artifacts.

And they console us in the face of death. But when we no longer deceive ourselves with the consolation brought forth by paradigms, we become aware of the violence and the lie, and we are nearly defeated by the fascination of radical shapelessness and its plea for radical intellectual honesty, which Nietzsche called *Redlichkeit*. It is only by virtue of a kind of nostalgia for order that we resist the fascination and stick to the idea that order is our *patria* in spite of all. But even then the narrative "consonance" superimposed on temporal "dissonance" remains the work of that force which should be called the violence of interpretation. The narrative "solution," accordingly, is the offshoot of this violence.

I do not deny that this dramatization of the dialectic between narrativity and temporality quite appropriately reveals the discordant concordance of the very relation between narrative consonance and temporal dissonance. But if we start with such undialectical forms as consonance for narratives and dissonance for temporality, we miss the dialectical character of the relationship.

First, the experience of temporality is not reducible to mere discordance. As we saw with Augustine, there is a level of authenticity where distention and intention are at odds with each other. The paradox of time must itself be preserved from being leveled off by its reduction to mere discordance. The question then would be whether the plea for the radical shapelessness of our basic experience of time is not itself a product, a result of the general fascination with meaninglessness characteristic of our modernity. Therefore, when literary critics or thinkers seem to yield to nostalgia, or worse, to fear of chaos, what motivates them ultimately is the authentic recognition of the paradoxes of time over against the loss of meaningfulness characteristic of a particular culture—ours.

Second, the alleged "consonance" brought forth by narrative emplotment has also to be qualified in many ways. Above all, we must not mistakenly overrationalize the intelligibility by which, following Aristotle, we characterized the inner connection secured by emplotment. The kind of intelligibility that is here at stake has more to do with imagination than with reason. Emplotment, to my mind, is one of the most striking expressions of the power of schematization that Kant ascribes to the "productive imagination." This deeply rooted kinship between narrative structures and productive imagination means that emplotment always works within the framework of cultural tradition. Whereas a logic of all possible narratives, if there is any, would be transcultural in the sense that it should be foreign to cultural change, the power of schematization that is at work in emplotment is transcultural in a quite different way, that is, in the way that it takes shape through paradigms that are transmitted through traditions. Such paradigms, understood as typical modes of emplotment, proceed from the sedimentation of the work of productive imagination and provide rules for further experimentation in the field of storytelling. Thus, they change under the pressure of new inventions, since they proceed from this ongoing process of emplotting, but they change slowly and even resist change, since they are the sedimental forms of this process. Invention and sedimentation are equally implied in the constitution of traditions. Storytelling satisfies this twofold structure of traditional paradigms. Accordingly, the balance between invention and sedimentation may be disturbed in two opposite ways: by servile application of rules or by systematic cultivation of deviance. Between these two extremes, calculated deformation characterizes the average relationship between paradigms and singular works. Deviance and schism are only the opposite of slavish application.

These remarks concerning the kind of intelligibility displayed by emplotment allow us to qualify accordingly the character of "consonance" that we are tempted to oppose in a nondialectical way to the character of "dissonance" of our time experience. Emplotment is never the sheer triumph of "order." Even the paradigm of Greek tragedy makes room for the disturbing role of *peripeteia*, the contingencies and reversals of fortune that elicit our fear and pity. Plots, too, coordinate distention and intention. The same should be said of the other paradigm that, according to Frank Kermode, has ruled the "sense of an ending" in our Western tradition. I mean the apocalyptic model, which so beautifully stresses the correspondence between the beginning, the Genesis, and the end, the Apocalypse. But Kermode himself does not fail to underscore the innumerable tensions generated by this model concerning the status of every event occurring "between the times" and, above all, in the "last times."

Peripety is enhanced by the apocalyptic model because the end is the concluding catastrophe that abolishes time and is foreshadowed by the "woes of the last days." But the apocalyptic model, in spite of its enduring power (attested to by its repeated resurgences in modern utopias), is only *one* paradigm and does not exhaust the formative function of narratives in general. Paradigms keep being generated by the very process of tradition forming that I have ascribed to the power of schematization proper to the productive imagination. "Concordance" thus follows the fate of the paradigmatic order of plot structures. Even the defiance of any paradigm, exhibited by the antinovels of our time, belongs to the paradoxical history of "concordance." Through the frustrations generated by their ironic disregard for paradigms, and thanks to the more or less perverse pleasure that the reader takes in being teased and fooled, these modern works satisfy both the tradition that they defeat and the disconnected experiences that they finally imitate by not imitating the inherited paradigms. This extreme use, exactly opposed to the ultimate triumph of order in the apocalyptic model, shows in its own way that the formal notion of narrative order is capable of infinite variations, including the ironic denial of all inherited paradigms. Even in this case, it remains true that in all storytelling *some* order finally prevails.

It is at this point that the opposite interpretation of the poetical solution of the time paradoxes occurs as a threat to all the previous arguments. It could be argued that when "concordance" is not violently superimposed onto the "discordance" of our time experience, the ironic disregard for all paradigms ultimately imitates and even enhances this discordant experience. Then the alleged "discordance" of our time experience may be suspected of being itself a literary artifact. After having been confronted with the violence of interpretation, we have to come to grips with the opposite possibility, the redundancy of interpretation. In both cases the circularity of the whole argument looks dubious, if not vicious.

The redundancy of interpretation is not only implied by the extreme case of discordance generated in the midst of our lives by literary works at odds with any kind of paradigm. It is suggested by the more ordinary fact that there is no human experience that is not already mediated by symbolic systems, and, among them, by narratives. Thus, the very notion of a "narrative quality of experience," advocated by Stephen Crites, seems to suffer from the same vicious circularity that the literary artifact of "discordance" displays. How could we say that "the form of active consciousness, i.e., the form of its experiencing, is in at least some rudimentary sense narrative" and even "that it is in itself an *incipient story*,"[5] since we have no access to the "time drama" of human life and experience without the stories told about ourselves by others or by ourselves?

Nevertheless, the objection does not do justice to a phenomenon that is very intriguing and that is, to my mind, the compelling reason for ascribing an incipient or inchoate narrativity to experience as such. Are we not inclined to look at periods or episodes of our life as untold stories: stories that have still to be told but that offer clues for telling them? I am well aware of the incongruity of the term "untold story." Are not stories told by definition? It is indisputable if we are speaking of actual stories. But is the notion of potential story unacceptable?

I point to two situations in which the expression makes sense. The patient who goes to the psychoanalyst brings him bits of life stories, dreams, "primitive scenes," episodes of conflict, or what have you, and the psychoanalytical sessions may be seen as aiming toward a telling by the analysand of a story that would be both more bearable and more intelligible. Roy Schafer has taught us to consider the whole set of metapsychological theories in Freud as a system of guidelines for retelling the story in a more wholesome way. This narrative reinterpretation of psychoanalytical theory implies that a life story moves from untold and even repressed stories to actual stories assumed by the subject as constitutive of his personal identity. It is the search for this personal identity that secures the continuity from the potential or incipient story to the full-blown story for which we assume responsibility.

The notion of untold story also seems to be appropriate in another situation. There is a book by W. Schapp called *In Geschichten Verstrickt* ("Entangled in Stories"). The author, a former judge, points to situations where we try to understand a person's course of action or character by sorting out the snarl of intrigues in which he is caught. The emphasis here is on "being entangled" (*verstrickt-sein*).[6] We can no longer say that it is because a story is told that people are entangled in stories. This entanglement appears rather as the "prehistory" (*Vorgeschichte*)[7] of the story, which has a beginning chosen by the storyteller. The prehistory is what connects the story with a broader whole and gives the story a "background." The background is made of the "living connectedness"[8] of all life stories with one another. Stories, therefore, in the sense of told stories, have to "emerge" (*auftauchen*) from this background. With this emergence, the one here involved emerges too. Then we can say, "The story stands for the man" (*die Geschichte steht für den Mann*).[9] The main consequence of this existential analysis of man as "being entangled in stories" is that telling is a secondary process, the process of "the story's becoming known" (*das Bekanntwerden der Geschichte*).[10] Telling, following, and understanding stories are only the "continuation" (*Fortsetzung*)[11] of the stories. This continuation in storytelling is the concrete modality of what I just called the emergence of the story and, with it, the emergence of the one for whom the story stands.

The literary critic trained in the Aristotelian tradition, for whom the story is an artifact made by the playwright, will not be happy with this notion of a told story "continuous" with the passive entanglement of people in stories that fade into a cloudy horizon. Nevertheless, the priority here given to the not-yet-told story may serve as a critical instance against any overemphasis on the artificial character of storytelling. We tell stories because ultimately human lives need and deserve to be told. This remark finds its strength when we invoke the need to rescue the stories of the vanquished and the losers. A whole story of suffering cries to be told.

But literary criticism might be less reluctant to welcome this notion of stories as what we are entangled in if it took into account some related hints pertaining to its own field of competence. In *The Genesis of Secrecy*, Frank Kermode has introduced us to the idea that narratives not only disclose but also obscure and conceal. It is not only parables according to Mark's Interpretation which are told in order not to be understood by the outsiders: Mark, he says, "is a strong witness to the enigmatic and exclusive character of narrative, to its property of banishing interpreters from its secret places."[12] These secret places are, of course, places in the text. They point to the inexhaustibility of the text. But could we not say that this "hermeneutic potential"[13] of narratives finds, if not a consonance, at least a resonance in the untold stories of our lives? Is there not a hidden complicity between the "secrecy" generated by the narrative itself—or at least by narratives akin to Mark's and Kafka's stories—and the not-yet-told stories of our lives that constitute the prehistory, the background, the living connectedness from which the told story emerges? In other words, is there not a hidden affinity between the secrecy *from which* the story emerges and the secrecy *to which* the story heads?

Whatever may be the compelling force of this last suggestion, it should be taken as an addition to my main argument that the circularity that is obvious in any analysis of narrative in terms of the inherent form of temporal experience, and in any analysis of this form of temporality in terms of narrative structure, is not dead tautology. We are, rather, dealing with a wholesome circular argument in which the points made from both sides of the problem are mutually supportive.

Notes

1. Monroe C. Beardsley, *Aesthetics: Problems in the Philosophy of Criticism* (New York, 1958), p. 115.

2. Paul Ricoeur, "The Hermeneutical Function of Distanciation," *Philosophy Today* 17 (1973): 129–41.

3. Augustine, *Confessions* Bk. 11, Ch. 20.

4. Ibid., Bk. 11, Ch. 27.

5. Stephen Crites, "The Narrative Quality of Experience," *Journal of the American Academy of Religion* (1971): 297.

6. W. Schapp, *in Geschichten verstrickt* (Hamburg, 1953), p. 85.

7. Ibid., p. 89.

8. Ibid., p. 96.

9. Ibid., p. 100.

10. Ibid., p. 101.

11. Ibid.

12. Frank Kermode, *The Genesis of Secrecy: On the Interpretation of Narrative* (Cambridge, Mass., 1979), pp. 33–34.

13. Ibid., p. 40.

11

On the Notion of Theme in Narrative

SEYMOUR CHATMAN

"Theme," like many terms in literary history, is uncomfortably vague. For many critics "theme" and "thematic" are simply synonyms for aspects of content; a thematic analysis is whatever one does with a text that does not relate to its expression. Under this definition, to investigate the theme of a narrative is to inquire into the meanings of its events, to speculate on the motives of its characters, to interpret their relationships, to work out "authorial intentions"—but always with respect to the named characters and the specific actions in the fiction itself.

Structuralist critics too have used the term in this way: Jonathan Culler notes that for some structuralists "theme is not the result of a specific set of elements but rather the name we give to the forms of unity which we can discern in the text or to the ways we succeed in making various codes come together and cohere."[1] On this view theme is the coalescing and cohering of codes, not a code itself. To grasp the theme is to have followed the story. It is narrative content seen under its aspect of unity. This view would specifically deny that theme is "a general law which the novel proposes, or the kind of knowledge which would permit us to predict what will happen in situations like those presented" (where, presumably, "those presented" are situations in the text, and "situations like" them are those that occur in the real world).[2]

But there is critical precedent for considering theme precisely this way, as "general law," and divining the theme is seen as extrapolating, as assigning a "general function" to textual elements. The term in this latter sense—as predictive, abstracting, generalizing, pointing from the fiction to the real world—is particularly common in American poetics, and it is that sense of the term that I should like to examine. The other sense of "theme," which equates it simply with fictive content as seen in its unity, I shall call the "subject" of the narrative, following Monroe Beardsley, whose sensible discussion will be detailed in a moment. To anticipate, "theme" will be considered as a term that relates elements within a fiction to meanings in the real world. It will not be seen as the intersection of codes, but as a code like any other.

According to Monroe Beardsley, a theme is a general idea or concept that the reader can abstract from the literary text and relate to the real world at large. A thesis is similar in its external reference to the real world, but unlike theme, it is a general statement that the text may be said to afford or contain; in other words, it is a doctrine that a text implicitly or explicitly asserts. Themes and theses are understood by readers through a process of "interpretation," that word being used in a sharply technical sense by Beardsley, in contrast to two other reading processes that he names "explication" and "elucidation." Let us consider these preliminary processes first.

"Explication" is Beardsley's term for the discovery of meanings in a text, either denotative or connotative. It works on "relatively localized parts of a poem, the meaning of a metaphor, the connotations of a word, the implications of a fragment of ambiguous syntax."[3] Elucidation in Beardsley's view is more global. It concerns the formation of hypotheses about the meaning of the whole text and thus entails "filling out our knowledge of what is going on, beyond what is overtly presented."[4] So it has a more or less elaborate inferential structure. With respect to narratives, explication corresponds to what in *Story and Discourse* I called simply "reading" the narrative, that is, making sense of the words or other medial structures that convey it, whereas elucidation I called "reading out" the deep narrative structure itself, beyond the mere surface tissue: understanding the connections among events and between events and the characters that perform them, figuring out motivations, assigning traits to the characters, and so on.[5] For example, one elucidation finds the governess in *The Turn of the Screw* sane and the ghosts real; another elucidation insists that she is mad and the ghosts illusory.

The process of interpretation, on the other hand, results in the extraction of another kind of concept at a much more abstract level, which relates the work's content to the real world, the world at large. Explication and elucidation concern only elements internal to the work, within its own fictive world. The preoccupation of explication is the immediate surface of the text: words, visual images, movements or postures of the body, in whatever medium (novel, film, pantomime, ballet) capable of actualizing narrative meanings. Elucidation is concerned with the broader network: not what the work says but what it means, as a whole, though still only within its own fictive sphere. Beginning students can often expli-

cate in a fashion, figuring out what the words and sentences in a
narrative text say; yet they cannot really understand what the text
means. Imagine, for example, a child who does not yet know about
sex watching or reading *Oedipus the King*: he might be an idiot savant capable of a brilliant explication, but he cannot elucidate.

To interpret, Beardsley argues, is to take elucidation a further
step, to go beyond the world of the work and to relate abstractions
suggested by it to truths, notions, or experiences met elsewhere in
life: "To say that a poem has a certain theme or a certain thesis is to
affirm . . . that the poem does not merely construct its own world
but refers to the real world."[6] "Refers," of course, means "refers conceptually," not just tangentially. A real historical figure like Napoleon may be a character in *War and Peace*, but that presence is
not itself sufficient grounds for attributing a theme or thesis to the
novel.

Because theme goes outward from the fictive text to the real
world, some theoreticians—Jonathan Culler, for example—have
argued that "the problem of thematic extrapolation is very closely
related to that of symbolic reading."[7] It is true that the search for a
theme on the one hand and for the tenor of a symbol on the other
may lead the reader from the fictive text to the world at large. But
the differences between the two remain crucial. The symbol bears a
more concrete aspect, and it is not one of kind. Its interpretation
entails an act of imagination, a certain leap that is quite different
from the interpretation of theme. A configuration of events, characters, behaviors, and so on in a narrative, on the other hand, does
resemble situations in the outside world, in a consubstantial way. In
fact, it is an instance of the class of such situations, albeit a fictive
instance. Its relation to real instances, therefore, is at most analogical, not symbolic or metaphoric. There is another important difference: Culler argues that "symbolic recuperation . . . operates
where causal connections are absent or where those which could be
called upon seem insufficient to account for the stress which an object or event receives in the text, or even when we do not know
what else to do with a detail."[8] But surely this is not true of theme: I
experience theme precisely in the act of comprehending the full
ramifications of factors like causality, not by virtue of their defi-
ciency. So for what might be called the American sense of "theme,"
there is little profit in investigating theme through symbol, and
the sections of Roland Barthes's *S/Z* alluding to theme (like that
called "The Birth of Thematics") seem singularly unfulfilled and
unfulfilling.[9]

Beardsley distinguishes between themes and theses as follows:

"A theme is something named by an abstract noun or phrase": the theme of *Wuthering Heights* (he suggests) is "the quest for spiritual contentment through harmony with both good and evil forces of nature."[10] Abstract enough, and to be distinguished from the *subject* of *Wuthering Heights*, which we might phrase as "the effect of maltreatment on a given gypsy waif brought up to expect the life of a gentleman and the revenge he wreaks on two families whom he holds responsible for demeaning him." Notice: "a given gypsy waif," which is almost as concrete as referring to him by name, "Heathcliff." Since the "subject" is not thematically abstracted from the narrative per se, its elements remain fictional: "a certain gypsy waif," but one who never actually lived. Nor would one maintain that *Wuthering Heights* pretends to argue the relative likelihood of gypsy waifs' meeting that fate. The theme (of *Wuthering Heights*) comes into existence only to the extent that something more general is abstractable as a site of contemplation or as an issue in the world at large. The emergence of such a generality depends upon our capacity to *place* it in active historical experience, against our network of cultural codes. The subject of *Oedipus the King* includes certain events: the murder of a certain father, the mating of his son with his widow, the blinding of the son, the fate, in short, of certain characters whose proper names certify their fictionality. But the themes, Beardsley argues, are abstractions like "pride, divine power, fate, irremediable evil, the driving spirit of man";[11] these abstractions are only recognized as such when they intersect with codes ready to handle them.

A narrative theme, then, is an abstract concept, that is, a concept of a high degree of generality extractable from the work of fiction and relatable to coded human experiences, experiences of other real and fictional worlds. And if Beardsley is to be believed, what distinguishes theme from thesis is that it is not a proposition. "Pride" is a theme, but "Man is proud" is a thesis; "divine power" is a theme, but "Divine power exists," another way of saying that "God exists," is a thesis. The distinction is more than merely syntactic, though the use of a noun phrase as opposed to a complete sentence conveniently marks the different conceptual statuses of the two objects of our thought. However expressed, themes, unlike theses, make no claims. They "can be thought about, or dwelt upon," Beardsley says, but they cannot be called true or false or characterized as assertions in any way. It makes perfect sense to say, "I am thinking about divine power, though I don't believe that God exists." But it is meaningless to say, "I think that divine power exists, though I don't believe that God exists." Like other propositions, however, theses predicate; they say that one thing is or does another thing. They do not merely cite or allude to something, as do themes. Beardsley's example is Faulkner's *The Sound and the Fury*: its subject is the Compson family, fictional examples of Southern aristocracy; its theme is the decline of Southern aristocracy; its thesis (if it has one) is that the decline of Southern aristocracy is regrettable, or inevitable.

Theorists, especially those with linguistic backgrounds, must be careful not to think of theses simply as themes that have undergone grammatical transformations. In certain grammatical theories "the decline of Southern aristocracy" might be understood to bear some transformational relation to "Southern aristocracy is declining" or the like. But, obviously, Beardsley's distinction would disappear if such transformations were insisted upon. Clearly one can contemplate the decline of Southern aristocracy without taking a position that it has or has not declined. It is precisely that provocative quality, in fact, that makes themes more subtle and demanding than theses. Themes permit fictions to raise profound moral and metaphysical questions without formally stating those questions and without presupposing the possibility of easy answers, or of any answers at all.

In short, the syntactic difference is trivial, or at best the mere mark of a profounder distinction, that between open issues and closed assertions. Themes confront the reader with age-old philosophical questions like "What is one's responsibility to family, to oneself, to one's work, to one's country?" Or "What is the purpose of life? Does it have a meaning?" And the greater the work, the less likely the reader is to propose a ready answer. Theses do not confront; they inform, remind, assert, and, in their extremest form, urge. They may lend themselves to or become themselves the moral of the tale.

Let us pursue the syntactic issue a bit farther. An interesting demonstration of how useless it is to insist on the mere formulation of sentences occurs in *Story and Structure*,[12] an undergraduate textbook that is very popular in America. To capture the theme of a narrative, its author argues, one must shape it as a sentence. He defines theme as "the controlling idea or central insight" or "unifying generalization about life stated or implied by the story."[13] Now, whatever you may think about "controlling idea" or "insight," the expression "generalization" means more than mere "object of contemplation"; it means a statement, if not an assertion. For Perrine, the conditions for theme are twofold: "Theme exists only (1) when an author has seriously attempted to record life accurately or to re-

veal some truth about it, or (2) when he has mechanically introduced some concept or theory of life into it that he uses as a unifying element and that his story is meant to illustrate."[14] Albeit
heavyhandedly, this seems to acknowledge a distinction between
stories that elicit only contemplation and those that offer positive
assertions of how things are: roughly, again, the distinction between theme and thesis.

The requirement that themes always be formulated as sentences, however, lands Perrine in various difficulties. Though the
theme of Othello "may be expressed as 'Jealousy exacts a terrible
cost,'" he says, "such a statement does not begin to suggest the
range and depth of Shakespeare's play." It is not the missing range
or depth that bothers me, but the moral imperative lurking behind
such an assertion, an imperative not implicit in the corresponding
noun phrase. Unlike "the terrible cost of jealousy," the sentence
"Jealousy exacts a terrible cost" sounds like the conclusion of a syllogism: Since jealousy exacts a terrible cost, and no one is eager to
entertain terrible costs, therefore do not be jealous. How annoying!
Whatever my thoughts about jealousy are after a performance of
Othello, one that certainly does not occur is that Shakespeare prayed
me to eschew that emotion. My response seems much more complicated. What stands out most is a sense of tolerance and even sympathy for jealous ones, including, and especially (so blessed is the
instruction of art), myself. Perrine senses the danger of the imperative, for he warns his student readers not to look for "morals" in
what they read, that is, "rules of conduct that they regard as applicable to their lives."[15] Yes, one does not look for rules, but one
cannot help being affected by Othello's example. And the word "example" evokes the notion of contemplation suggested by Beardsley's
definition.

Perrine squeezes sentences out of themes zealously. He writes,
"It is insufficient to say that the theme of a story is motherhood or
loyalty to country. Motherhood and loyalty are simply subjects.
Theme must be a statement about the subject. For instance, 'Motherhood sometimes has more frustrations than rewards' or 'Loyalty to
country often inspires heroic self-sacrifice.'"[16] The studied use of
partial adverbs like "sometimes" and "often" is especially worth
noting: they are Perrine's escape hatch, his way of avoiding total
assertions, since a total assertion would be a thesis, and might lead
back again to direct moral instruction. After all, "It's the early bird
that gets the worm" tolerates no such mitigation as "sometimes" or
"often." A parable asserts an absolute opinion; it does not mince
actuarial tables. Perrine offers a whole collection of mitigations—

for instance, placing qualifications and restrictions on the individuals (represented by characters) who are the generalized agents or patients of the abstracted contemplation. All mankind must resonate to the terrible cost of jealousy. But Perrine wants us to narrow theme-sentences to read like legal contracts.

Consider his analysis of the theme of a story by Elizabeth Bowen called "Tears, Idle Tears," whose plot may be outlined as follows. A young boy, Frederick, bursts into tears in Regent's Park, as he often does, to his mother's exasperation. He is too big to cry, and his mother, a "gallant-looking correct woman," the plucky widow of an RAF hero, avenges herself on Frederick in small ways. He feels the justice of her wrath and condemns himself for his weakness. Forgetting his tears momentarily, Frederick tries to touch the tail of a duck; a girl comments, warning him about the parkkeeper. She sees his swollen eyes, casually offers him an apple, and asks him about his teary problem, nonjudgmentally, out of mere curiosity, comparing him to another boy who cries like that and who is even older. Then she says, ever so simply, "You snap out of that, if you can, before you are George's age. It does you no good." Then she extends a friendly hand to Frederick, shaking his "cheerfully," and with "tough decision." "You and George," she says. "Funny to meet two of you. Well, good-bye . . . cheer up." Frederick gives a great skip and rejoins his mother. "Years later, he could still remember, with ease, pleasure and with a sense of lonely shame being gone, that calm white duck swimming off round the bank. But George's friend . . . and George's trouble, fell through a cleft in his memory and were forgotten soon."

According to Perrine, the theme of this story should be expressed as follows: "A boy whose irrational behavior is only aggravated by attempts to make him feel guilty and ashamed may be cured when his behavior is accepted calmly and he learns that it is not unique."[17] Why is it that this statement sounds less like a theme than a psychotherapeutic recipe? Is it not partly because of its insistence on the predicate, and partly because of its excessive delimitation? "We must be careful," he warns, "not to make the generalization larger than is justified by the terms of the story. Terms like *every, all, always* should be used very cautiously; terms like *some, sometimes, may* are often more accurate."[18] But such restrictions keep the theme from referring to the outside world in many ways that are relevant to readers who are not demographers or social workers. If we follow Beardsley's broader view, it is not unreasonable to note the following themes in "Tears, Idle Tears." There are a variety of themes of pain: the pain of being small and helpless, the pain of being misunderstood, the pain of being held up to impossible standards, the pain of seeming fated to do the thing that most humiliates you, the pain of regularly disappointing someone you love. And pleasure themes too: the pleasure of being treated casually, like anyone else, after being told all your life that you are special, the pleasure of being the object of friendly curiosity, the pleasure of being given an unsolicited gift, the pleasure of the casual sympathy of a stranger, the pleasure of changing easily from a loser to a winner, the pleasure of overcoming childhood problems. These are only some of the themes of the story, and it is interesting how they interlock, into a kind of master theme, which (at the risk of doing still worse than Perrine) I venture to phrase as "the sense of comfort that derives from being nothing more (or less) than a member of the human race and the special grace that descends upon us when we see our fallibilities mirrored in and on occasion exceeded by others'."

Insofar as he insists on limiting the theme of the story to irrationally behaving boys, boys whose guilt may be cured by being calmly reassured of its nonuniqueness, Perrine excludes possible thematic resonances among all sorts of other readers: say, a woman who does not and never did behave irrationally, who, on the contrary has always been the soul of rationality, who is highly accomplished and revered by others but in that very reverence finds herself alone and even a bit estranged, and thus takes comfort (that is, pleasure) in Frederick's story, because sometimes, when she goes to the supermarket or the beauty parlor, for example, she is treated by shopgirls and manicurists as just another person . . . and so on. Perrine's insistence on qualifications narrows the audience and hence the universality of experience that one associates with thematic extrapolation into the real world. If I do not find a bit of myself in that extrapolation, the text remains locked into its subject (in Beardsley's sense) and cannot issue forth into true thematic generality.

Mine is a better statement of the theme, I feel, not merely because it is expressed in nominalized form, but because it thereby more thoroughly universalizes the story. It moves further away from immediate subject to larger implication. Perrine's instructions for abstraction just do not go far enough: "In stating theme we do not use the names of the characters in the story, for to do so is to make a specific rather than a general statement. The theme of 'Tears, Idle Tears' is not that 'Frederick is cured of his irrational fits of crying after talking with the girl on the park bench.'"[19] But going from "Frederick" to "a boy whose irrational behavior is only aggravated by attempts to make him feel guilty" is not much of a trip. Perrine

remains too specific, perhaps because he believes that "in many stories the theme may be equivalent to the revelation of human character. If a story has as its central purpose to exhibit a certain kind of
human being, our statement of theme may be no more than a concentrated description of the person revealed, with the addition,
'Some people are like this.'"[20] To me that stretches "theme" out of
all useful shape. The theme must not only refer to experiences that
I and other readers have had in the real world; it must also exhibit
genuine human significance. It must possess some survival value.
That is, through personal association it must emerge into meaningful public contemplation. Like other public statements, the validity
of a theme's phrasing can be argued, and readers can be persuaded
of its applicability to the text. "Some people are like this" just
doesn't make it: it is too banal; it does not distinguish a narrative
theme from the description of a particular patient in a case history.

Beardsley associates the thematic aspect of literature with
what he calls the Revelation Theory of Art. Though he has reservations about the viability of this theory for the other arts, he seems
willing enough to accept it for literature: a work of literature "is said
to reveal . . . something in the objective physical world outside the
artist, or a reality behind the physical world."[21] It has the capacity
to do so because of a focusing power peculiar to it: "When the general characteristic—say, vanity in human ambition [as in Ibsen's
Master Builder]—pointed up by the work is one that can also be
found in life, though seldom in so clear and pure a form, it is natural to describe this fact by saying that the work 'reveals' human vanity."[22] But, he warns, the word must be used with caution. When
we speak of themes, "We are speaking not of predications but of the
matching of characteristics."[23]

To say that a theme "reveals" means that it shows the fictive
situation to be an instance of a tendency abroad in the real world
(this is the mode of "the text shows x as" or "the text is true to the
real world"). A thesis, on the other hand, argues that the fictive
situation reveals the way the real world goes (this is the mode of
"the text says that x is the case," or "the text is true about the real
world"). Revelation sentences tout court state theme or thesis ambiguously: "This play reveals the vanity of human ambition." In its
stronger, or thesis, form, the sentence says, "This play argues that
human ambition is vain (or sometimes vain)." In its weaker version, as theme, it simply ascribes the abstract topic of vain ambition
to the play, something like: "This play shows an instance of vain
ambition upon which the reader is invited to meditate and with
which he can compare his own experience." Beardsley argues that a

literary work with a theme but no thesis may be said to be more or less true to human nature; but it cannot be said to be false to it:

> A predication [that is, a thesis] that all is vanity is true or false; it makes sense to call it either. But a quality of human nature exemplified in a literary work is not in the same position; if it can also be traced in real people, we call it true to human nature; if it cannot, it is not false to human nature, but simply a new invention.[24]

In this way, Beardsley concludes, literature can reveal—that is, exist in the mode of a kind of aesthetic revelation—in the sense that "some of the universals it exhibits are . . . the same universals we find about us, only more intense."[25]

How the reader contemplates such intense universals is beyond my capacity to formalize (though I will make a few stabs at a practical thematic analysis in the pages that follow). Still, elements of a descriptive vocabulary come to mind. "Resonating" is perhaps an apt verb to explain the psychological response to a theme: it conveys the idea of sympathetic interaction with the text without any sense of completion—the theme keeps on stimulating me to speculations, personal comparisons, and whatever, as long as I continue to think about it. There is no moment of sharp comprehension, although, I suppose, the general process can be described as one of insight, to revert to Perrine's term. For the thesis, alternatively, I propose the verb "grasping"—if there is a specific assertion made, it is reasonable to ask whether the reader has or has not grasped it. It seems much more feasible to argue with others about the validity of one's interpretation of a thesis than of a theme, and for some narratives, like fables, to reach a virtual consensus.

Putting one's finger on those universals, and especially the process by which the reading mind perceives them, is easier said than done. Let me try to exemplify with two stories by authors whose works are known for their thematic richness: Anton Chekhov and Franz Kafka. Chekhov's "A Dull [or Dreary] Story" seems a good example of a narrative with a theme, whereas the Kafka story, "First Sorrow," I think, strongly urges a thesis. I will take up the latter first and with greater brevity.

The concept of thesis naturally suggests narrative forms like the parable, narratives *expressly* designed to illustrate some assertion. Even the most difficult case, the parables of Kafka, can be explained along these lines. For what makes them difficult is not so much their failure to offer a closed assertion as their tendency to offer several and sometimes contradictory ones. But even though we have trouble formulating the appropriate assertion, somehow, we feel, there is one implied.

"First Sorrow" is only a few pages long. It recounts the tale of a nameless trapeze artist who has arranged to spend his time mostly aloft, in complete absorption in his work. His manager, a man of infinite patience, has done his best to guarantee this secluded life, speeding the artist around from engagement to engagement in racing cars in the middle of the night. One day it occurs to the trapeze artist that he must have two trapezes rather than one to work on. The manager immediately agrees but realizes that the seeds of frustration, of "first sorrow," have been born in the artist's mind. They are already reflected on his "smooth, childlike forehead."

Here are some of the possible formulations of the thesis:

1. Artists, in their struggle for perfection, ensure their own ultimate frustration.
2. Excessive devotion to any work will lead to a crisis of perfectionism. (A weaker form is "All work and no play makes Jack a dull boy.")
3. Society harms its artists by protecting them from the necessary humdrum abrasions of life, abrasions that help the rest of us mature because they teach us to cope with frustration, including necessary delays in the gratification of our desires.
4. Artists, and geniuses in general, are very much like children. They become totally involved in their work, which they do not differentiate from play; the consequence is a narcissism that ultimately poisons their lives.
5. Art, or indeed any work that aspires to greater degrees of perfection, is not only absorbing but isolating.
6. Since art is the quest for perfection, artists refuse to compromise with reality and so they find obstacles everywhere.

Obviously one could write many such sentences. What strikes me is not the futility of the task but its inevitability, given the character and powers of Kafka's art. His parables are not designed to elicit single formulations: any statement is likely to sound partial. But that does not mean that his parables do not "say" something, do not imply some specific assertion. And it is the search for that assertion that makes the parables the haunting texts they are. I am invited to feel that the code of parable is invoked, and that a specific moral observation lies hidden in the perplexing words. That the sentences proliferate may make me uneasy, but not about Kafka's ultimately assertive intentions. This is a richness quite different from that which I experience when perusing a story like Chekhov's.

I picked "A Dull Story" because I found its theme stated explicitly by a critic. Narratology as a branch of general poetics does well to study not only texts, but also the behavior of critics with respect to texts. It is useful to examine published critical statements identifying themes, and then to conjecture how these came to be formulated.

"A Dull Story" (*"Skushnáya Istóriya"*) appeared in 1889 and was subtitled "From the Notebook of an Old Man." A famous professor of medicine, Nikolai Stepanovich, writes despondently of the boredom and deterioration of his life, his declining intellectual and physical powers, his insomnia, the domestic tedium around him, his wife's obsessive concern with money and with his health, his daughter's distance and vague difficulties, her unpalatable suitor, with whom he must so often sit at dinner, the pedantic mediocrity of his assistant, and so on. He describes a typical day, replete with predictable visits—a colleague, an idler who comes to plead that he be given a passing grade on his examination, a silent doctor who presses him for a meaningless dissertation topic. Then he recalls the history of his ward, Katya, her bright curiosity and promise as a child, and how she became obsessed by the theater and ran away to join a theatrical company, only to be seduced and abandoned by an actor and to return disillusioned and withdrawn from life, a withdrawal that, she finally admits, derives from self-contempt about her lack of acting talent. Nikolai describes his nightly visits to Katya's house, where he is always upset by the bored cynicism she shares with a university colleague, Mikhail Fyodorovich. He compares them to a pair of toads and finds to his disgust that he sounds more and more like them. Even when he is on vacation, his life is miserable: his age and illness do not stop his wife from persuading him to visit Kharkov to check on his daughter's suitor's credentials. Further, she upsets him terribly by demanding that he stop seeing Katya because of her bad reputation in the neighborhood.

One night Nikolai wakes up certain that he is on the verge of death. But in the midst of this fit, he is called by his wife to attend his daughter, who is also experiencing a bout of intense and inexplicable misery. He tries helplessly to comfort her; there is nothing he can do, nothing he can say to help. He returns to his room, only to hear Katya tapping at his window. She implores him to take all her money and go to a doctor to be cured of the illness that he has predicted from the outset will kill him in a few months. He refuses, saying that her money is of no use to him now. In Kharkov the search for credentials proves idle, for he receives a telegram from his wife informing him that the couple have already eloped. The story ends as he prepares to leave his mean hotel room: Katya comes to him again and implores him to tell her what to do with her life. Despite her sobs and protestations that he, her only friend, her spiritual father, must not refuse such a request, he protests that he does not know what to say. He asks her to join him for breakfast and admits his fears that he will soon be dead. She is too preoccupied with her own problem to listen: "What shall I do?" she pleads. She refuses breakfast coldly and leaves him without looking back.

The following is a statement of the theme of "A Dull Story" by W. H. Bruford in his study of Chekhov's stories.[26] I quote it in its entirety:

> So in "A Dreary Story" (1889) Chekhov gives us the life of a famous scholar, a Russian professor of medicine of international reputation, movingly told by himself as he nears the retiring age and realises more and more clearly the tragic consequences of his inability to share the inner life of those dearest to him. Through his successful concentration on the intellectual life, the springs of human feeling have dried up in him, and at the same time he has lost all conception of "a common idea, or the God of a living man." This study of the effect of increasing age and intellectual desiccation, a world where "God is dead," gives in ninety pages a surprisingly full picture of contemporary academic life in Russia, through several contrasted figures and the family circle of the professor, with its own peculiar tensions. The central theme is as usual the unbridgeable separateness of the lives of sensitive and intelligent men and women, for whom, however, a self-contained stoical equanimity is represented as being not an ideal, but a kind of living death.[27]

Before taking up why and how I consent to this as a fair statement of the theme of "A Dull Story," let me consider an issue of some significance to thematics that I have only touched upon, namely, that implied by the qualifier "*central* theme." Can a narrative evoke a sense of several themes, and, indeed, a hierarchy among them—a sense that one or a few themes may be central or major, and supported by a constellation of minor or peripheral themes? Nothing seems easier to accept or more in keeping with intuition. What is a peripheral theme in this story? Bruford does not label any as such, but in the third sentence of the passage quoted he implies it, in the phrase "the effect of increasing age and intellectual desiccation." First let us confirm that it *is* a theme. Later we can see that it is a peripheral one. The phrase is clearly thematic, though ambiguous: it could mean "an effect which I shall now name," in which case it is not so much peripheral to but a narrowing of the central theme. Such a reading would go "*one effect* of increasing age and intellectual desiccation is the unbridgeable separateness" and so on. But for the sake of my own argument, I shall interpret "*the effects* of increasing age and intellectual desiccation," thus treating it as related to but not synonymous with the theme of "unbridgeable separateness." Earlier parts of the story do in fact depict a variety of the effects of aging, long before we get to that of increased difficulty in communication. Early on, I clearly remember resonating, through my bifocals, to the general problem of aging and loss of powers, a theme that I would phrase "the tragic consciousness felt by older people of the decline in their basic vital powers and the special poignancy of that consciousness to the gifted person." Presumably Professor Bruford's phrase came to him, as mine did to me, in response to Nikolai Stepanovich's description of his appearance (shaking hands and head, neck like the fingerboard of a double bass), of the impairment of his ability to write, of his insomnia, of his sense that life is unbearably *déjà vu*, of his recognition that those whom he has loved, like his wife, once beautiful, are now as ugly as he, and so on.

Consciousness of decline in powers through aging is by no means the only peripheral theme of the story. Let me note a few others that occurred to me, simply to fill out the picture. Apropos the doorman Nikolai: the mysterious capacity of service personnel, mere factota, to know more about what is happening in an institution than principals; apropos his "learned clod" of an assistant, Pyotr Ignatyevitch, the sad paradox that the gifted man suffers doubts and disillusionments about his work that would never occur to the steady, unimaginative plodder; apropos the professor's lecture: on the one hand, lecturing as a form of power, and on the other the sense of shame at a job badly done; apropos his dismissed thoughts of retiring: knowing what one should do and knowing that one should do it, but not being able to do it. And so on.

But let us get back to Bruford's statement of the central theme. Why is it easy to agree to its centrality? The answer, I believe, is encoded in the text, and as such open to a test of agreement among readers. First, there is the proof of redundancy. Not one but many instances of Nikolai's difficulty in communication occur—the poor lecture, the cross-purposive arguments with his wife

about visiting Kharkov and spending time with Katya, the differences with colleagues, assistants, his daughter's suitor, and so on.
In every case he is not only uncommunicative but rendered helpless
by the breakdown, and hence even less able to communicate the
next time. Most significant are those failures that reflect the special
poignancy that would be felt by an aging intellectual, a man of
wisdom, who, if anyone, should be able to help young people in
search of meaningful ways to live. Three cases stand out, and they
occur in a curve of mounting intensity: Nikolai's angry unwillingness, and later his confused and bad-faith agreement, to provide
dissertation topics to young doctors who silently wait for him to get
over his temper tantrums; his inability to help his daughter come to
grips with or even understand the vague malaise she feels; and,
most important, his failure to offer his beloved ward, Katya, any
solace, any hope, even the slightest hint of how to deal with the
agonies of her life. Obviously Chekhov's ordering of these failures is
not accidental. Indeed, ending with Katya illustrates a second
powerful code of interpretation, that which Barbara Herrnstein
Smith has taught us to call "closure."[28] Coincidence of closure with
redundancy renders the final scene and the theme attaching to it
exponentially heavy in significance. At least three young people,
including the one most important in his life, ask Nikolai in one way
or another: "Tell me what to do." To preserve his "self-contained
stoical equanimity," in Bruford's phrase, he refuses. The fact that
such stoicism may be honest, that it allows one to stay faithful to
deep convictions about one's real responsibilities to others in a
meaningless universe—that, in brief, to say nothing is better than
to lie, since any optimism necessarily entails lies—these do not
ameliorate the situation, but, on the contrary, rob one of the last
thing worth living for, human friendship and contact.

　　Having proven to my own satisfaction the thematic centrality
of noncommunication, I can better understand the peripherality of
the theme of aging and its discontents. Tragic failures to communicate can exist without the concomitant of aging; Bruford rightly
points out its general thematic prevalence in Chekhov's work. Even
a young father might well sense the puzzling counterproductiveness
of giving advice to his imploring, frustrated child and yet the emotionally desiccating effect of refusing to do so. Thus, the central
theme concerns not so much an old man's withholding advice as a
mature man's doing so. The theme of aging, with its nodding head
and scrawny neck, supports and renders more poignant that of the
ultimate if painful wisdom of silence, but it is not crucial. It vali-
dates, renders verisimilar—in the popular structuralist expression,

it "naturalizes"—the doctor's central problem, but is not logically essential to it.

The main reason for my consent to Bruford's formulation is that it coincides with aspects of my own experience that resonate with the story. Though I am not a physician and have no medical wisdom, I have often found myself being asked for help by a variety of people with one or another claim on my attention; they, too, often ask in a vague and unclear way. Indeed, the biggest problem is their inability to articulate the problem: a daughter suffering from rejection at employment offices, students who cannot sufficiently get their lives together to do their work, an ailing and dependent parent of the old school. My professional expertise and memories of various messes I have gotten myself into have made me wary and hypersensitive about the delicacy of the line I must walk when giving advice. So I get a strong—that is, a resonant—sense of Professor Nikolai's feelings: of his understanding the problem very well, of understanding that one cannot help, much as one would like to, because the problem of existence is relentlessly for each person to solve for himself.

I am not arguing that one needs to be professionally in demand for advice to understand the theme of "A Dull Story." Even a simple laborer will experience, if he is honest, the frustrations of counseling young loved ones. Whether he is able on his own to understand that that is the theme of this story is another but an irrelevant question; the fact that he *could* understand and accept it if one explained it to him is enough for me to perceive its universality.

Notice too that the resonance increases as I go further into the implications of the theme. It becomes even more a problematic. For instance, I cannot help feeling, with Bruford, that Professor Nikolai may be wrong: it may in fact be better to comfort, even though you are lying, than to say nothing. What makes the problematic, what keeps the story resonating in my mind long after I put it down, is precisely the openness of the question: is it better to comfort or not to comfort? That is the question. That is the theme.

One cannot help being personal, since it is precisely the nature of the thematic appeal to call up deep personal associations, personal instances: they serve as guarantors, if you will, of the genuine universality of the theme. A fictional narrative with weak thematic appeal, an ordinary spy novel, for example, evokes few such associations. I can read John Buchan's *The Thirty-Nine Steps* with considerable absorption and even vicarious identification with the hero as he flees from the German spies and the misguided British police, but I am not reminded in a significant way of my own real fears. And even less do I feel that sense of open resonance in the face of the insoluble and perennial problems of life.

A final question concerning theme: is it a component of narrative? That is, does it belong in Saussure-Hjelmslev-type diagrams of the sort I offered in *Story and Discourse?*[29]

	Expression	Content
Substance	Media insofar as they can communicate stories (some media are semiotic systems in their own right)	Representations of objects and actions in real and imagined worlds that can be imitated in a narrative medium, as filtered through the codes of the author's society
Form	Narrative discourse (the structure of narrative transmission) consisting of elements shared by narratives in any medium whatsoever	Narrative story components: events, existents, and their connections

The answer depends on whether we can demonstrate that every narrative does in fact have a theme. At a certain level perhaps that is true: since every narrative draws on the full set of coded representations of real or possible worlds, one could say minimally that any narrative, whatever else it does, demonstrates that "life is or could be like that." Such a formulation has the same insipid validity as the argument of some semioticians that everything is a sign because at the very least it signifies itself. As abstractions, both are so weakly general that they lose explanatory value. In other words, there may be genuinely "themeless" narratives; but a narrative—by definition—cannot exist without a chrono-logic of events, events whose sequence is radically and manifestly temporal, and a character or characters set against a background of some kind. Hence, theme may not belong in the diagram at all.

A better formulation, perhaps, is to consider the narrative text a second-order system made up of first-order semiotic elements, which can go on itself to serve a third-order system of expository texts. This view accommodates the common-sense intuition that narratives exist either for their own sake or to support, supplement, bolster, or document other kinds of texts: a sermon can use a narrative as an exemplum, a newspaper editorial arguing a change in public policy can use a narrative as an illustration of the inadequacy of present policy, a television voice urging one to buy a certain product can be accompanied by a narrative in visual images that shows how happy people are after they have bought the product. This exemplum-use of narratives can be seen as the explicit side of a coin whose reverse, implicit side is theme- and thesis-use. From the perspective of a general text theory, narratives with strongly marked themes or theses may be said to function as exempla for open-issue texts or assertion texts that happen not to be stated as such. In both the explicit and the implicit cases, such narratives serve an ancillary rather than a basic function. This is not to suggest that the great thematic or thesis novels are any the less literary for their evocation of general issues or arguments in the real world. Literariness is quite another matter.

Notes

1. Jonathan Culler, *Structuralist Poetics: Structuralism, Linguistics and the Study of Literature* (Ithaca, 1975), p. 224.
2. Ibid.
3. Monroe C. Beardsley, *Aesthetics: Problems in the Philosophy of Criticism* (New York, 1958), p. 130.
4. Ibid., p. 242.
5. Seymour Chatman, *Story and Discourse* (Ithaca, 1978).
6. Beardsley, *Aesthetics*, p. 403.
7. Culler, *Structuralist Poetics*, p. 225.
8. Ibid.
9. Roland Barthes, *S/Z* (New York, 1974).
10. Beardsley, *Aesthetics*, p. 403.
11. Ibid., p. 404.
12. Laurence Perrine, *Story and Structure* (New York, 1974), fourth edition.
13. Ibid., p. 102.
14. Ibid., p. 103.
15. Ibid., p. 104.
16. Ibid., p. 107.
17. Ibid.
18. Ibid.
19. Ibid.
20. Ibid., p. 103.
21. Beardsley, *Aesthetics*, p. 379.
22. Ibid., p. 408.
23. Ibid.
24. Ibid., p. 409.
25. Ibid.
26. W. H. Bruford, *Anton Chekhov* (New Haven, 1957).

27. Reprinted in *Discussions of the Short Story*, ed. Hollis Summer (Boston, 1963), p. 75.

28. Barbara Herrnstein Smith, *Poetic Closure* (Chicago, 1968).

29. *Story and Discourse*, p. 24.

12

Mythology
The Theory of Plot

ALEXANDER NEHAMAS

The essay that follows is, I fear, not significant enough to constitute the sort of grateful emancipation Nietzsche may have had in
mind when he wrote, in *Thus Spoke Zarathustra*, that "one repays a
teacher badly if one always remains nothing but a pupil." And
though I take issue with a particular position that Monroe Beardsley
has defended, my approach is, happily, deeply under his influence.
In trying to present a reasoned alternative to his views, I hope that
I will be offering both a celebration and a continuation of one of
Beardsley's main contributions to the intellectual climate over the
past thirty-five years: the rational discussion of the arts.

Are literary works and their plots identical? And, if they are
not, are literary works more than, and not exhausted by, their
plots?

A natural reaction to these questions is to claim that a literary
work (say, a novel) is more than its plot for the very same reasons
that the two are not identical. By contrast, I shall argue that a
novel is not more than its plot, although it is not identical with it,
either. I shall therefore have to show that the answers to the two
questions with which we began are independent of each other.

Standard discussions of the plot, which consider it as the story
told in a novel or as the sequence of events narrated in it, construe
it as one of the parts (or elements or aspects) of the novel to which
it belongs. Along with parts like the characterization and the setting, it forms one of the levels of which novels are often said to
consist, while still other elements, like the themes or the novel's
world view, belong to distinct levels. Now, if the plot is one of a
novel's parts, it seems clear that the two cannot be identical. And
though popular works may come close to being "nothing but plot,"
it also seems clear that, for the same reason, novels must in general
be more than their plot.

Many critics and philosophers consider the plot as the most elementary part of a novel in that it is absolutely basic: in the words of E. M. Forster, "it runs like a backbone"; it is the skeleton around which every narrative work is constructed.[1] Some also think, as we shall see below, that it is elementary also in that it hardly belongs to literary works considered as aesthetic objects. But whatever their views on its aesthetic significance, most literary theorists agree with Aristotle that the plot is something that belongs to literary works, that it is an object to be discovered, isolated, discussed, and evaluated, in itself as well as in relation to other parts of its novel and to similar parts of other novels.[2]

The plot, I shall argue, is not a part of a novel that can be described in its own right. To describe a novel's plot is not to describe an elementary aspect of that novel, but to give an elementary description of the novel itself. Part (but only part) of the reason we think otherwise is the surface form of expressions like "a description of the plot," which, like "a picture of Pegasus," suggests that there is an object there to be described or pictured.[3] My own view is that the expression "a description of the plot" should be construed rather as "a plot-description," signifying not so much a description of a particular part of a novel as a particular type of description of the novel itself. Later in this essay, I shall try to give some indication of what characteristics constitute the type to which plot-descriptions of novels belong. In short, I shall claim that it is a mistake to think that the plot belongs to literary works, that it is an object, rather than an instrument, of criticism. Moreover, this mistake is at least partly responsible for the anarchy that characterizes the theory of the plot; the moment discussions of that notion leave behind them the intuitions that they attempt to systematize, they become idiosyncratic, uninformative, or both. The reason for this, I shall suggest, is that there is no such thing as the theory of plot. It may be due to the fact that "criticism is not a physical, not even a psychological science" and that "any hope . . . for the kind of basic agreement in criticism that we have learned to expect in the exact sciences is doomed to disappointment"[4] that there is no such thing as theory in criticism. But a more likely explanation, I shall claim, is that there is no such thing as the plot in literature.

The plot is held to be distinct from the characters who participate in the events that constitute it and from the setting of these events, though it is commonly admitted, often in the process of drawing it, that the distinction cannot be pressed very far.[5] To take a particular discussion, René Wellek and Austin Warren have claimed that by "plot" we should not understand just a tight or gripping story; we should instead speak of "types of plots, of looser and more intricate, of 'romantic' plots and 'realistic.'" For example, "one of the oldest and most universal plots is that of the Journey, by land or water."[6]

Inspired by Aristotle, this structuralist scheme invites description in Aristotelian terms. Within this "stratum" ("the fictional world") of a literary work, the plot functions like a category distinct from characterization and setting, while the Journey is a genus belonging to it, with land and water Journeys as two of its species. Land and water are, accordingly, differentiae.

Now it is standard Aristotelian doctrine that all the elements in a definition (genus, species, and differentiae) belong to the same category. Yet land and water specify the environment of journeys, and "setting is environment";[7] they are thus illegitimate as plot-differentiae. Even if it is conceded that "Journey" applies only to events and not to their setting, the distinction between plot and setting appears, right at the outset, very unclear. Even graver difficulties face the specification of lower plot-species, like the "peaceful" or the "adventurous" journey by land, where psychological notions more appropriate to characterization become essentially involved. The distinction is further threatened if we agree that "environments can be viewed as metonymic, or metaphoric, expressions of character. . . . A stormy, tempestuous hero rushes out into the storm. A sunny disposition likes sunlight. . . . The great city . . . is the most real character in many a modern novel."[8] Actually such connections are not even metaphoric; rushing out into storms is what makes some characters tempestuous and some journeys adventurous. Odysseus' being caught in a storm (the event), the way he reacts to it (the characterization), and the proximity of Phaeacia (the setting) are all equally essential to the plot of the *Odyssey* (and to the *Odyssey* itself).

What, in the *Odyssey*, does the phrase "an adventurous journey by water" describe? Does it describe one of its parts, and is the description complete or incomplete? Does it refer to the same part to which Aristotle refers when he writes that "the story of the *Odyssey* is not long: a man is away from home for many years, Poseidon pursues him, and he is alone; at home, his wealth is being squandered, and his son's life endangered, by his wife's suitors; after suffering much he arrives, reveals himself, attacks and destroys his enemies, and preserves his own"?[9] It seems to me that these questions are moot. Such statements do not give a description of a part of the *Odyssey*, but only a partial description of the *Odyssey* itself.

Wayne Booth gives the plot of a tale by Boccacio by writing,

"There was once a young lover, Federigo, who impoverished himself courting a chaste married woman, Monna Giovanna."[10] But
this, as well as our quotation from Aristotle, seems to me to constitute yet another story, with its own rudimentary plot, characterization, and setting. And though this story has no literary merit, it is
very valuable in providing a short, clear, and manageable outline of
the work that it describes, on the basis of which discussion can proceed further. But an outline is an elementary description of a work,
and not a description of one of its elementary parts.

The failure of such examples is important, for there are no
helpful general definitions of "plot." Wellek and Warren, for example, claim that the plot is "the narrative structure of play, tale, or
novel."[11] The value of this definition is doubtful because of the fundamental obscurity of its key term, "narrative." The term is originally introduced so as to "imply the contrast of enacted action, i.e.,
drama," and narrative fiction is then defined as fiction that combines dialogue with some version of third-person discourse.[12]

But if "narrative" is introduced as a predicate of fiction, distinguishing the drama from the novel or the romance, what is the
sense of the expression "narrative structure" that applies to all fiction with the exception of lyric poetry? Perhaps the plot is to be
taken as just the structure of the dialogue and the third-person discourse, if any, to be found in any literary work. But, first, we must
know what sort of structure we should look for. Second, this definition leaves the notion of setting, "the literary element of description as opposed to narration,"[13] quite obscure. Finally, we still do
not know which element of a literary work its plot constitutes. For
the dialogue and the third-person discourse of a literary work together either constitute the work itself, in which case the plot turns
out to be "the" structure of the work itself; or else they determine
everything that the work is about, in which case the plot is "the"
structure of everything the work is about. In either case, we are far
removed, and to no obvious gain, from the original intuition that
the plot is just the story told in a literary work. Notice that I am not
claiming that novels cannot be, in some sense or another, about
events. What I am claiming is that neither these events, somehow
distinguished from their setting or their significance, nor the novel's
description of them, again distinguished similarly, can be considered a part or aspect of the novel in question. Thus, we can describe
such events, or the novel's description of them. But to do so is simply to give a partial description of the novel.

We should not give up yet the widely accepted connection
between narration and plot. Monroe Beardsley, in his influential

book *Aesthetics*, appeals to it in identifying the plot, the sequence of events a work is about, with that work's narrative structure.[14] Beardsley admits that "narration" cannot be accurately defined. He quotes Gertrude Stein's aphorism, "Narration is what anybody has to say in any way about anything that can happen, that has happened, or that will happen in any way," and Thornton Wilder's praise of Stein's "almost terrifying exactness."[15]

The trouble here, it seems to me, is that if this is being terrifyingly exact about narration, then there is no being exact about it. And the implication of this for the theory of criticism is not that a vague notion of narration is adequate, but that the notion is unlikely to be of systematic significance. In addition, a crucial ambiguity in this concept of narration diminishes its value even further.

The plot is held to be the narrative structure of literary works. Narration consists of someone's (*a*) saying (*b*) something about (*c*) something. Is the plot now the structure of what is said about something (i.e., *b*), or is it the structure of that about which something is said (i.e., *c*)? Is it the structure of the words and sentences in a literary work, or is it the structure of what they, and the work, are about? And what, if any, is the relationship between these two?

In saying that the plot is the narrative structure of play, tale, or novel, Wellek and Warren imply that it is to be found in the linguistic elements—dialogue and descriptions—that constitute literary works. But such a syntactical breakdown can be accomplished, as we shall presently see, without reference to what, intuitively, any work is about. When they write, by contrast, that the Journey is a plot, they remain close to that intuition but are prevented from reaching theoretical understanding. For, as we shall also see, the story a work tells is independent of its breakdown into words, sentences, episodes, dialogue, and description—in short, of its formal analysis.

Discussing, for the sake of simplicity, the narrative structure of "The Three Little Pigs," Beardsley writes that it "consists of two linear sequences of episodes, most of them scenes-with-dialogue, and a final episode"; he goes on to say that "in Part I there are three events that parallel each other—the wolf goes to each of the houses."[16] Now, the first quotation gives a formal analysis of the tale that has in itself no connection with the actual story. It may reflect formal relationships between the events of which that story consists, but it is clear that such relationships may obtain between the events constituting any number of stories with different subject matter. Conversely, the actual story, intuitively conceived, cannot determine the formal composition of a work that relates it.

Two works can thus have the same plot, that is, the same narrative structure, and completely different plots, that is, stories. Many Greek tragedies, for example, consist of similar sequences of prologue, choral odes, episodes, and epilogue, though each tells a totally different story. Conversely, two works that tell the same story may be structured quite differently. The narrative structures of *The Pilgrim's Progress* and *The Pickwick Papers* are dissimilar though they are both instances, according to Wellek and Warren, of the plot-type Journey.

Northrop Frye has tried to bridge this gap, but his effort, I think, fails.[17] He distinguishes between the "literal" and the "descriptive" phase, or level, of literary works ("poems"). He writes that "understanding a poem literally means understanding the whole of it, as a poem, and as it is," while "descriptively, a poem is not primarily a work of art, but primarily a *verbal* structure or set of representative words." To this uneasy distinction correspond two senses of "narrative" or "plot." Literally the narrative is a work's "rhythm or movement of words," the very arrangement of all its linguistic components: "even if [a writer] alters 'came a day' to 'a day came' he has still made a tiny alteration of sequence, and so, literally, of his rhythm and narrative." Descriptively, however, "narrative means the relation of the order of words to events resembling the events in 'life' outside," and "we no longer think of the narrative as literally embracing every word and letter. We rather think of a sequence of gross events, of the obvious and externally striking elements in the word-order."[18]

On such a scheme, considered literally the plot is just the work itself, independently (if that is possible) of any content. Considered descriptively, it seems to be a rough description either of the words constituting the work or of what the work is about, and in neither of these two cases does it isolate an element in the work. Moreover, the connection between the work's formal breakdown and its subject matter is not made any clearer than it was before.

Wellek and Warren, Beardsley, and Frye are committed to thinking of the plot as one of the structures of which literary works have been thought to consist by early twentieth-century formalists as well as by more recent structuralist critics. Yet neither their examples of particular plots nor their theoretical attempts to define the plot seem to succeed in isolating one element within literary works. Moreover, they do not answer (since they do not raise) the more general question in which we are here interested, namely, whether an elementary description of an object need be construed as a description of one of that object's elementary parts.

The ambiguity that we have been discussing can be traced back ultimately to Aristotle's original definition of the plot as "an imitation of an action."[19] Is the plot the *imitation* of the action, or is it the *action* imitated?

On the first alternative, which makes it very difficult for two distinct works to share a plot, the plot can hardly be distinguished from the characterization and the setting. The manner in which, for example, Hans Castorp's adventure in the snow is represented in Mann's *The Magic Mountain* is essentially connected with the manner in which his reaction to it, the geography of the mountainside, and the duration of the storm are described. Any change in these would change the representation of the event, and thus the plot of the novel.

The second alternative, given how many different ways there may be of specifying the same action, may allow extraordinarily many works to share a plot. In addition, it relies even more heavily than the first on the dubious distinction between the events that a literary work represents and the manner of their representation. It presupposes that we can somehow gain access to those events independently and that we can therefore contrast them with the version we find in some particular work. Aristotle may have thought this because Greek tragedy usually drew its material from known legends (or myths—hence his word *"mythos"* for plot), though he knew that some plays, like Agathon's *Atheus*, involved totally invented situations.[20] And though it might seem that we could refer to the events described in Sophocles' *Electra* through their descriptions in Euripides' play by the same title, we shall see that even in the few cases where this expedient is available, it does not justify the distinction based upon it.

The assumption that we can in any way compare an author's description of events with those events betrays a lack of awareness of one of fiction's fundamental conventions—a convention, moreover, that it has been until recently conventional to disguise; for, as Margaret Macdonald has written, "a storyteller performs; he does not—or not primarily—inform or misinform. To tell a story is to originate, not to report."[21] It seems artificial, if not plain wrong, to claim that *what* Thomas Mann represents in *The Magic Mountain* is Castorp's getting lost in the snow, while *how* he represents this is as a crucial though significantly short-lived event that changes the life of his "civilian" hero. The difference here, I think, is not between what and how, core and periphery, but rather between a very general and a slightly more specific description of this part (that is, this chapter) of the novel. Given that we accept the first description, we tend to consider its content as the subject and to characterize the second, on which disagreement is still possible, as the treatment that the subject receives.

We have said that the distinction between what is described and how it is described in particular cases is made in connection with genres like Greek tragedy. For example, Richmond Lattimore writes that "the stories told in tragedies were not pure fictions invented by the tragic poets. Mostly, the general outlines of these stories were secure as given: details might vary considerably; in choosing his variants, or in shaping and weighing the invariable, the poet made his plot."[22] The plot, in this case, is the particular treatment a story or "Legend," which exists somehow independently, receives in different plays:

> What did the Legend require, permit, forbid? Oedipus was king of Thebes. He solved, foiled, and abolished the Sphinx. He killed Laius, his father. He married his widowed mother, without knowing who she was; but the secrets of the family were discovered. He quarreled with his sons. All this, to the Greek of the fifth century was "so." . . . But we hear far more about Oedipus than this, and further details give scope for variation.[23]

The strategy here is to begin with the plays concerning a character, Oedipus. We then take the points on which they agree, put them together, and find in them the Legend of Oedipus, to which we attribute a causal and regulative function, and thus an independent status: it requires some things, it permits some, it forbids others. We now have a subject, the Legend of Oedipus, for both *Oedipus the King* and *Oedipus at Colonus* to be about. We contrast the Legend with the points on which these and other works also about the Legend differ and conclude that these points are not essential to the Legend and thus belong to the particular treatment it receives in different works.

But suppose we discover a play in which an Oedipus foils a Sphinx but, instead of becoming king of Thebes, runs away with his mother. I claim that this would be as good an instance of the Legend of Oedipus as any we now have, and that no noncircular argument can be made against it. For though our hypothetical work contradicts the Legend, the Legend is just those points on which *extant* Oedipus-plays agree. It is easy to say that the Legend permits and requires just what is and what is not variable in these plays. But precisely because of this, the Legend permits and requires nothing.

The same situation could occur in relation to all the points

that constitute the Legend of Oedipus. Some of these hypothetical
works would be strange Oedipus-stories, but they would be Oedipus-
stories nevertheless. The Legend is not an independent object, a literary Platonic Form, common to all and only Oedipus-works. It is,
rather, the content of a description true of a number of works of
literature. It does not permit, forbid, or require anything; on the
contrary, it is these individual works that permit, forbid, or require
particular useful groupings. "The Legend of Oedipus," like "the
plot-type Journey," is not a referring, but a distributive, singular
term. It does not denote a single object that is in some works or is
what some works are about, but a number of individual works about
which it supplies general information.[24]

The same is true, I suggest, of plots in general. A novel's plot
is not one of its parts. To specify the plot of a novel is to specify that
novel in an elementary way. It is to give an outline, and thus a very
simple interpretation, of that novel. The more general the specification, the more the works of which it is true, and the more the
plot looks like a type that can be shared by different works. This is
the reason definitions of the plot fail to isolate an element of literary works, and why, as we shall now see, the decision whether the
plot of a work has or has not been specified is essentially arbitrary.

Suppose we say that the plot of *The Magic Mountain* is the
story of a young man around the time of the First World War. Have
we now specified the plot of the novel? If so, is the plot of *The
Magic Mountain* identical with the plot of *The Man without Qualities*, which can also be described in these same terms? The natural
reaction is to say that only a slightly more detailed description will
show that it is not. For it is equally right to say that the plot of *The
Magic Mountain*, in contrast to that of Musil's novel, is the story of a
young German whose original three-week visit to his consumptive
military cousin's sanatorium ends only when he returns to fight in
the war seven years later. And, of course, we can easily amplify this
specification, which already involves characterization and setting.
For we can go on to say that we have here the story of a very ordinary, bourgeois, "civilian" German youth who goes to visit his sick
"military" cousin; this visit, however, is prolonged for seven years,
during which the cousin leaves, returns, and dies; the hero, who
turns out to be ill himself, falls in love with a sick Russian woman
and, on her account, with disease itself (or is it the other way
around?); he attaches himself to two intellectual mentors, each of
whom represents a basic tendency in European culture; he becomes
interested in anatomy, painting, chemistry, astronomy, psycho-
analysis, spiritualism, and music, each of which he considers to be

somehow relevant to his own condition; he finally leaves all this behind in order to return to the "flatland" and (perhaps) to die well rather than to live ill.

Such descriptions, it seems to me, can go on indefinitely, and at no point do we exhaust the plot and proceed to another "part," "phase," or level of the work. In two senses, it is not clear what does and what does not belong to a novel's plot. First, it is not clear how the plot is to be distinguished from characterization, setting, and, as I shall argue presently, theme or meaning. Second, it is not clear which aspects of a novel are relevant to deciding whether two novels do or do not share the same plot. The practice of critics seems to show that such decisions are arbitrary (though not, just for that reason, without value). Their theory seems to suggest that this arbitrariness is due to the fact that to specify a plot is to give an elementary specification of a novel, which, depending on how detailed it is, may be true of more than one work. "The plot," according to this hypothesis, is a term conventionally applying to the content of a group of relatively partial and simple descriptions of novels, often revealingly called plot-outlines or plot-summaries. And if this is true, then a novel is related to its plot not as a whole is related to one of its parts nor as a complex is related to one of its elements, but as an object is related to one (or some) of its descriptions. This explains why a novel is not identical with its plot and also why it is not more than its plot as we usually understand that idea. Such a comparison is the wrong comparison to make between an object and a description of it.

In saying this, however, we may seem to have done away with the crucial distinction between plot and theme, between what a novel is about and what it means. This latter, deeper, level is by many taken to be the main object of literary interpretation, "the business of 'getting at the message' of a text, and of decoding and making explicit its meaning . . . [which] may to some extent lie 'beyond' or 'below' the surface."[25] Different plots, it might be argued, can express similar themes, and different themes can be expressed by similar plots. In answer to this I shall argue that this distinction, as commonly made, is yet another version of the illegitimate contrast between what a work represents and how it represents it. Nothing may be intuitively wrong with saying that *Jaws*, *The Old Man and the Sea*, and *Moby-Dick* have the same plot but differ in their meaning; but this intuition cannot be systematically elaborated.

In the context of this discussion, plot, characterization, and setting are grouped together as what a work is obviously or explicitly about, what any reader who asks "How is this story going to turn out?" is concerned with. They are, as a whole, contrasted with the concern of the reader who asks, "What is the point of this story?"—the theme[26] or the "metaphysical qualities"[27] of the work. The plot is explicit and particular; the theme, which the plot expresses, is implicit and general: "In *Anna Karenina* the parallel plots stress that the heroine's fate, while typical and necessary, is yet an extremely individual one. Obviously her fate reveals the inner contradictions of modern bourgeois marriage in the most powerful terms."[28]

"Poetry," says Aristotle, "is more philosophical and more important than history; for poetry deals more with the universal, while history, with the particular."[29] A literary work is on its surface an account of particular situations of particular (though mostly imaginary) people. This account is identified with the plot, which is supposed to be understandable with little, perhaps even with no, interpretation. In some works, however, it seems that the plot suggests something more general, more abstract, and, perhaps, more important; something that is not immediately given and whose understanding requires interpretation.[30] Popular works, which generally lack themes, merely entertain. Serious works, however, do more than this and are more than they appear to be on the surface: they use their explicit subject matter for a further purpose. As Erich Kahler has remarked, "The great novels of the twentieth century, its essential books, are without exception terminal books, apotheoses of the narrative form. . . . Each, in theme, is an inventory of our spiritual holdings, a moral, aesthetic, and metaphysical reckoning up of our human estate."[31]

The effect of this attitude is to create a gulf between popular and serious literature, mere reading and literary criticism, entertainment and the aesthetic experience—and thus to render all of them less comprehensible. It disposes us to think that *Jaws*, *The Old Man and the Sea*, and *Moby-Dick* have the same "simple" plot, a man pursues a fish, but that though this is all that *Jaws* is, at least successfully, about, Hemingway's novel is also about our relationship to nature and the ironies of ideals. It stands, on such a view, between *Jaws* and *Moby-Dick*, which also tells the same story, but does even more with it. *Jaws* only entertains, but the other two novels work on more, and more complicated, levels. Though they also entertain, they provoke additional reactions as well and are therefore suitable objects of literary criticism.

On this approach, the critic begins where the mere reader stops. The latter only cares whether the fish will be caught. The critic is also interested in why it is or is not caught, in what that signifies, in what hints the texture of the novel gives about it, in what the chase does to the chaser, in metaphor, imagery, and symbolism. And thus we end up with what we might call a layer-cake view of literature, according to which "a literary work of art is not a simple object, but rather a highly complex organization of a stratified character with multiple meanings and relationships."[32] And literature is made even less accessible to its readers when, considering the plot as one of the lowest "strata" of a literary work, a philosopher like Roman Ingarden concludes that "the vicissitudes of the characters depicted in the work . . . [are] a matter of extra-literary fact" and that reading "with the object of informing oneself" about them is an activity "performed in the service of some extra-aesthetic preoccupation"![33]

Proponents of this view readily admit that the distinction between plot and theme is as elusive as that between plot and characterization. No novel is totally without plot, and none is totally without theme, though *Siddhartha* and *Jaws* may come close to these extremes.[34] But where, even roughly, do we leave plot, mere reading, and entertainment behind and become involved with theme, criticism, and the aesthetic experience?

It is not easy to identify the theme with what is implicit in literary works,[35] first because an adequate account of the relevant relation of implication is yet to be given,[36] and second because such an identification is not likely to succeed in any case. For example, Naphta's homosexuality (by all accounts, a part of the plot) is at best hinted at in *The Magic Mountain*, while the nature of time (one of its central themes) is explicitly discussed on a number of occasions.

Beardsley suggests another alternative when he writes that "the subject of *Oedipus Rex* includes Oedipus, Jocasta, Thebes . . . or the investigation of the cause of a plague. . . . But the themes are pride, divine power, fate, irremediable evil, the driving spirit of man"[37] and that, therefore, plot may be distinguished from theme as particular from general. Oedipus' particular pride represents human pride because in Oedipus Sophocles has captured a universal human type: Oedipus' pride represents human pride because Oedipus has a universal character.

But who is this individual, Oedipus, who represents a human type? Sophocles did not create an individual: "a storyteller, like a dramatist, is not said to create persons, human beings, but characters. Characters, together with their setting and situations, are parts of a story."[38] Characters, moreover, are one and all not individuals but types. This fact, which Pirandello exploits so artfully in *Six Characters in Search of an Author*, shows that Oedipus does not

represent or symbolize a human type—he *is* a human type; his pride
does not represent a type of pride—it *is* a type of pride. Oedipus
does not *have* a (universal) character; he *is* a character, which we
may recognize as (part of) our own. Aristotle was right when he
wrote that "what is universal is what sort of thing a sort of person
will probably or necessarily do—*this* is what poetry deals with,
though it uses individual names."[39]

If the central idea of this essay, that in specifying a work's plot
we are describing the whole work in a relatively elementary manner, is correct, then the fact that the plot is difficult to distinguish
from the theme no longer represents a problem. The limits, and the
conditions of identity, of the plot are unclear because the plot is in
each case taken to be constituted by those features of the work that
are, in that case, assumed not to be controversial. And what is not
controversial differs from case to case. Most literary works being accounts of imaginary events, most plot-specifications are simple descriptions of these events, and it is here that the connection between the plot and the story told in literary works originates. Plots
are outlines, and outlines describe objects in terms of easily deter-
minable features; but such features, which differ according to one's
audience, are not the referents of these descriptions.

Similarly, in specifying a theme, we do not refer to a part or
level of the work of which it is the theme, but to the whole work;
though such a description will in general be more elaborate than
that of the plot. In describing a theme we usually assume that a
more elementary description of the work in terms acceptable to us
and to our audience is available. In describing the theme we give a
more detailed, specific description of the work, and that is why
works with similar plots can have different themes. Where a more
general description may be true of two works, a more detailed one
may be true only of one.

Thus, in stating a theme we offer an interpretation of a work
given an antecedently accepted description; this description is, in
that case, the work's plot, which (as readers of Thomas Pynchon or
Alain Robbe-Grillet soon discover) may itself have required significant interpretation to be arrived at. In a way, we may liken the difference between plot and theme to the difference between seeing an
object as a dark bird hovering over the ground and seeing it as a
zone-tailed hawk on the hunt. These are not distinct aspects (much
less parts) of the bird; both descriptions refer to the bird itself,
though each tells us something different about it. Similarly, if plot
and theme are in any way levels, they are not levels of literary
works but levels of discrimination in our understanding of such

works. If we can agree more easily on the plot than on the meaning of a novel, this is because the plot consists of features chosen precisely so that agreement on them can be easily reached, while the theme-description specifies further features to which we appeal in order to account for those features that we already agree are there.

In each particular case, then, the theme plays an explanatory role. It is used to explain features of a work, specified through its plot, which may have needed to be accounted for in their own right at some earlier time. Accordingly, we do not once and for all settle the plot of a novel and then go on to its meaning. In asking "What is the point of this story?" we are not moving on to a new level, but we are trying to give a more detailed interpretation of that story; we try to account not only for its broad features, but also for its texture, for the more intricate interrelationships of its parts.

For example, having said that the plot of Moby-Dick is Ahab's pursuit of a whale, we may go on to say that its point is to exhibit his revengefulness. But why is Ahab revengeful? He lost, we reply, his leg and his pride to the whale. Yet this does not account for Ahab's all-consuming passion. So we appeal to the fact that Moby-Dick symbolizes all evil to Ahab; this may help to account for the strength of Ahab's feelings, and for his crew's willingness to follow him in his insane pursuit. At this point we may no longer think that the plot of Moby-Dick is Ahab's pursuit of a whale; it is now the story of "crazy Ahab" to whom "all that most maddens and torments; all that stirs up the lees of things; all truth with malice in it; all that cracks the sinews and cakes the brain; all the subtle demonisms of life and thought; all evil . . . were visibly personified and made practically assailable in Moby Dick." And it is the story of his crew, for whom the whiteness of the whale (discussed in a chapter that seems to, but ultimately does not, interrupt the development of the plot) functions in a similar way. This description raises new questions: Why is the whale's whiteness important? Why is Ahab consistently described by fire imagery? To answer these questions we must continue to interpret the novel: answered questions tend to be considered as part of the plot when a critic and his audience are agreed about them; unanswered ones, or those answers about which agreement is yet to be reached, tend to remain parts of its meaning.

This interdependence between plot and theme may explain why many direct statements of a work's theme, though correct, can be uninformative. To tell an audience unacquainted with Moby-Dick and Oedipus the King that both works are concerned with human pride presupposes that the audience knows more about these works than it does. To revert to our earlier simile, it is like telling someone who does not know what a bird is that he is seeing a zone-tailed hawk.

Why, then, is it so natural to consider the plot as a part of literary works rather than as a partial interpretation of them? The answer may lie in our tendency, as Nelson Goodman writes, to "sometimes mistake features of discourse for features of the subject of discourse. . . . We seldom conclude," Goodman continues, "that the world consists of words just because a true description of it does, but we sometimes suppose that the structure of the world is the same as the structure of the description."[40] Such an error is even more likely in criticism, whose subject of discourse is discourse, whose world is words.

The plot, as we have said, is the content of a partial interpretation of a literary work. But since both the work and its interpretation consist of words, and sometimes of overlapping sets of words, we tend to take features of our interpretation—its being elementary, easy to reach, sometimes true of other works as well—and project them onto the work itself. But since, in many cases, such features are not true of the work as a whole, we postulate the existence of a part of the work that we claim to be elementary, easy to grasp, and capable of being shared by a number of different works.[41]

In doing so we confuse the literary work, which (at least in this respect like a natural object) is there to be understood and interpreted, with our own interpretation and understanding. If my view is correct, questions about how the plot is to be defined, why we can never completely isolate the plot of a work, and what, if any, aesthetic significance it has, lose their ugency.

More important, we can now see that interest in a work's plot is not, as Ingarden thinks, an extra-aesthetic preoccupation, but part of our preoccupation with any literary work. Given our construal of the plot, to be exclusively interested in a work's plot is not unaesthetic but very naive: it is to be interested in the most elementary features of that work, to have the least interest we can have if we are to have any. What is "extra-aesthetic" here is not our interest in the plot, but that our interest in it is exclusive. And even here the charge is unjustified. To be concerned with the plot does not exclude the aesthetic experience, whatever that is, but all it means is that we are only pursuing a very small part of what we can get out of literature.

"Popular" works, according to this view, do not lack any levels that "serious" works possess. They are just very simple works, even if they consist, as they often do, of scores of characters multiply related. They are not very interesting, for interest is not measured

simply by our inability "to put a book down," but also by how long
we can occupy ourselves with it, what other parts of our life it has
an influence on, and how often we can return to it. Staying up all
night to finish a book that we throw into the trash in the morning is
not the essence of interest. Popular literature does not sustain prolonged or detailed attention; it cannot be read well, "slowly, deeply,
with consideration and caution" (or looking backward and forward:
rück- und vorsichtig).[42] What exhausts such works is not their plot,
but their inability to hold more than minimal attention.

Ingarden accepted a psychological distinction between mere
entertainment on the one hand and the aesthetic experience on the
other as a parallel to his ontological distinction between the different parts, strata, or levels of literary works. In this he has been
followed by numerous writers on criticism and the philosophy of
art. But as we are now becoming suspicious of the latter distinction,
we may begin to question the former one as well. Instead of contrasting the aesthetic experience with entertainment, we may now
try to see it as entertainment of a more discriminating, complex,
and demanding sort. Great literary works do not give their readers
something in addition to entertainment, but entertainment of the
highest sort. They do not require interpretation in addition to reading, but, rather, more discriminating and attentive—more active—reading. In short, they require criticism, which turns out to
be not an alternative to, but a refinement of, reading.

A literary work, then, is distinct from its plot not because the
work is a whole of which the plot is a part, but because the plot is
the content of an elementary description of that work. For the same
reason, a literary work is not more than its plot, nor again is it exhausted by it; this is the wrong comparison to make: nothing can be
more than a description that is true of it, and no description, however detailed, can exhaust its object.[43]

Notes

An earlier version of this paper was read to the Pacific Division of
the American Society for Aesthetics in March 1979. I thank Gary Isem-
inger and Catherine Lord for their comments on that occasion. Robert
Brandom, John Cooper, Cynthia Freeland, and Peter Machamer read
drafts of the paper and their criticisms were very valuable. The financial
assistance of the National Endowment for the Humanities is gratefully
acknowledged.
1. E. M. Forster, *Aspects of the Novel* (New York, 1927), p. 26. Forster makes this statement of the story, "a narrative of events," which he
distinguishes from the plot, "also a narrative of events, the emphasis fall-

ing on causality" (p. 86), but this distinction is unclear. For an interesting, though incidental, discussion of this issue, see Mary Louise Pratt, *Toward a Speech Act Theory of Literary Discourse* (Bloomington, Ind., 1977), pp. 44–45, 70–72.

2. See Aristotle, *Poetics*, 1449[b]36–1450[a]4; translation by S. H. Butcher in *Aristotle's Theory of Poetry and Fine Art* (New York, 1951). A different view of the plot as a part of the *art* of composing tragedies, not primarily of the tragedies themselves, is given by Gerald F. Else, *Aristotle's Poetics: The Argument* (Cambridge, Mass., 1967), p. 263.

3. See Nelson Goodman, *Languages of Art* (Indianapolis, 1968), pp. 21–26.

4. M. H. Abrams, *The Mirror and the Lamp: Romantic Theory and the Critical Tradition* (London, 1953), p. 4.

5. E., René Wellek and Austin Warren, *Theory of Literature* (New York, 1942), pp. 216–25. It is worth noting that both these authors, and also Robert Scholes and Robert Kellogg, *The Nature of Narrative* (New York, 1966), p. 160, quote the very same aphorism by Henry James in discussing this question: "What is character but the determination of incident? What is incident but the illustration of character?"

6. Wellek and Warren, *Theory of Literature*, p. 217.

7. Ibid., p. 221.

8. Ibid.

9. *Poetics*, 1455[b]17–23.

10. Wayne C. Booth, *The Rhetoric of Fiction* (Chicago, 1961), p. 9.

11. Wellek and Warren, *Theory of Literature*, p. 216.

12. Ibid., pp. 215–16.

13. Ibid., p. 221.

14. Monroe C. Beardsley, *Aesthetics: Problems in the Philosophy of Criticism* (New York, 1958), p. 240.

15. Ibid., p. 249 and n.

16. Ibid., p. 250.

17. Northrop Frye, *Anatomy of Criticism* (Princeton, 1971), pp. 73–82.

18. Ibid., pp. 77–79.

19. *Poetics*, 1450[a]4.

20. Ibid., 1451[b]20–25.

21. Margaret Macdonald, "The Language of Fiction," in *Philosophy Looks at the Arts*, ed. Joseph Margolis (New York, 1962), p. 190.

22. Richmond Lattimore, *Story-Patterns in Greek Tragedy* (Ann Arbor, Mich., 1964), pp. 2–3.

23. Ibid., p. 3.

24. See Wilfrid Sellars, "Abstract Entities," in *Philosophical Perspectives* (Springfield, Ill., 1967), pp. 232–36.

25. Quentin Skinner, "Motives, Intentions, and the Interpretation of Texts," *New Literary History* 3 (1972): 394. See also Richard Kuhns, "Criticism and the Problem of Intention," *Journal of Philosophy* 57 (1960):

7, and Monroe C. Beardsley, "Some Problems of Critical Interpretation: A Commentary," *Journal of Aesthetics and Art Criticism* 36 (1977–1978): 352.

26. Frye, *Anatomy of Criticism*, p. 52.

27. Wellek and Warren, *Theory of Literature*, p. 225.

28. Georg Lukacs, *The Historical Novel* (London, 1962), p. 142.

29. *Poetics*, 1451^b5-7.

30. Beardsley, *Aesthetics*, p. 403.

31. Erich Kahler, "The Devil Secularized: Thomas Mann's Faust," in *Thomas Mann: A Collection of Critical Essays*, ed. Henry Hatfield (Englewood Cliffs, N.J., 1964), p. 109.

32. Wellek and Warren, *Theory of Literature*, p. 27.

33. Roman Ingarden, "Artistic and Aesthetic Values," in *Aesthetics*, ed. Harold Osborne (Oxford, 1972), p. 41.

34. Cf. Frye, *Anatomy of Criticism*, p. 53; Wellek and Warren, *Theory of Literature*, p. 225.

35. Beardsley, *Aesthetics*, pp. 403–11.

36. John Hospers, "Implied Truths in Literature," in Margolis, *Philosophy Looks at the Arts*, pp. 199–214, discusses a number of (unsuccessful) attempts to define that relation.

37. Beardsley, *Aesthetics*, pp. 403–4.

38. Macdonald, "The Language of Fiction," p. 190.

39. *Poetics*, 1451^b8-10.

40. Nelson Goodman, "The Way the World Is," in *Problems and Projects* (Indianapolis, 1972), p. 24.

41. Jack Meiland, in "Interpretation as a Cognitive Discipline," *Philosophy and Literature* 2 (1978): 23–45, performs the same maneuver in distinguishing what he calls "textual" meaning ("*Romeo and Juliet* portrays a struggle for happiness on the part of two individuals against certain social forces," p. 30) from "literary" meaning, as an example of which he cites what a Marxist interpreter of the play would take the significance of the textual meaning to be (p. 35). Meiland concludes that there can be numerous interpretations of the same work, since the same textual meaning is compatible with many literary meanings. The latter claim is true, but only because the "textual" meaning (like the plot) is defined as the referent of the most general and elementary description (or interpretation) of the play. Any such description of any object is *compatible* with numerous more specific descriptions of the same object.

42. Friedrich Nietzsche, preface to the new edition of *The Dawn*, quoted by Walter Kaufmann in *Basic Works of Nietzsche* (New York, 1968), p. 458, n. 5.

43. See Stanley Cavell, "Aesthetic Problems of Modern Philosophy," in *Must We Mean What We Say?* (New York, 1969), pp. 74–78.

Literature and Language

13

Linguistic Competence and Literary Theory

ANN BANFIELD

The greater the objective certainty that a stylistic explanation can claim the more we will have overcome that impressionism which, until recently, has seemed the only alternative to the positivistic treatment of literature.

Leo Spitzer, *Linguistics and Literary Theory*

It is a great and necessary proof of wisdom and sagacity to know what questions may be reasonably asked. For if a question is absurd in itself and calls for an answer where there is no answer, it does not only throw disgrace on the questioner, but often tempts an incautious listener into absurd answers, thus presenting, as the ancients said, the spectacle of one person milking a he-goat, and of another holding the sieve.

Kant, *Critique of Pure Reason*

In Chomsky's distinction between competence and performance, competence signifies that part of the speaker's internalized linguistic knowledge representable within a formal theory. Isolating the object of study within generative linguistics is thus equivalent to formulating a model of competence by eliminating performance factors. This initial gesture of separating the two abstract categories of competence and performance theoretically allows some data to be set aside as irrelevant—indeed, requires it—although what belongs to one category or another in specific cases depends upon the hypothetical grammar proposed to account for competence.

Linguistic competence, then, is not simply the equivalent of the speaker's internalized linguistic knowledge; it is an idealization of it, an abstraction of what is in theory formalizable in it from what is not. It is thus fully grasped only in contrast to the notion of performance. Formalization becomes possible precisely because there is something which is acknowledged to escape it. In practice, it is often difficult to separate positive discoveries from the intuitive recognition of what is irrelevant to the theory. The isolation of compe-

201

tence as the object of linguistic inquiry is the conceptual act that guarantees the possibility of that formal grammar that is the model of the speaker's knowledge, so conceived. At the same time, it enables the linguist to give a *structural* account of this knowledge, that is, one that is independent of linguistic functions, such as communication. Furthermore, the primacy of a theory of competence over one of performance is asserted; no theory of performance can be postulated until a theory of competence has been constructed.

Once the causal connection between the notion of competence as it functions in generative grammar and the possibility of a formal, nonfunctionalistic linguistic theory with predictive power (i.e., of a linguistic science) is seized, the analogy between linguistic competence and some other cognitive competence can have fruitful consequences. (Any other analogical notion of competence only adds pseudoscientific terminology to the discussion of cognition in general.) In any precise domain in which the analogy operates, a similar isolation of the object of formal theory from factors that escape formalization must take place; there must be a counterpart not just to the notion of competence, but also to what falls under the heading of "performance." Furthermore, this counterpart to the competence/performance distinction must have a precise enough empirical content to render the analogy and its actual relation to the linguistic notion testable, in order to decide whether there is a general category of cognitive competence of which linguistic or any other analogical competence is only a special case, or whether there are structurally independent competencies. Such an initial gesture idealizing away from certain literary phenomena is not unprecedented in literary theory. In the famous formulation of the Intentional and Affective Fallacies, Monroe Beardsley and W. K. Wimsatt, Jr., define the object of the literary theorist's inquiry by identifying what it is not. "The Intentional Fallacy," Beardsley and Wimsatt maintain,

> is a confusion between the poem and its origins. . . . It begins by trying to derive the standard of criticism from the psychological *causes* of the poem and ends in biography and relativism. The Affective Fallacy is a confusion between the poem and its *results*. . . . It begins by trying to derive the standard of criticism from the psychological effects of the poem and ends in impressionism and relativism. The outcome of either Fallacy, the Intentional or the Affective, is that the poem itself, as an object of specifically critical judgment, tends to disappear.[1]

But what is the object of inquiry in literary theory? On the crudest level of analogy with linguistic theory, the literary theorist presumably seeks to discover the formal principles that account for the ability of some speakers (authors) to produce literary works recognizable as such and for that of other speakers (readers and audiences) to interpret them. Anyone who has confronted the evidence of the text will soon realize, however, that this conception of literary competence is too wide: many factors involved in the creation and interpretation of texts do not display the kinds of regularities that can be represented within a formal theory by a symbolic notation. What is required is an idealization of the text that—if inspired by the linguistic analogy—is as adapted to the particular qualities of the literary as was Chomsky's idealization from the utterance to the sentence.

Thus, only by conceiving of its object as something other than texts can poetics constitute a formal theory. For literary texts are instances of linguistic performance and only furnish the data for literary theory. It is some such idealization of the text that Beardsley and Wimsatt have in mind when they specify that "since no reader will ever read the work in exactly the same way, it must be said that the meaning of the work lies within an area of readings, and is, like the pronunciation of language sounds, a norm."[2] In his *Aesthetics*, Beardsley points out that the object of aesthetic theory is not a single "presentation" or performance. Nor is it some statistically combinable sum of all its presentations, but an idealization.[3]

Style is one such idealization of the text.[4] As the object of literary theory and the model of literary competence, style is what the theorist seeks to account for by a set of rules and principles whose output is literary sentences and texts. The formulation of these rules and principles implies a more precise articulation of the notions "literary sentence" and "text" themselves. This has its counterpart in linguistics, where the notion "sentence" is both an intuitive concept of the speaker and, as such, a part of the linguist's data, and a hypothetical construct of grammatical theory defined by the grammar itself.

Style as the idealization of the text is discernible as a conceptual whole in contradistinction to what is nonstyle. This latter, negatively defined category, however, like the category of linguistic performance, is not necessarily definable as a unified construct. When a theory of it or some part of it can be developed, it might be shown to contain more than one system. In the domain of style to be considered here, the category that escapes the formalization style permits—the category analogous to linguistic performance—

can be more precisely identified. At the general level, however, we can equate what falls—chaotically—outside the domains of style with what is conceived traditionally as the proper object of literary criticism, as opposed to literary theory:[5] questions concerning individual writers' creative selection and combination of forms latent in language, questions concerning the relation between biography (the "life") and history (the "times") and the work itself, analyses of the compatibility of style and meaning, questions of interpretation, and judgments of literary value. Any systematic answers to these questions will be dependent on a formal theory of style.

In the remainder of the paper, I examine a subcategory of style that provides empirical content for this conception of literary competence. This discussion of point of view will allow the elaboration of an empirically precise analogue in literary theory of the linguistic distinction between competence and performance, between what is expressible in a formal notation and what is not: the distinction between "linguistic" and "pragmatic" point of view. This has unexpected additional consequences. It strengthens the case for a structural as opposed to a functional account of point of view by providing syntactic—that is, linguistic—arguments against the communications model of language to implement the pragmatic ones given by Chomsky.[6] Finally, from the treatment of style as the proper idealization of the text, we will discover that literary competence, far from being distinct from linguistic competence, that is, formalizable literary phenomena—reduces to a subpart of the latter. For this reason linguistics is the appropriate methodological model for literary theory, which is not to say that literature is indistinguishable from language or literary language from the nonliterary. Indeed, the theory of style adopted here makes it possible to locate the sources of the specifically literary.

1. Linguistic and Pragmatic Point of View

The crucial importance of eliminating performance factors for any progress toward theory can be best demonstrated in practice, and this I propose to do for point of view. This notion is a special challenge to formal theory because it brings under investigation what epitomizes the asystematic and unpredictable: the subjective. If point of view, long a central concept in the criticism of narrative fiction, is to be incorporated into a theory of competence, then it must be formalizable. The intuitions of literary criticism, like those of the native speaker, are relevant, but a formal theory of point of view must go beyond them. Since point of view is a phenomenon of language, we look for grammatical evidence in terms of constructions and lexical items that cannot be fully explained without recourse to this notion. These are its linguistic realizations. But because the notion of point of view is, initially, only an intuitive one, its final definition may exclude phenomena that qualify in some intuitive sense as "subjective" if they are judged to involve factors irrelevant to the object of the theory.

Recent linguistics has turned to the investigation of various aspects of point of view: Ross's study of the special behavior of the first and second person, Quang Phuc Dong's account of exclamations and epithets, Kuroda's discussions of Japanese sensation words and the reflexive *zibun*, my own treatment of nonembeddable constructions excluded from direct speech and the style I call "represented speech and thought," Fillmore's lectures on deixis, and Milner's account of insults and exclamations.[7] Around this evidence a coherent theory is already being elaborated. This is possible, Milner argues, because the constructions forming the syntactic evidence for point of view show the kind of regularities nonsubjective constructions do and can be described without the intervention of the speaking subject, although they must ultimately be referred to the subject for interpretation:

> comment douter en effet que l'exclamation et l'insulte n'excèdent la portée de la linguistique formalisante? Cette dernière, quelle que soit sa justification d'autre part, est rendue simplement possible par ceci: les données de langue se laissent décrire, pour peu qu'on y tienne, sans qu'intervienne le fait brutal qu'elles ne se soutiennent que d'être énoncées par un sujet. De ce fait, l'écriture à quoi pour les modernes se réduit en fin de compte une science n'a pas à intégrer un terme que se définit justement de ne pas s'écrire dans la science.
>
> Mais l'exclamation et l'insulte, une fois qu'on en reconnaît l'appartenance à la langue, exigent, on le verra, d'être référées à ce terme exorbitant. Pourtant, et c'est là que le tour de la langue se boucle, ces movements où parfois tant de passion s'investit sont loin d'être sans forme distinguable. Bien au contraire, leurs expressions s'inscrivent dans des régularités et donnent lieu à une écriture en tout point comparable à toute écriture syntaxique.[8]

Just this conviction that point of view shows syntactic regularities describable by the same formal mechanisms used for other, nonsubjective syntactic phenomena has been challenged by certain literary critics and linguists. Among the latter, Kuno and Kaburaki have been insistent. Their objections, as I shall argue, are based upon a confusion of linguistic and pragmatic point of view.

Kuno and Kaburaki deny that a formal syntactic account can be given for phenomena classified under what they call "empathy." In fact, Kuno, in a general critique of the rigorous, or what Kuno and Kaburaki term the "rigid,"[9] takes empathy as a crucial case for demonstrating the inadequacy of formal syntactic explanations. For Kuno the notion "syntactic" is interchangeable with the notion "precisely formulated,"[10] just as for Kuno and Kaburaki the qualifier "rigid" accompanies "syntactic": "a rigid syntactic constraint." However "nonsyntactic" is defined for Kuno, its domain is not only the narrowly semantic but also the pragmatic; finally, it is to be equated with the unformalizable itself.

> Among generative grammarians, there is a widely held view that linguistic phenomena are primarily controlled by precisely formulatable syntactic conditions, and that nonsyntactic factors that interact with syntax, such as the speaker's belief about the universe that he lives in, presupposition, discourse influences, perceptual strategies, and so forth, play, if ever, only minor roles in producing varying degrees of grammaticality of acceptability of sentences. It is widely believed that a nonsyntactic explanation is a vice that one should take recourse to only if all attempts for precise syntactic formulations fail, and that nonsyntactic factors that cannot be precisely formulated are of little value in the theory of grammar.[11]

What Kuno wants to reclaim as a legitimate object of linguistics is performance itself. "Perceptual strategies" are, in fact, constructs of a proposed theory of performance.[12] But Kuno does not argue for the inclusion in the theory of grammar such "performance factors" because he has found a way to represent generalizations underlying them formally. Rather, he concludes that they call into question the whole possibility of formal explanation and therefore of the very distinction between competence and performance:

> I believe that I have presented undeniable evidence that concepts such as "theme," "exhaustive listing," "old, predictable information" and "new predictable information" play major roles in determining the degree of grammaticality or acceptability of sentences in wide varieties of so-called syntactic phenomena. The fact that these concepts are not precisely

formulatable is unfortunate, but it does not mean that they should be rejected. With these intuitively-plausible, although vague, concepts, we have a clue to understanding what is going on in wide varieties of phenomena some of which I have discussed above. Without these concepts, most of these phenomena would remain random phenomena.[13]

This applies also to the notion of empathy, for it includes "processes . . . so heavily dependent upon discourse factors and the speaker's point of view, that it is simply impossible to explain them on a purely syntactic basis."[14] Contributing to Kuno's conviction that the vague is preferable to the precisely formulatable is the assumption that any phenomena of language that can be observed constitute the data of linguistic theory. This is why he can conclude that until it is possible to construct a formal theory of all aspects of language use, "it seems most plausible to keep working on real linguistic data in order to discover and catalogue various factors, be they syntactic, semantic, discourse-based, or pragmatic."[15] He has not grasped that the "real linguistic data" never exist prior to any hypothesis about the data. If the processes he calls "so-called syntactic phenomena" are not syntactic at all, but pragmatic, perhaps they must be excluded from the data of linguistic theory.

These general criticisms of Kuno and Kaburaki must be supported by an analysis that demonstrates, in the particular case of what they call "empathy," that an enlightening formal account *can* be provided for this phenomenon. But this cannot be done unless one discriminates between relevant and irrelevant data. Kuno's conclusion is a trivial one: formal syntactic explanations are inadequate for "so-called syntactic phenomena." But if the so-called syntactic phenomena are winnowed out from the real, a formal account of point of view becomes achievable. The criteria for separating out the formalizable—the distinction between linguistic and pragmatic point of view—will be defined by the theory of point of view proposed here.

Kuno and Kaburaki's notion of empathy *seems* to correspond to the notion of point of view or "subjectivity," the terms traditionally used to cover the phenomena treated by Quang Phuc Dong, Ross, Kuroda, Fillmore, Milner, and me. Kuno, in fact, explicitly equates empathy with point of view: "The concept of empathy is not new: it is a part of what has been referred to in literary criticism as 'point of view'"[16]

We can assess a theoretical construct both on its internal coherence and on its ability to refer to and explain similar isolatable linguistic phenomena. What links the various constructions and lexical items identified as phenomena of point of view is the necessity of referring them in ordinary discourse to the speaking subject for full interpretation. For example, because (1a) contains an "epithet," a noun of the type Milner calls *noms de qualité*, it necessarily invokes the speaker and his value judgments, while the interpretation of (1b), with an ordinary noun substituted, does not involve the speaker at all.

(1)   a. John was examined by that idiot (fool) of a doctor.
        b. John was examined by that student of the doctor.

Kuno and Kaburaki's formulation of empathy, on the other hand, is heavily dependent on evidence of a very different kind. They open their discussion of empathy with the following examples:

(2)   a. John hit Mary.   = Kuno and Kaburaki's (1)
        b. John hit his wife.
        c. Mary's husband hit her.
(3)   a. Mary was hit by John.   = Kuno and Kaburaki's (2)
        b. ??John's wife was hit by   ??His wife was hit by John.
        him.
        c. Mary was hit by her husband.

They comment as follows:

> All the above sentences are identical in their logical content, but they differ from each other with respect to "camera angles." In (1a), it is most likely that the speaker is describing the event objectively, with the camera placed at some distance from both John and Mary. In (1b), on the other hand, the camera is placed closer to John than to Mary. This can be seen by the fact that the speaker has referred to John as *John*, and to Mary as *John's wife*. The situation is reversed in (1c), where the camera is placed closer to Mary than to John. (1b) and (1c) show one way (choice of descriptors) by which the speaker can overtly show from whose angle he is describing the event.[17]

Evidence of empathy, then, in (2) and (3) is provided by what Kuno and Kaburaki call "choice of descriptors." Is this equivalent to the way point of view in (1a) was indicated by the presence of an epithet? Comparing the two notions, point of view and empathy, as they are brought into play in (1) and in (2) and (3), respectively, we find that they include two distinct sets of claims.

2. The Assignment of Point of View

To enable us to distinguish the two classes of evidence, we must distinguish the two theoretical constructs, "point of view" and "empathy," which define the limits of the evidence for each theory. The notion of linguistic point of view isolates one class of subjective constructions from other constructions not only by their special interpretation, but also by their structure. These are the exclamations, exclamatory sentences, and the constructions I have discussed elsewhere.[18] They appear either leftmost in the sentence or alone as an "incomplete" or "amorphous" sentence, as in (4).

(4)   Damn the torpedoes!
      Off with her head!
      What a lark!
      Oh, how happy we'll be!
      God, am I crazy!
      Poor baby!
      Damn fool!
      Fuck you!
      Up with the republic!
      To the barricades with those bricks!
      Down with tyrants!
      One more remark like that and I'll quit!

The nonembeddable aspect of these elements and constructions suggests a revision of Chomsky's 1973 paper, "Conditions on Transformations,"[19] but one in conformity with the account of base structure presented there through the bar notation. The consequence is to provide the mechanism for relating all subjective expressions, both embeddable and nonembeddable. In this revision, the initial symbol of the base grammar is replaced by a nonrecursive node E ("Expression"): $\bar{S}$ is introduced in a rule expanding E which also introduces to its left those nonembeddable constructions, like those in (4), which express the speaker's point of view. Thus, the grammar can quite naturally relate point of view in the syntax uniquely to the node E. We have only to make the relation between the E and point of view explicit. Because an embedded sentence ($\bar{S}$)—that is, crucially, the subordinate clause of indirect speech— cannot contain exclamations and other nonembeddable expressive elements and, therefore, can only represent the quoting speaker's point of view, the number of points of view must be restricted to one. The following principle thus assigns point of view uniquely to the speaker.

(5)   1 E/1 Speaker: For every expression (E), there is a unique referent of I (the Speaker), to whom all expressive elements are attributed.

We have only to specify that these expressive elements are all immediately dominated by E. Milner suggests the formulation in (6).

(6)   dans une structure [$_E\omega$], ou $\omega \neq$ S, ω ne peut être interprété que comme l'expression d'un affect du sujet de l'énonciation désigné par E.[20]

The distinction between E and $\bar{S}$ permits the grammar quite naturally to explain another aspect of these subjective expressions, one that enables us to make (6) redundant, or, at least, to relate it to a more general interpretative principle. In themselves, Es cannot be assigned a truth value, although they may contain an $\bar{S}$ that has one. There is no state of affairs affirmed or denied by "Damn the torpedoes!" or "One more remark like that and I'll quit." In each case the speaker expresses his point of view without asserting or denying anything. If truth value is a property of propositions, the lack of a truth value for subjective expressions follows from their syntax—only $\bar{S}$ can be plausibly argued to have the logical form of a proposition. And if we assume, following Frege,[21] that the truth value of a sentence constitutes its reference, then, as Milner suggests, we might treat the subjectivity of Es, or of what is outside of $\bar{S}$ in E, the syntactic residue of what determines the truth value of an $\bar{S}$ in E, as constituting their proper reference. The E refers to the speaking subject. (6) then becomes only the subpart of the general rules for reference that concerns the E.

But point of view, especially as understood in literary criticism, is not always coextensive with the speaker. There is an extensive critical literature on the phenomenon of "third-person point of view," which Kuno seems to be unaware of. This interpretive category has a precise manifestation in syntax, in the style called *style indirect libre*, *erlebte Rede*, or represented speech and thought, illustrated in (7).

(7)   "Oh, how extraordinarily nice workmen were, she thought."
        (Katherine Mansfield, "The Garden-Party," p. 287)

"Where were her paints, she wondered. Her paints, yes." (Virginia Woolf, *To the Lighthouse*, p. 167)

"Why couldn't she have workmen for friends rather than the silly boys who came to Sunday night supper?" ("The Garden-Party," p. 287)

"And now that he did think of it, he began to remember that he *hadn't* seen Christopher Robin about so much lately. Not in the mornings. Afternoons, yes; evenings, yes; before breakfast, yes; just after breakfast, yes. And then, perhaps, 'see you again, Pooh,' and off he'd go." (A. A. Milne, *The House at Pooh Corner*, p. 84)

This literary style requires a revision of 1 E/1 Speaker, for in it point of view is assigned, not to the E's first person, but to a consciousness designated by a third-person pronoun. But the E is still restricted to expressing a single point of view, so we need only substitute for the term "SPEAKER" a more general one including both SPEAKER and third-person consciousness, which I call the "SELF." (5) now reads:

(8)   1 E/1 SELF: For every node E, there is a unique referent, called the SELF, to whom all expressive elements are attributed.

Because no sentence can be interpreted with a third-person SELF if it contains a first person (* Where were my$_i$ paints, she$_j$ wondered), a further principle must specify that in a sentence containing a first person, only the I is interpretable as the SELF.

(9)   Priority of Speaker. If there is an I, I is the SELF.

I have offered a more elaborate justification of these principles elsewhere.[22]

In contrast to the account of point of view outlined here, Kuno and Kaburaki's notion of empathy leaves unclear the relation between the speaker and a nonspeaker's point of view. The definition of empathy in (10) might be taken to imply (vaguely) that the term covers exclusively the phenomenon of third-person point of view or represented speech and thought.

(10)   Empathy. Empathy is the speaker's identification, *with varying degrees* (ranging from degree 0 to 1), with a person who participates in the event that he describes.[23]

Or, if it allows the possibility of "zero identification" on the speaker's part, there is no formal way to distinguish the cases where, according to Kuno and Kaburaki, the point of view is "objective" (e.g., [2a]) from those where the point of view is the speaker's, unless the latter is a case of what they call the "speaker empathizing with himself."[24] In Kuno's brief discussion of represented thought, which he calls, following Kuroda, "the nonreportive style," he explicitly opts for analyzing an other than first-person point of view as characterized by the absence of the speaker.

> It is not the case that the narrator is *reporting*, as an observer, on what John knew. The sentence is the direct representation of John's own point of view, without the narrator's mediating interpretation. It is a *nonreportive* sentence in which the narrator has identified himself with John, and is putting out what John felt in the new form.[25]

Kuno gives only two very similar examples of this style; one (given in [11]) is preceded by a sentence with a first person, a sequence that is not in fact uniformly acceptable in this style, if the second sentence is to be interpreted with a third-person SELF.

(11)   Mary$_i$ tried to convince both Tom and me to go. As for herself$_i$, she$_i$ wasn't sure what she$_i$ would do.

Nor do the other cases where the speaker "empathizes with a third person" qualify as examples of represented speech or thought.

There is an inconsistency between this description of represented thought, where the narrator is held to be absent, and the later definition of empathy (10), presumably meant to explain it, where the speaker mediates another point of view. Because Kuno and Kaburaki's formulation is so vague, it is difficult to determine how to test their claims empirically. If their restrictions for third-person point of view are only as precise as the statement that "if the speaker is not expressing his own internal feeling, but someone else's, then that person must be close enough to the speaker for him to be able to tell what is going on in his mind,"[26] one wonders what linguistics has to offer literary criticism, which is certainly far more sophisticated on this subject. When they offer a trivial "Humanness Hierarchy"—"Human > Animate Nonhuman > Thing"[27]—to specify the order of closeness required for successful mind reading (empathy), one is no doubt meant to conclude that it is easier to get close enough to tell what is going on in a human mind than to see into a rock's mind. Kuno and Kaburaki are right in concluding that formal linguistics cannot say how close one needs to get to read minds; they are wrong only in assuming it should.

The notion of empathy adds its vagueness to the principles

utilizing it. For instance, the "Ban on Conflicting Empathy Foci," which specifies that

(12)   "A single sentence cannot contain logical conflicts in empathy relationships,"[28]

could be interpreted as a notational variant of 1 E/1 SELF, lending it a rigor it does not have. Its terms are too imprecise to determine why the cases Kuno and Kaburaki cite as counterexamples are such and others are not. For example, one might assume that (2a) violates this Ban, because in it the speaker empathizes with both John and Mary, since he uses the proper noun for both. Clearly this is not what Kuno and Kaburaki have in mind; but by being sufficiently ambivalent about how to identify "logical conflicts in empathy relationships" as well as how the subjectivity of lexical items like proper nouns is "neutralized" in contexts where descriptive nouns like "wife" and "husband" do not appear, they can suggest that they have isolated evidence confirming (12). The indeterminateness of the crucial terms in it—"empathy," "logical conflicts"—is compounded by the fact that the apparent violations seem perfectly acceptable sentences. This is the case with (13a and b), labeled "??" by Kuno and Kaburaki.

(13)   a. ??John$_i$ heard from Jane$_j$ what she$_j$ had heard from him$_i$ two days before.
         b. ??John$_i$ received back from Mary$_j$ the package that she$_j$ had received from him$_i$.

In any case, these sentences are no different from their counterparts with the supposedly "empathetic" verbs "hear from" and "receive from" removed.

(14)   John$_i$ $\begin{Bmatrix}\text{told} \\ \text{was told by}\end{Bmatrix}$ Jane$_j$ what she$_j$ $\begin{Bmatrix}\text{had told} \\ \text{had been told by}\end{Bmatrix}$ him$_i$ two days before.

In other cases what Kuno and Kaburaki mark as a violations of (12) and therefore classify as nonsyntactic case of empathy is part of a much broader phenomenon widely recognized in the literature. They give (15 a and b) as violations of (12).

(15)   a. *Then Mary$_i$'s husband$_j$ hit his$_j$ wife$_i$.
         b. *Then John$_i$'s teacher$_j$ hit his$_j$ student$_i$.

(15) includes only special cases of what Chomsky calls "Disjoint Reference."[29] The principle governing disjoint reference simply states that no two NPs in the same syntactic domain can intersect

in reference (except for bound anaphora). In (15) the two intersecting NPs are *Mary* and *his wife*. Chomsky points out that non-anaphoric NPs (e.g., NP$_i$ in 15) cannot intersect even across sentences.[30] Notice that in (16) only "empathetically neutral" descriptive nouns appear; so the sentences should be, according to Kuno and Kaburaki's standards, decidedly superior in acceptability to those in (15). But this is not the case.

(16)　* Then the woman$_i$'s husband$_j$ hit his$_j$ wife$_i$.
　　　* Then the boy$_i$'s teacher$_j$ hit his$_j$ student$_i$.

The linguistic reality of the phenomena described under the heading "empathy" seems to vanish once more when exposed to the light of analysis. (12) is unnecessary unless read as a notational variant of (8).

　　　The same observations hold for (17), the "Speech-Act Empathy Hierarchy," and (18), the "Surface Structure Empathy Hierarchy." (No connection between these two "empathy hierarchies" is made by Kuno and Kaburaki.)

(17)　Speech-Act Empathy Hierarchy
　　　It is not possible for the speaker to empathize more with someone else than with himself.[31]

　　　Speech-Act Participant Hierarchy (Revised)
　　　It is easiest for the speaker to empathize with himself; it is next easiest for him to empathize with the hearer; it is most difficult for him to express more empathy with third persons than with himself or with the hearer;
　　　　　　Speaker > Hearer > Third Person.[32]

(18)　Surface Structure Empathy Hierarchy
　　　It is easiest for the speaker to empathize with the referent of the subject; it is next easiest for him to empathize with the referent of the object. . . . It is next to impossible for the speaker to empathize with the referent of the *by*-passive agentive:
　　　　　　Subject > Object > By-passive Agentive.[33]

　　　The supposed violations of (18) Kuno and Kaburaki give are once again dependent on judgments not shared by native speakers: for example, (19).

(19)　??Mary was criticized by me.

(19), it is claimed, "is unacceptable because by applying Passivization, the speaker is saying that he is not expressing his own point of view while describing his own action."[34] The complete acceptability of these and similar examples is established by Kato with examples taken from published prose, which includes transcriptions of actual speech. I cite only three cases from Kato to demonstrate the acceptability of (19).[35]

(20) a. I said "*Me* watch it! Fuck that! Let *him* watch it!" He was hired by me. I could fire him if I didn't like him. (Studs Terkel, *Working*)

  b. When somebody says to me, "You're great, how come you're *just* a waitress?" *Just* a waitress. I'd say, "Why, don't you think you deserve to be served by me?" (*Ibid.*)

  c. Gore [Vidal] never lacked love, nor was he abandoned by me. (*Time*, 5 April 1976)

These constraints are complicated in a series of further ad hoc principles, often brought up only as the more general constraints fail to cover the evidence. For example:

> The low acceptability of (43e) in isolation requires explanation. By placing an indefinite noun phrase in the subject position for *married*, the speaker is expressing his empathy with its referent rather than with John. However, it is generally the case that it is easier for the speaker to empathize with someone he has been talking about than with someone he has just introduced into the discourse for the first time.[36]

The comparative "easier," used here and in (17) and (18), sets up constraints that are only relative and thus anticipates any possible counterexamples. For what explains the preference for the relative and the vague over the absolute and the rigorous is that the former dismisses all objections. This is why Kuno and Kaburaki can conclude their essay by complacently remarking that

> violations of empathy constraints sometimes yield totally unacceptable sentences; at other times, especially when other factors make up for the violations, they yield only awkward or *even acceptable* [my italics] sentences. This leaves the impression that empathy constraints apply only "selectively." It is not clear at present what kind of violations are unsalvageable, and what kind can be tolerated. . . . An explanation for what appears to be a "selective" application of empathy constraints will require careful examination of the relative strengths of all these rules.[37]

The inconsistency of their methodology is that they demand something more than a "selective" application of syntactic rules and constraints from those they attack. Only a nonformal approach

is impervious to such criticisms, it seems, although it owes its justification to the validity of such criteria for the opposition. Kuno and
Kaburaki's constraints are only interesting and falsifiable when
given their strongest, most precise interpretation as notational variants of constraints I proposed in "Narrative Style."[38] But then much
of the data that they treat must be excluded from the jurisdiction of
these constraints as linguistically irrelevant. Far from being a defect
of this approach, it is the first requirement for formalization. Let us
compare the evidence for the two positions.

2. Empathetic versus Subjective Lexical Items

2.1. Naming as a Problem of Linguistic Point of View: Proper Nouns versus Noms de Qualité

Consider again the claim that (2b and c) adopt John's and
Mary's respective points of view, which depends on the presumed
difference in subjectivity between "John" or "Mary" and "husband"
or "wife." What do we then conclude about the following sentences, where the speaker, who controls empathy according to (10),
is explicit?

(21) a. Mary hit my husband.
      b. My husband hit Mary.
      c. I hit Mary. Mary hit me.

If the sentences of (21) do not represent violations of (19) and (20),
do we really assign point of view to the referent of Mary in them?
The fact that the speaker in (21a and b) refers to the person designated by the noun "husband" and not by a proper noun might be
accounted for by any number of reasons—her addressee does not
know her husband by name or does not know that he is her husband, and so on. But the grammar can hardly incorporate these
pragmatic reasons as grammatical regularities. That the use of "husband" instead of the proper noun does not imply that the speaker
empathizes with Mary is clear if we add an adjective like "poor," to
be discussed in 2.2.

(22) Mary hit my poor husband.

An argument similar to Kuno and Kaburaki's with respect to
naming as an expression of point of view is given by Uspensky. In a
discussion of the various names applied to Napoleon in Tolstoy's
War and Peace—"Napoleon," "Bonaparte," "Buonaparte," "General
Bonaparte," "the consul," "emperor," "le grand homme," "Bona-
party," "Napoleon Bonaparte"[39]—Uspensky argues that the selec-

tion of a name for Napoleon indicates the point of view from which the statement containing it is made. For instance, in the following passage, the change in names, according to Uspensky, signals a "shift from one point of view to another."

> Both Emperors dismounted from their horses and took each other by the hands. Napoleon's face wore an unpleasantly hypocritical smile. Alexander was saying something to him with a cordial expression.[40]

While choice of names in a novel poses interesting problems for the study of point of view in literature, it does not form part of the evidence for linguistic point of view. The difference between "Bonaparte," "Buonaparte," and "Napoleon" as names for the individual so designated is not inherent and absolute but relative and dependent on extralinguistic factors like the history of Napoleon's Russian campaign or class relations and political attitudes in Russia in 1812. A linguistic theory of point of view could not account for the phenomenon of naming described by Uspensky, because it could not incorporate a theory of history. Again we are dealing with a case of "pragmatic point of view." No critical reading of *War and Peace* would be complete without taking into account Tolstoy's selection of names for Napoleon, but this problem belongs to the domain of pragmatics and literary criticism.

There are, however, nouns whose presence in the sentence indicates a point of view and so requires the notion SELF. One important class is that which Milner calls *noms de qualité* or epithets. (23) implies, by the noun it uses for the object of the verb, the presence of the SELF in a way that (2b and c) do not.

(23) Mary hit that $\begin{Bmatrix} \text{darling} \\ \text{idiot} \end{Bmatrix}$ of a husband of hers.

Other epithets in English include "fool," "bastard," "bitch," "whore," "sweetheart," "sucker," "liar," "prick," "ass," "crook," "devil," and "angel," and, in French, "*crème*," "*crétin*," "*idiot*," "*diable*," "*imbécile*," "*fripouille*," "*moule*," "*laideron*," "*amour*," and "*merveille*." In ordinary speech, the noun represents the speaker's estimation of an object or person. In literary texts, it can represent a third person's point of view, as in (24).

(24) *Ce pauvre diable d'ouvrier*, perdu sur les routes, l'intéressait. (Emile Zola, *Germinal*, Fasquelle, p. 30)

Another class of nouns that invoke the SELF are kinship nouns.[41] They include "papa," "mommy," "Uncle X," "Comrade

X," "grandma," and so on. Thus, (25) invokes a point of view, whereas (4b and c) do not.

(25)   John hit mommy.

In literary contexts, such nouns may represent a third-person SELF, as in the case of epithets.

(26)   It hadn't been put to her, and she couldn't, or at any rate, didn't, put it to herself, that she liked Miss Overmore better than she liked *papa*, but it would have sustained her under such an imputation to feel herself able to reply that *papa* too liked Miss Overmore exactly as much. (Henry James, *What Maisie Knew*, Anchor, p. 33)

Because of the presence of "papa," we must read (26) from Maisie's point of view, but if "her father" were substituted for this noun, it could read as objective narration.

Milner assigns epithets a feature +Quality.[42] On the basis of their behavior and interpretation, Milner establishes the characteristics of +Quality nouns that distinguish them from ordinary nouns, which I partly summarize here. The ordinary lexical noun has virtual reference, which limits its actual reference, acquired only in context. It cannot normally be used as an anaphoric substitute, dependent referentially on an antecedent. The epithet, on the other hand, has no virtual (lexical) reference, but only actual reference in use in a speech act. It can be used nonautonomously and anaphorically related to a previous (ordinary) noun: "John$_i$ can't be counted on. The idiot$_i$ always forgets the instructions." A proposition in which ordinary nouns appear in predicate attribute position is interpreted as a judgment subsuming an element into a class or an object under a concept, both of which—class and concept—are defined independently of the particular speech acts in which they appear. The judgment assigning membership in a class that the attributive proposition expresses can be negative as well as positive: "x is not a y" is the symmetrical inverse of "x is a y." In other words, the ordinary noun is *classificatory*: it can designate a subset of its virtual reference, and this fact bestows on the noun its referential autonomy.

The epithet is not classificatory. There is no class of "idiots" or "bastards" whose members can be identified by common objective characteristics. The only common property they have is what Milner calls a "performative" one. Idiots, as well as bastards, are those of whom one says "idiot" or "bastard." For the same reason, the negation of an attributive proposition like "You are an idiot" is not "You are not an idiot."[43]

The referential nonautonomy of the epithet or *nom de qualité*, Milner argues, is a function of its subjectivity. Subjectivity is again the residue of reference. We can integrate this account of two classes of nouns, categorized on the basis of their nonpossession or possession of the feature Quality, which can be taken as equivalent to the property of being "classificatory," into the account of Es and $\bar{S}$s given earlier, itself based on Milner's system. There, we recall, subjectivity was assigned all phrases outside the node $\bar{S}$—that is, everything other than $\bar{S}$ directly generated under E (cf. [6]). Adopting, following Milner, Frege's notion that propositions have reference (their truth value), we can now extend the division between reference or, strictly speaking, referential autonomy, and subjectivity to noun phrases as well. Those nouns that are +Quality and hence cannot contribute to determining reference are then interpreted subjectively—that is, with reference to the SELF—as are constructions other than $\bar{S}$ immediately dominated by E, which have no truth value. The absence of a truth value for Es is thus equivalent to the lack of virtual reference for the *nom de qualité*.

Again it can be seen that proper nouns pattern with ordinary nouns, although they are generally used to designate an individual. The proper noun, like the ordinary noun, has virtual reference lexically; but it also has actual reference lexically. This distinguishes it from both ordinary nouns and epithets. This is most readily seen with a noun like "Palestine" or "Bertrand Russell," but is no less true of one like "John" or "Paradise." Of course, everybody's cognitive system is somewhat different in the links between the words "John" or "Palestine" and "reality." A proper noun does not require actual reference by some further use of the determiner, although we can further specify with "the John from Cambridge" or "the Palestine of ancient times" or "the Palestine of the British Mandate" or "the Palestine Israel refuses to recognize." None of these specifications change the fact that the proper noun is not assigned subjectivity because it is classificatory by means of having virtual reference.

On the other hand, kinship nouns like "papa" and "uncle" differ from proper nouns in that they have no virtual reference; this suffices to confer subjectivity on them. Some—for example, "papa"—might be held to have actual reference lexically, but others require co-occurrence with a proper noun for actual reference: "Uncle Tom," "Comrade Trotsky." If they do not appear in many contexts in which epithets appear (they are found in vocatives, but this they share with proper nouns as well as epithets), their appearance in a sentence invokes the SELF as epithets do.

The subjectivity of epithets and kinship nouns is interpreted with respect to the SELF, associated with the node E. To further establish the relation between epithets and the E, Milner points out that they also appear in certain constructions immediately dominated by E where ordinary nouns cannot appear:

(27)   Bastard!
         Fool!
      * Husband! (as an epithet)
         That idiot of a husband of hers!
      * That brother of a husband of hers!
         The darling!
      * The husband!

Their direct connection to the E for interpretation is apparent from the fact that in the embedded clause of indirect speech, epithets and kinship nouns are always attributed to the quoting speaker's point of view and not the quoted speaker's, as in (28).

(28)   John said that the idiot was close to a genius.

We can relate the behavior of the personal pronouns to this treatment of subjective, nonreferentially autonomous nouns. In ordinary discourse the nonsubjective third-person pronouns may be anaphoric or deictic,[44] like *noms de qualité*, coreferential in the former case with another noun phrase in the linguistic context. But the first- and second-person pronouns in their central usage refer implicitly to the speaker and addressee/hearer. We can explain this by referring the first and second person to the ordered pair E and SELF (and, for the E of ordinary discourse, ADDRESSEE/HEARER), making them coreferential with SELF and ADDRESSEE/HEARER, respectively. They have only a pronoun realization because they are anaphorically related to the constructs SELF and ADDRESSEE/HEARER.

A central feature of represented speech and thought is that the third-person pronoun behaves in specific ways like the first person, although it does not, like the first person, enter into a relationship with an interlocutor. That is, the first person is not exhaustively defined by the communication relationship, as the second person is; *I* is also the SELF. In a sentence of narrative, the SELF may appear independently of the SPEAKER. Whether the SELF has a third- or a first-person realization, it is nevertheless still restricted to a pronoun. Such a third-person pronoun is not an ordinary anaphoric pronoun having a relation with an antecedent noun in the discourse. It does not require an antecedent, but may appear first in a discourse, as in these opening sentences:

(29) "His wife was talking to two other women." (D. H. Lawrence, "The Overtone")

"He was working on the edge of the common." (Lawrence, "England, My England")

The sentences in (29) are acceptable only if the third-person pronoun in them is understood as the sentences' SELF.[45] But such behavior is normal for the first person; it never requires an antecedent noun in the discourse. So stories may begin, like those in (29), with "Longtemps je me suis couché de bonne heure" or "I was born . . . ."

It is in a grammar with the SELF as a formal construct for a syntactically based notion of point of view that the restriction of the third-person SELF to a pronoun becomes predictable: it patterns with the first person because both are realizations of SELF and anaphorically related to the E node. The *nom de qualité* and kinship nouns share certain features with personal pronouns; they do not refer to the SELF, but to someone the SELF names. In this way, subjective noun phrases receive a systematic treatment within a formal grammar where the data Kuno and Kaburaki present are judged irrelevant.

3.2. Empathetic versus Evaluative Adjectives

Proper nouns are not the only lexical items Kuno and Kaburaki identify as "empathetic." They also treat certain adjectives and verbs as evidence of empathy. Again we find a clear division between lexical items that represent linguistic point of view and those that provide no evidence relevant to the grammar of point of view but belong to pragmatics.

The adjectives they give as examples of empathetic ones are "beloved," "dear old," and "embarrassing." The only evidence presented that these adjectives form a class is a set of sentences purportedly demonstrating their interaction with empathetic expressions of other lexical categories. None of the sentences marked as unacceptable or questionable are clearly so; certainly they are no different with the empathetic adjective removed.

(30) ??Mary was told by John about his (beloved) wife.
??Mary was told by John about his (dear old) friend.

In (31), it is claimed that *his* "can be coreferential only with *John*," but this is certainly not the case.

(31) John heard from Bill about his *dear old* friend.

Here the problems whose solution purportedly requires the notion of empathy are nonexistent.

In place of any syntactic evidence justifying the inclusion of "beloved," "dear old," and "embarrassing" in a category of "subjective expressions,"[46] Kuno and Kaburaki offer the following "explanation" for the supposedly peculiar behavior of these adjectives:

> It is clear why *beloved, dear old,* and *embarrassing* behave the way they do. As adjectives that describe internal feelings that do not usually have an external manifestation, they are best suited for describing the speaker's own feeling, as in *my beloved wife* and *my dear old friend.* If the speaker is not expressing his own internal feeling, but someone else's, then that person must be close enough to the speaker for him to be able to tell what is going on in his mind.[47]

We can observe first that "Milton's beloved wife" and "a stranger's dear old friend" are as acceptable as the first-person versions. And contrary to Kuno and Kaburaki's claim that these adjectives "cannot be used in the nonsarcastic sense with nonanaphoric noun phrases as experiencers,"[48] we find perfectly acceptable counterexamples like those in (32) to match with the examples they give in (33), which, if they are indeed questionable, Kuno and Kaburaki make no attempt to explain.

(32) Nothing is more heart-warming than to see a dear old (beloved) friend.
One is always embarrassed when one forgets the name of a dear old friend.

(33) a. ??Someone talked to me about his beloved wife.
      b. ??One should not brag about one's beloved wife.
      c. ??A stranger talked to me about his dear old friend.

The fact is that Kuno and Kaburaki's explanation for the supposed behavior of these adjectives is only a statement about their lexical meaning. Lexical meaning, if it is all relevant to a word's being subjective or not, is not the determining factor. There are lexical items of different categories to "describe internal feelings that do not usually have an external manifestation" but that in no way represent the expression of point of view. "Love," "suffer," "dream," "happy," "troubled," "sentimental," "tender," are all terms for describing mental states or acts. The crucial difference is between *describing* states, internal or external, and *expressing* them.[49] There are, in fact, adjectives *describing* external states that are, nevertheless, subjective, because they may be said also to express an internal one (although not one internal to the referent of the noun it qualifies). It is their expression of the SELF's attitude, not their meaning, that relates subjective adjectives. One such adjective is "poor" in (34).

(34)   Mary left her poor husband.

In its figurative reading, it is synonymous with "unfortunate." Both words have the same lexical meaning, but the latter is not, or not usually, subjective or evaluative. The meaning of *poor*, which is de-scriptive of the referent of the noun it modifies, is independent of its subjectivity, which expresses the attitude of the SELF toward this referent. Subjectivity, as we have seen, does not contribute to the determination of truth value, as lexical meaning in the strict sense does. This is why dictionaries do not typically record information about subjectivity. But the linguistic lexicon relates meaning to form in all ways that are not predictable for a given lexical entry; information of this sort may itself be part of a system: for instance, a feature system. Subjectivity is this kind of lexical information—it invariably relates a word so marked to the SELF.

   The class of what I call "evaluative adjectives," [50] to which "poor" belongs, includes also "blasted," "bloody," "damn(ed)," "darling," "darn," "divine," "dirty," "confounded," "fine" ($\neq$ "suit-able" or "undamaged"), "fucking," "great," "incredible," and "weird." French examples, discussed by Milner, [51] include "*abomina-ble*," "*affreux*," "*divin*," "*époustouflant*," "*exécrable*," "*fichu*," "*horri-ble*," "*incroyable*," "*sacré*," "*sale*," "*satané*," and "*stupéfiant*." Many are evaluative with a figurative reading and have literal, noneval-uative counterparts. "Damned" has a morphological variant—"damn"—permitted only in evaluative contexts ("darn" is another such variant). The subjective or evaluative and nonevaluative ver-sions of the same adjective have partly different distributions. While more than one evaluative adjective may precede the noun, they can never be conjoined:

(35)   The child was a poor and small orphan.
       My heart went out to the poor darling child in the Rolls-
          Royce.
       My heart went out to the poor and darling child in the Rolls-
          Royce. (Literal)
       Joan showed me some damn fine trout she had caught.
     * Joan showed me some damn and fine trout she had caught.
       I'm tired of this $\left\{ \begin{array}{l} \text{counfounded, blasted} \\ {}^{*}\text{confounded and blasted} \end{array} \right\}$ work.

Many evaluative adjectives cannot appear in predicate attribute position except with a literal reading; in the case of those that are only evaluative, they are excluded entirely:

(36)   Her poor cousin can't get the Rolls-Royce to start. *versus* Her
            cousin is poor.
        What happened to the damn key? *versus* *The key is damn
            (darn).
        It was a fine specimen. *versus* The specimen was fine.

Some evaluative adjectives *can* appear in this position in main
clauses, but the sentence is always exclamatory. They are, nevertheless, excluded from restrictive relatives with the definite article.
Compare the meaning of the adjective in (37).

(37)   That book was great!
        I stayed up all night to finish that book, which was great.
        * The book that was great was donated to the library, but
            the other kept.
        Her dress is darling!
        I saw the dress, which is darling.
        * I saw only the dress that is darling.

Evaluative adjectives, as Milner observes, often cannot be
compared:

(38)   * The poorer thing!
        * What a greater book!
        * I never met a more fucking idiot!

That "embarrassing" is not an evaluative adjective can be
readily ascertained; it appears in all the contexts listed above from
which evaluative adjectives are excluded:

(39)   Don't tell the story that was embarrassing.
        Rude and embarrassing remarks should be avoided.
        That interview was more embarrassing than the last.

"Dear old" and "beloved" are more problematic. Both can be
conjoined:

(40)   She is a kind and dear old friend.
        An old and beloved teacher of mine died last year.

But they are excluded from the predicate attribute position:

(40)   * That friend is $\begin{Bmatrix} \text{beloved} \\ \text{dear old} \end{Bmatrix}$.

They can, however, appear in this position with "one," while evaluative adjectives cannot:

(41)   That friend is a beloved one.

Cf. *Their friend is a $\begin{Bmatrix} \text{great} \\ \text{poor} \\ \text{damn} \end{Bmatrix}$ one.

"Dear old" appears in this context only in its conjoined alternate form:

(42) That friend is a dear and old one.

"Beloved" can be compared:

(43) No one is more beloved to me than you.

But "dear old" can only be compared in its conjoined form:

(44) I have no dearer or older friend than you.

I therefore conclude that neither "beloved" nor "dear old" is a true evaluative adjective.

This conclusion is further verified by the relevant interpretive facts. In the subordinate clause of indirect speech, all evaluative adjectives represent the point of view of the quoting and not the quoted speaker—that is, of the E's unique SELF. This is not the case with the adjectives Kuno and Kaburaki give, as can be seen from the contrast in (45).

(45) a. John said that he had been looking for the damn thing all day.
      b. John explained that he was meeting a dear old friend.

In (45a) at least the quoting speaker asserts that the adjective "damn" is warranted; in (45b) John is asserting that his friend is "dear and old," independently of the quoting speaker.

In Milner's analysis, evaluative adjectives are incorporated into the *système de qualité* proposed for the *noms de qualité*. Evaluative adjectives receive the feature +Quality, which makes them interpretable with respect to the pair E and SELF. Like epithets, they are "nonclassificatory." There is, Milner points out, no well-defined class whose members have the property of being "fine," "damn," "poor," or "blasted." Or, what amounts to the same thing, the only common property one could attribute to them is that, using them, one can call something "fine" or "damn" or "poor" or "blasted." While for the ordinary adjective the truth of a given attributive utterance depends on the inclusion in a class, for the evaluative adjective it is the class that depends on the particular attributive utterance.[52] Thus, the evaluative adjective belongs to a well-defined class of lexical items that are linguistically subjective, and their behavior can be predicted from the properties of this class. But there is no evidence that the adjectives Kuno and Kaburaki give as in-

dications of empathy form a well-defined class, nor is there much
hint of what the properties of this putative class might be.

3.3. Subject- and Object-Centered Verbs versus Deictic Verbs

The verbs Kuno and Kaburaki identify as "subject-centered"
and "object-centered" again represent categories without a clear
linguistic basis. For instance, they claim that "*marry* requires that
the speaker's empathy be placed on the referent of the subject."
Thus, "John married Jane" and "Jane married John" "differ in where
the speaker's empathy lies."[53] But the sentences marked as questionable seem perfectly acceptable:

(46)   a.   ?John's present wife married him in 1960.
       b.   ?A 17-year-old girl married John.
       c.   ??A 17-year-old girl married me.

As in a number of other cases, Kuno and Kaburaki claim that
(46b) "requires a context that would force the use of *married John* as
the predicate" and give (47) as a case of such a context:

(47)   Speaker A: No one seems to want to marry John.
       Speaker B: Oh, no. A 17-year-old girl has just married John.

(47) only confirms the acceptability of (46b). Kuno and Kaburaki
misunderstand the argument from context. Certain sentences may
stand in isolation better than others that require a certain discourse
context. This may be a problem for discourse grammar, but it does
not lessen their acceptability as sentences.

Likewise, none of the acceptability judgments or impossibili-
ties of interpretation forming the evidence for the claims Kuno and
Kaburaki make about the verbs "meet" ("in the sense of accidental
encounter"),[54] "run into," "hear from," and "receive from" are accurate, but it is hardly necessary to cite all the cases where their
judgments are wrong. Their presentation at times reads like a par-
ody of linguistic argumentation, as when they remark in a footnote
of the supposedly questionable "??Tom received a package from me"
(their [51b]):

> Linda Shumaker (personal communication) has told us
> that (51b) is acceptable if there is something strange about the
> package (for example, it contains a bomb). Although we do
> not fully understand what is going on here, it seems that in
> such a situation, *a package* receives the focus of attention, and
> the conflict in the empathy foci is weakened or ignored.[55]

The only verb Kuno and Kaburaki examine that requires reference to the SELF and thus is truly subjective is the verbal locution "come up to," which they contrast with "go up to." They deny that the subjectivity of "come up to" is a function of the presence in it of the deictic verb "come," completely ignore its treatment in Fillmore's work,[56] and give as their evidence a difference in acceptability between (48a) and (48b).

(48)   a.   * I came up to John and told him that he had insulted me.
       b.   I came to see John.

But the relevant contrast is not between (48a) and (48b), but between (48a) and the equally unacceptable (49).

(49)   * I came to John.

Of course, (48b) is only acceptable if read as an announcement of purpose (to his secretary, for instance) and not as a narrative statement. The point is that the general rules governing the use of "come" as opposed to "go" apply to (48a) in a predictable way.

Deictic verbs, like all subjective elements, must be referred to the E and its associated SELF (and, in oral discourse, its ADDRESSEE/HEARER) for interpretation. But their subjectivity differs from that of the +Quality nouns and adjectives. They do not so much "express a point of view" as they are "from a point of view." In this they most closely resemble the first and second person or the third-person SELF of represented speech and thought, and so traditionally they are all grouped together under "deixis." They can also be related to the kinship nouns, which, instead of expressing the SELF's attitude toward the individual so designated, as do epithets, indicate a relation the SELF holds to the individuals he calls by these names, just as the deictic verbs indicate a spatial relation with the SELF at the moment of utterance.

3.4. The Inadequacy of the Informal Method

In their proposal of various "nonsyntactic," "nonformal" constraints utilizing the notion of empathy, Kuno and Kaburaki have assumed the existence of a coherent set of lexical items whose similarity can only be captured through this notion. We have just seen that there is no evidence that such a class of words exists apart from those requiring the constructs E and SELF for interpretation. There are further problems in maintaining the existence of a class of empathetic words because point of view would be assigned in different ways for the different lexical items.

For instance, the use of a proper noun—"John" or "Mary"—when in contrast with a descriptive noun would require, according to Kuno and Kaburaki, assigning point of view to the reference of the proper noun. This is in contrast with the assignment of point of view in sentences containing epithets or kinship nouns. In both these cases, however, the point of view represented is not that of the person designated by the noun but that of the sentence's SELF, as in every subjective statement.

In the case of empathetic adjectives like "beloved," it is more difficult to generalize about how point of view would be assigned. Kuno and Kaburaki state that "they are best suited for describing the speaker's own feeling,"[57] but when they do not, the only directive we have for assigning point of view is dependent on determining who is close enough to the speaker to have his mind read. Presumably in "That boy wrote his beloved mother," the point of view is that of the referent of the possessive preceding the adjective. But this is not sufficient for "The doctor saw a beloved friend" or "John told Bill about his beloved wife." In the case of "John told Bill about the president's embarrassing slip," the adjective might mean "embarrassing to the nation at large." Again this is in contrast to the interpretation of evaluative adjectives, which, like epithets and kinship nouns, invariably express the point of view of the SELF, regardless of what position the adjective takes in the sentence.

Finally, subject- and object-centered verbs specify that "the speaker's empathy be placed on the referent" of the subject and object, respectively. Their definition thus differs from that of deictic verbs like "come," which always represent the spatial position of the SELF, regardless of the grammatical relation any pronoun representing the SELF has in the sentence.

Thus, the proposed members of the class of empathetic expressions are not related by where they assign point of view. No similarity in "where empathy is placed" unites the various lexical items Kuno and Kaburaki treat. If there had been independent evidence for the proposed class of empathetic words, this irregularity might be taken as a fact of their behavior. But lacking such empirical justification, the existence of this class in the competence of speakers, and so in the grammar that is its model, is further disconfirmed by the irregular way its putative members assign point of view. But the uniform interpretation of all subjective expressions as the representation of the SELF's point of view corroborates the evidence already presented that this class is the relevant one for a theory of linguistic point of view.

3. Conclusion

It is by the fact that utterances—which we have represented in our formal grammar by the symbol E—can be referred to the SELF that subjectivity enters language. The SELF, which is not reducible to Chomsky's idealized speaker-hearer, "symétrisable et non désirant," as Milner puts it,[58] but is rather "capable de désir et non symétrisable," points to all that exceeds the grasp of formal theory. But this does not prevent the subjective, once it has entered language as insults, exclamations, evaluations, etc., from being submitted by language itself to an organization that is syntactic and to rules of the same form as those that produce syntactic structures in general—"leurs expressions s'inscrivent dans des regularités et donnent lieu à une écriture en tout point comparable à toute écriture syntaxique."[59] This constitutes the representation of feeling and divides it from feeling itself. The referring E is the mediating node between the formal grammar and the conscious subject. It is this nonsymmetrical SELF, and not Chomsky's ideal speaker-hearer, that finds its natural place in Chomsky's own notion of language, where "communication is only one function of language, and by no means an essential one."[60]

Chomsky's evidence for his view is pragmatic, and one might still maintain in the face of it that although, as Chomsky asserts, "I can be using language in the strictest sense with no intention of communicating,"[61] language itself retains a formal structure shaped by the communicative function. This is the position taken by those who maintain that soliloquy is "self-communication." But though Chomsky maintains that that is to "trivialize the issue,"[62] it is not logically excluded that one could speak a language that is marked by the presence of the hearer in the absence of an audience—Chomsky's example of language used with no intention of communicating. It is the existence of a literary style—"represented speech and thought"—that provides the crucial evidence that language is not *structurally* reducible to its communicative function. In this style the SELF is realized independently if its function as SPEAKER, which is the symmetrical relation the SELF adopts with the addressee/hearer in communication.

Such conclusions have been reached through an examination of syntactic evidence that yields to formal analysis, and this is achievable because there is a prior assumption that there are theoretical limits to what is properly considered evidence, though in practice what these limits are is an empirical question.

Finally, literary competence, formalized here as linguistic point of view, cannot be distinguished from linguistic competence, for the grammar must contain the theoretical constructs E and SELF. Literary style, which has distinct grammatical forms, can be created and interpreted anew by independently working writers and readers because it exists *in potentia* in linguistic competence. There can, therefore, be no *formal* literary theory that is not in some sense a linguistic theory. But accepting the linguistic model entails acknowledging the absolute distance between the formalizable and the nonformalizable, even if what constitues each is, in practice, always changing. All the richness of the text cannot be contained within linguistic competence and the grammar that represents it or within the idealization of the text that style represents. Concomitantly, all the formal elegancies discoverable within this proliferation of facts can be brought into focus only when a background is allowed to blur and become confused. Caught between these alternatives, the reader, the interpreter of the text, who begins perforce by experiencing it in all its infinite richness, can only exercise the capacities of theorist, of scientist, if you will, and enjoy in the savant's epiphany the visions of a hidden order, if the attempt to explain all is abandoned.

But all that is abandoned, that is labeled "performance" or "pragmatics" or "criticism," cannot be forgotten, because it is dependent for its existence on its continual formulation and reformulation.

Notes

I wish to express my appreciation to the Linguistics Section of the University College, London, and especially to Geoffrey Pullum, for the facilities provided to produce the final version of this paper.

1. Monroe Beardsley and W. K. Wimsatt, Jr., "Intention," in *The Dictionary of World Literature* (Paterson, N.J., 1962), pp. 229–32.
2. Ibid., p. 229.
3. Monroe Beardsley, *Aesthetics: Problems in the Philosophy of Criticism* (New York, 1958), pp. 44–46.
4. Of course, any discussion of literary competence would have to eventually include meter, and the following works have contributed much to a formal theory of this aspect of poetic competence: M. Halle and J. S. Keyer, *English Stress: Its Form, Its Growth, and Its Role in Verse* (New York, 1971); P. Kiparsky, "Stress Syntax, and Meter," *Language* 51 (1975): 576–616, and "The Rhythmic Structure of English Verse," *Linguistic Inquiry* 8 (1977): 189–248; J. C. Milner, "Refléxions sur le fonctionnement du vers français," *Cahiers de Poétique Comparée* 1, fasc. 3 (1974): 2–21; and M.

Ronat, "Métrico-Phono-Syntaxe: le vers français alexandrin," *Cahiers de Poétique Comparée* 2, fasc. 2 (1975): 11–45.

5. This conforms to the traditional division of labor between aesthetic or literary theory and criticism. For a discussion of this distinction in the light of Chomsky's theory of language, see Beardsley, *Aesthetics* and Roland Barthes, *Critique et vérité* (Paris, 1966).

6. Noam Chomsky, *Aspects of the Theory of Syntax* (Cambridge, Mass., 1965).

7. John Ross, "On Declaring Sentences," in *Readings in English Transformational Grammar*, ed. R. Jacobs and P. Rosenbaum (Waltham, Mass., 1970), pp. 222–72; Quang Phuc Dong, "English Sentences without Overt Grammatical Subject," in *Studies Out in Left Field*, ed. A. M. Zwicky, et al. (Edmonton, Alberta, 1971), pp. 3–10; S-Y Kuroda, "Where Epistemology, Style, and Grammar Meet: A Case Study from the Japanese," in *A Festschrift for Morris Halle*, ed. P. Kiparsky and S. Anderson (New York, 1973), pp. 377–91, and "Reflections on the Foundations of Narrative Theory from a Linguistic Point of View," in *Pragmatics of Language and Literature*, ed. Teun van Dijk (New York, 1976), pp. 108–40; Ann Banfield, "Narrative Style and the Grammar of Direct and Indirect Speech," *Foundations of Language* 10 (1973): 1–39; Charles Fillmore, "May We Come In?" and "Coming and Going," Santa Cruz Lectures, Indiana University Linguistics Club, 1975; Jean-Claude Milner, *De la syntaxe à l'interprétation* (Paris, 1978).

8. Milner, *De la syntaxe*, pp. 17–18.

9. Susuma Kuno and Etsuko Kaburaki, "Empathy and Syntax," *Linguistic Inquiry* 8 (1977): 666.

10. Kuno, "Three Perspectives in the Functional Approach to Syntax," in *Papers from the Functionalism Parasession*, Eleventh Meeting of the Chicago Linguistics Society (Chicago, 1975), p. 276.

11. Ibid.

12. The relevant source for the notion of "perceptual strategies" is Thomas G. Bever, "The Cognitive Basis for Linguistic Structures," in *Cognition and the Development of Language*, ed. John R. Hayes (New York, 1970), pp. 279–362.

13. Kuno, "Three Perspectives," p. 308.

14. Ibid., p. 325.

15. Ibid., p. 326.

16. Ibid., p. 321. But one might think it was new—Kuno never cites a single literary theorist on point of view and cites only two of the many linguists who have written on the subject.

17. Kuno and Kaburaki, "Empathy and Syntax," p. 627.

18. Banfield, "Narrative Style."

19. Noam Chomsky, "Conditions on Transformations," in S. Anderson and P. Kiparsky, *A Festschrift for Morris Halle*, (New York, 1973), pp. 232–86.

20. Milner, *De la syntaxe*, p. 230.

21. Gottlob Frege, *Translations from the Philosophical Writings of Gottlob Frege*, ed. and trans. P. Geach and M. Black (Oxford, 1977), p. 63.

22. See Ann Banfield, "Narrative Style," pp. 1–39; "Where Epistemology and Grammar Meet Literary History," *New Literary History* 9 (1978): 415–54; "The Nature of Evidence in a Falsifiable Literary Theory," in *The Concept of Style*, ed. Berel Lang (Philadelphia, 1979), pp. 183–210.

23. Kuno and Kaburaki, "Empathy and Syntax," p. 628.

24. Ibid., p. 631.

25. Kuno, "Three Perspectives," p. 310.

26. Kuno and Kaburaki, "Empathy and Syntax," p. 649.

27. Ibid., p. 653.

28. Ibid., p. 632.

29. Noam Chomsky, "Conditions on Transformations" and "Conditions on Rules of Grammar" in Essays on Form and Interpretation (New York, 1977).

30. Noam Chomsky, *Reflections on Language* (New York, 1975).

31. Kuno and Kaburaki, "Empathy and Syntax," p. 631.

32. Ibid., p. 652.

33. Ibid., p. 647. If the Speech Act Empathy Hierarchy is interpreted as equivalent to "Priority of Speaker," then evidence for it can be amassed—namely, the impossibility of interpreting a sentence with a third-person SELF if it also contains a first person. But this evidence rules out the revision of (17), for the SELF in represented speech and thought is never the second person, and it is impossible to interpret a sentence containing a second person as representing any other than the speaker's point of view (see my "Narrative Style," "Epistemology and Grammar," "The Nature of Evidence"). The sentence below would only be interpreted as a question by the first person, unlike its counterpart with the third person in (7).

Why couldn't you have workmen for friends rather than the silly boys who came to Sunday night supper? (you asked).

If the parenthetical phrase is added, the reading becomes possible, but this kind of narrative in the second person is so rare that instances of it are always exceptional. In Michel Butor's *La Modification*, for instance, none of the cases of represented speech or thought appearing in it contain a second person, even though the narrative is recounted in the second person.

34. Kuno and Kaburaki, "Empathy and Syntax," p. 650.

35. Kazuo Kato, "Empathy and Passive Resistance," *Linguistic Inquiry* 8 (1979): 149–52.

36. Kuno and Kaburaki, "Empathy and Syntax," p. 641.

37. Ibid., p. 670.

38. See Banfield, "Narrative Style." This is the way George Dillon and Frederick Kirchhoff, "On the Form and Function of Free Indirect Style," *PTL* (1976): 431–40, read the account of empathy in Kuno, "Three Perspectives"; they present Kuno's account of represented speech

and thought as a less explicit version of the one given in my "Narrative Style."

39. Boris Uspensky, *A Poetics of Composition*, trans. V. Zavarin and S. Wittig (Berkeley and Los Angeles, 1973), pp. 27–32.

40. Ibid., p. 30.

41. Banfield, "Narrative Style."

42. Milner, *De la syntaxe*.

43. Ibid., pp. 294–98.

44. Alternative terms for "deixis" are "egocentric particulars," used in Bertrand Russell, *An Inquiry into Meaning and Truth* (London, 1940), pp. 109ff., and *Human Knowledge: Its Scope and Limits* (New York, 1948), pp. 84–93; Reichenbach's "token reflexive words," used in Hans Reichenbach, *Elements of Symbolic Logic* (London, 1947), pp. 244–87; Peirce's "indexical symbols," used in Charles Sanders Peirce, *Philosophical Writings of Charles Sanders Peirce*, ed. J. Buchler (New York, 1955); and Jakobson's "shifters," used in Roman Jakobson, "Two Aspects of Language and Two Types of Aphasic Disturbances," and in *Fundamentals of Language* (The Hague, 1956), pp. 55–82.

45. This ability of the third-person pronoun to appear without antecedent in narrative has its counterpart in the ability of the past progressive to appear in the first sentence of a narrative without an adverbial phrase of time. For example, "His wife was talking to two other women" is not normally acceptable in isolation, but requires an adverbial like "when he arrived" or "earlier this morning."

46. Kuno and Kaburaki, "Empathy and Syntax," p. 648.

47. Ibid., p. 649.

48. Ibid.

49. See Russell, *An Inquiry*.

50. Banfield, "Narrative Style."

51. Milner, *De la syntaxe*, pp. 209, 280ff., and 305–6.

52. Ibid., pp. 299–300.

53. Kuno and Kaburaki, "Empathy and Syntax," p. 640.

54. Ibid., p. 642.

55. Ibid., p. 643, n. 19.

56. Fillmore, Charles, "How to Know Whether You're Coming or Going," in ed. Hyldgard, Karl, *Linguistics* (New York, 1971), pp. 369–78, and idem., "Coming or Going."

57. Kuno and Kaburaki, "Empathy and Syntax," p. 649.

58. Milner, *L'Amour de la langue* (Paris, 1978), p. 46.

59. Milner, *De la syntaxe*, p. 18.

60. Chomsky, *Reflections on Language*, pp. 56–71.

61. Ibid., p. 61.

62. Ibid., p. 71.

Sources

James, Henry. *What Maisie Knew.* New York, 1954.

Lawrence, D. H. "England, My England," in *The Complete Short Stories*, vol. 2. New York, 1961.

————. "The Overture," in *The Mortal Coil and Other Stories*. Hammondsworth, Eng., 1972.

Mansfield, Katherine. "The Garden-Party," in *Stories*. New York, 1956.

Milne, A. A. *The House at Pooh Corner.* New York, 1946.

Terkel, Studs. *Working.* New York, 1974.

Woolf, Virginia. *To the Lighthouse.* London, 1974.

Zola, Emile. *Germinal.* Paris, n.d.

14

Metaphors and Counterfactuals

ALAN TORMEY

There is a game—in the 1950s it used to be played by members of the Iowa Writers' Workshop—called "Smoke." It works as follows. The player who is "it" chooses some famous person with whom everyone playing is surely acquainted (Harry Truman, Marlon Brando, Chairman Mao, Charles de Gaulle, for instance) and tells the other players, "I am a dead American," "I am a living American," "I am a dead Asian," "I am a dead European"; and then each of the other players in turn asks one question of the person who is "it," such as, "What kind of smoke are you?" (cigarette, pipe, cigar—or, more specifically, L&M, Dunhill, White Owl) or "What kind of weather are you?" "What kind of insect are you?" or "What kind of transportation?" The person who is "it" answers not in terms of what kind of smoke his character would *like*, if any, but what kind of smoke he would *be* if, instead of being human, he were a smoke, or what kind of weather, insect, transportation, and so forth, he would be if reincarnated as one of those. Thus, for example, Kate Smith if an insect would be a turquoise beetle; Marlon Brando, if weather, would be sultry and uncertain, with storm warnings out; and as a vehicle of transportation Harry Truman would be (whatever he may in fact have driven) a Model T Ford. What invariably happens when this game is played by fairly sensitive people is that the whole crowd of questioners builds a stronger and stronger feeling of the character, by unconscious association, until finally someone says the right name—"Kate Smith!" or "Chairman Mao!"—and everyone in the room feels instantly that that's right. There is obviously no way to play this game with the reasoning faculty, since it depends on unconscious associa- tions or intuition; and what the game proves conclusively for everyone playing is that our associations are remarkably similar. When one of the players falls into some mistake, for instance, saying that Mr. Brezhnev of the U.S.S.R. is a beaver instead of, more properly, a crafty old wood- chuck, all the players at the end of the game are sure to protest, "You mis- led us when you said 'beaver.'" The game proves more dramatically than any argument can suggest the mysterious rightness of a good metaphor— the one requisite for the poet, Aristotle says, that cannot be taught.

John Gardner, *On Moral Fiction*

I

Philosophical interest in metaphor has been remarkably constant from Aristotle on, and the questions that occur have been remarkably consistent. How can metaphorical language be distinguished from nonmetaphorical language? Do metaphors have truth values, or should they aspire only to "aptness" or "plausibility"? Can the meaning of a metaphor be elucidated in paraphrase? What sustains or supports metaphorical statements? Must a sentence be literally senseless to be eligible for metaphorical meaning?

All of these questions have received subtle and substantial treatment in recent years, and notably from Monroe Beardsley, whose contributions to the literature are one of its principal enhancements. I share with Professor Beardsley the conviction that "of the still disputed questions, perhaps the most salient from the philosophical point of view is one concerning the cognitive status of metaphors."[1]

It is reassuring to note that metaphor is no longer systematically ignored or disowned by philosophers of language and semantic theorists on the grounds that "it is either a pathological phenomenon that any account of normal language is right to disregard, or a rare and specialized extension of language, as in poetry, that can be safely left on one side for later analysis while the main task of explicating literal meaning proceeds."[2] But if metaphor is finally receiving an overdue respect as a central problem in the philosophy of language, its treatment still frequently suffers from an overly constricted sense of its place in a systematic review of the semantics of natural languages. It is in this context that I want to pursue what seem to me to be striking and provocative parallels between the effort to elucidate metaphorical meaning and certain contemporary attempts to understand and explicate counterfactual conditionals. As we shall see, many of the central issues surrounding metaphorical meaning have close counterparts in the debate over counterfactuals. In fact, as I shall argue, it may be profitable to export distinctions and analyses from one realm to the other and, in particular, to regard metaphors as elliptical counterfactuals. I should add that I do not believe there is such a thing as an ontology of meaning, such that in raising questions about metaphorical meaning, we also raise hopes of a metaphysical discovery. Rather, I would say of meanings what has been said of possible worlds: that they are not discovered but stipulated. What follows should, then, be regarded as a *recommendation*, and if there is good reason for adopting it, it will be found, as it is with successful metaphor, more in its power of illumination than in simple truth.

Before exploring this fusion of theories, let us consider an example. One much discussed instance of metaphorical attribution is the Shakespearian line "Juliet is the sun."[3] A tired and trivial metaphor, perhaps, but useful, since it is both simple and paradigmatic. Traditional theories of metaphor often deal with such locutions as semantically, if not syntactically, anomalous and proceed to restore significance to them by reference to "metaphorical attribution," which in turn is explicated via supposedly shared properties or analogical relations. Thus, both Juliet and the sun are warm, brilliant, life-sustaining, constant, central, and so on, the list being essentially open and variable, though not wholly arbitrary.

This approach may be (and has been) criticized on a variety of grounds for failing to give a satisfactory account of metaphorical meaning. Aside from the suspicion of circularity in construing metaphorical meaning in light of metaphorical attribution, it threatens to trivialize metaphor by counting it a clipped and cryptic way of saying something that could have been said more clearly and adequately in a nonmetaphorical manner. Moreover, the meaning of a metaphor on this view will remain incorrigibly ambiguous or indeterminate, given the "openness" of paraphrastic possibilities.

On the view that I am proposing, the issue of metaphorical meaning arises in quite a different way. If we consider a metaphor to be an *elliptical counterfactual*, the recasting of Romeo's line will yield something like "If Juliet were a celestial object she would be the sun" (and not, say, an asteroid or Jupiter or Pluto). To alter the example momentarily, the metaphorical import of the cliché "Man is a wolf" can be likewise recast as follows: "If man were an animal (that is, a different animal), he would be a wolf" (and not, say, a lemur or a giraffe or a rhino). In construing these metaphors as elliptical counterfactuals, we gain an immediate advantage in avoiding the problems generated by attempts to uncover metaphorical meaning in disjunctive, open-membered sets of paraphrases; and the familiar charge that any attempt to explain the meaning of a metaphor will commit the "heresy of paraphrase" is disarmed by this strategy.

So far, however, this is merely stage setting. It remains to be shown just why this view should be seriously entertained. In the remainder of the paper I shall argue that this theory helps to relocate metaphor near the center of a matrix of vital and unavoidable issues in the philosophy of language; that it explains why we should have

so much trouble deciding whether to assign truth values to metaphors; that it helps to explain the critical acceptance or rejection of
metaphor; and that ultimately it may assist us in choosing from
among competing accounts of counterfactual conditionals.

II

We need, first, to recall a few of the relevant problematic features of counterfactuals. Perhaps the least contestable thing that
can be said initially is that counterfactuals are concerned with what
would be, or would have been, the case if something or other were,
or had been, different from what it actually is or was. (This is an
intentionally crude formulation: refinements at this stage will generate irrelevant disputes.) Thus, for example, "If the surgeon had
not operated, the appendix would have ruptured." Despite the fa-
miliarity and frequency of such locutions, some philosophers have
protested that we do not know precisely how to interpret them, nor
do we have decisive procedures for assigning truth values to them.[4]
This may be a premature council of despair, but, again, it is not my
present purpose to resolve philosophical issues concerning counterfactuals per se, but rather to underscore parallels between that en-
terprise and efforts to elucidate the meaning of metaphor. A feature
that most philosophers have taken to be central to the issue is the
fact that nomological statements—for example, natural or causal
laws—sustain or entail counterfactuals, whereas accidental universals do not. From "Everyone in Saigon understands Vietnamese," it
does not follow that if I were now in Saigon I would understand
Vietnamese; whereas "Sodium is soluble in acetone" supports the
counterfactual "If this sample of sodium had been placed in acetone, it would have dissolved." Thus, nomologically sustained counterfactuals extend the scope of the laws that sustain them to encompass possible as well as actual states of affairs.

The second immediately relevant concern is, of course, truth.
The question has generally been seen as arising from the need to
construct an analysis of counterfactuals that would both explain
their import and establish criteria for determining the conditions, if
any, under which a counterfactual may be said to have a truth
value, a simple truth-functional analysis being unacceptable because a counterfactual construed as a material conditional will always yield a true statement. The arguments over this issue are extensive and inconclusive, but the point to be kept in mind here is
that both counterfactuals and metaphors generate a strong tempta-

tion to say that some, at least, are true, even in the absence of straightforward, determinate truth conditions.

Returning to metaphor, then, we may now explore the implications of the suggestion that metaphors are elliptical counterfactuals. First, the familiar difficulty of determining or assigning truth values to metaphors can now be viewed as inherited from the parent problem of ascertaining when, or if, counterfactuals are to be regarded as strictly true or false, or whether they are more properly regarded as, at best, tenable or plausible. The point here is not, again, to settle the issue but rather to point out that efforts to settle it with respect to *both* counterfactuals and metaphor must confront precisely the same difficulty, namely, the absence of straightforward, empirically determinate truth conditions.

Thus, on one prevalent view, counterfactual reasoning involves "fact-contravening supposition" and is addressed to the issue of "what would happen if something or other were different from what it actually is."

> Such considerations never require us to move outside the realm of hypothetical variations on the make-up of the actual. Throughout the counterfactual arena, our horizons are limited. . . . Hypothetical reasoning of the markedly *remote* variety, involving utterly nonexistent things . . . does not enter into the arena of counter*fact*.[5]

Thus, when entertaining fact-violating possibilities, we remain in the realm of the "seriously possible." Consequently, Rescher continues:

> counterfactual inference involves only the mildest form of hypothetical reasoning, that concerned with the possible variations of the actual: it does not venture into the sphere of what is utterly nonactual and *merely* possible. . . . *Counterfactual* supposition never takes us beyond the sphere of the proximately possible, where one is dealing throughout with possible alterations in the history of this actual world of ours.[6]

For example, the phrase "If Kennedy had survived in Dallas . . ." may serve to introduce a "serious" counterfactual, whereas "If Kennedy had been born in the Augustan age . . ." does not. However difficult it may be to set the limits, it seems clear that some such distinction between *serious* possibilities and merely hypothetical possibilities is needed if we are to discriminate between plausible and implausible counterfactual reasoning. Consonant with this view is that of John Mackie, for whom conditions are also a species of suppositional reasoning: of "asserting something within the scope of a supposition." This translates "If *P*, *Q*" as "Supposing that *P*, *Q*" Mackie adds:

> Granted that every (primary) use of a conditional is tanta-mount to asserting something within the scope of some sup-position, there may be different reasons for doing so. . . . If one is treating what is supposed as a genuine possibility—or in counterfactual cases as having been a genuine possibility—that is, as something not ruled out by the background assump-tions in the light of which one is considering it, but as some-thing which, in view of those background assumptions, would have—or would have had—some determinate outcome, then one will regard 'If P, Q' and 'If P, not-Q' as incompatible.[7]

Thus, for example, "If Hitler had invaded England in 1940, he would have won the war" and "If Hitler had invaded England in 1940, he would have been defeated" will be seen as incompatible conditionals by whoever regards the antecedent as expressing a gen-uine possibility within the scope of a fixed and plausible set of back-ground assumptions.

Now, in light of this distinction, let us return to the Shake-spearian metaphor and its counterfactual parsing. If "Juliet is the sun" is recast as "If Juliet were a celestial object, she would be the sun," it is quite obvious that the antecedent is *not* seriously possible, given our normal background assumptions about persons and plane-tary bodies. Taken as a counterfactual, the metaphor is decidedly implausible, and the result is instructive. The metaphor is an ellip-tical, implausible counterfactual offering us an antecedent supposi-tion that cannot literally and seriously be entertained.

It might be objected here that a strict reading of the generated counterfactual would produce absurdities: that, for example, if Ju-liet were the sun she would have sun spots, or that if man were a wolf he would have a bushy tail, these being ascriptions undoubt-edly unintended by the metaphor or the metaphorizer. This objec-tion can be pressed, however, only if one insists on attempting to *reliteralize* the metaphor, thereby rendering it unintelligible on any analysis; for a literal reading of a metaphorically intended statement would invoke a Leibnizian imposition of indiscernibility with its at-tendant coextension of properties. It would be as if, in playing the game "Smoke," the players were to identify Marlon Brando, *qua* weather, as "sultry and uncertain, with storm warnings out," and then expect to find a prediction of his future behavior in the evening forecast. The operations of selection and subjectivity are integral to the success of metaphor. Only *some* of the potentially shared or transferred properties count. Determining the boundaries of inclusion and exclusion is the domain of the critic, not the philosopher, since, alas, there exists no semantic theory of relevance sufficiently rigorous and rich to structure an *a priori* criterion. The expectation that a theory of metaphorical meaning should tell us precisely where these boundaries lie is on a par with the expectation that a theory of molecular motion should tell us where to find the molecules.

Consider a rather different example, a well-known line by Carl Sandburg, "The fog comes on little cat feet," which can be roughly parsed, counterfactually, as: "If the fog were animate, it would be a cat and move as cats move."[8] Again, we could not *seriously* suppose the antecedent to be possible without drastically restructuring our mundane conceptual schema, and that does not appear to be what is required for an understanding or appreciation of metaphor. I suspect, though I do not know, that most metaphors would yield similarly implausible counterfactuals in this way.

An ancillary virtue of this account is that it anticipates the need for the distinction between "dead" and "live" metaphors. If live metaphors—those that still inspire interest and provoke puzzlement—can be generically characterized as implausible counterfactuals, dead metaphors can be assimilated to plausible counterfactuals, it being commonly agreed that dead metaphors have been demoted to the ranks of the literal. There is also, inevitably, a penumbra in which there occur expressions that cannot easily or mechanically be identified as either metaphorical or literal. In light of the structure and history of natural languages, this should hardly be surprising, and any theory of metaphorical meaning that pretends to provide a decisive and exclusive distinction between metaphorical and literal language must be in open confrontation with both common and literary usage.

Obviously metaphors—or many of them—do *work*: they are powerful, novel, evocative, relevant, and, most remarkably, they may be apt, successful, and striking. But if metaphors are elliptical, implausible counterfactuals, their aptness or success must be accounted for in some further way. Thoroughly plausible counterfactuals—for example, "If this piece of platinum had been heated, it would have expanded"—are reasonably supposed to be sustained or supported by relevant causal laws or nomological relations. Meta-

phors, as implausible counterfactuals, can expect no support from
this quarter. Does it follow, then, that we should give up our intuitions that some metaphors are better, more apt (perhaps even
"truer") than others? I think not; for what distinguishes metaphors
from other subspecies of counterfactual will be found largely in the
difference in their *grounding*. Lawlike relations are usually irrelevant
to the probity or aptness of metaphors. Metaphors are sustained or
supported rather by familiar, but miscategorized, conditions. Briefly:
what is usually taken to be a means of illuminating the *meaning* of a
metaphor—namely, providing a "paraphrase"—is actually a procedure for grounding or sustaining the metaphor. The following remarks by Stanley Cavell are informative here:

> Now suppose I am asked what someone means who says,
> "Juliet is the sun." . . . I may say something like: Romeo
> means that Juliet is the warmth of his world; that his day be-
> gins with her; that only in her nourishment can he grow. And
> his declaration suggests that the moon, which other lovers use
> as emblems of their love, is merely her reflected light, and
> dead in comparison, and so on. In a word, *I paraphrase it*.
> Moreover, if I could not provide an explanation of this form,
> then that is a very good reason, a perfect reason, for supposing
> that I do not know what it means. *Metaphors are paraphras-
> able.*[9] (My italics)

"Paraphrase" is a misnomer, however, for what is being offered
here, and what is commonly offered by critics as the "explanation"
of a metaphor, is not a paraphrase but supportive grounding for the
metaphor. Strictly, to paraphrase is "to express the meaning of a
(word, phrase, passage, or work) in other words, usually with the
object of fuller and clearer exposition: to *render* or *translate* with lat-
itude" (*Oxford English Dictionary*, my italics). Surely, however, one
may be able to grasp the import of Romeo's line without being required to "provide an explanation of this form," and Cavell's putative paraphrase is no more a translation of the metaphor than a
citation of inductive evidence is a translation of the causal laws sustained by it. We can understand a metaphor without knowing what
sustains it, just as we can grasp the meaning of the conditional
statement "If you drink the water in Naples, you'll become ill"
without knowing its grounds (namely, that the water contains,
among other things, high levels of sodium trioxide).

What have been commonly mislabeled as paraphrases of metaphor are not crude and misguided efforts at translation, but serious

attempts to support or sustain the metaphor by citing, *inter alia*, shared properties and analogical resemblances. We have been victimized by a sort of logical dislocation in our readiness to promote the evidence or grounds for the aptness of metaphors to the position of a semantic surrogate for the metaphor. But metaphors do not mean whatever it is that sustains them. "Man is a wolf" does not translate: "Man is voracious, cunning, crafty, or cruel" (and so on), though these supposedly shared properties may be good reason for advancing the metaphor in the first place. Thus, on the view that metaphors are elliptical counterfactuals, there is no danger of committing the dread "heresy of paraphrase," for there is no paraphrase. To the extent that it is amenable to analysis, the meaning of a metaphor may be brought out by recasting it in counterfactual form, and purported paraphrases may be relocated where they belong, providing grounds for the metaphor and supplying arguments for its appropriateness.

Thus, it should not be surprising if, as Max Black has famously remarked, the paraphrase of a metaphor "fails to be a translation because it fails to give the insight that the metaphor did."[10] I should say that it fails to be a translation of the metaphor for a more decisive reason: it occupies a different logical space—not that of translation to text, but that of grounding to statement.

At this point we may confront another issue concerning the question of metaphorical "truth." Ina Loewenberg, among others, has been critical of what she calls "the strange use of the concept of truth" in Beardsley's theory of metaphor, which she interprets as entailing that "the metaphorical sentence is simultaneously true and false. It is, on the one hand, either absurd or false or self-contradictory, and, on the other, in some sense, true."[11] Now, holding a metaphorical statement to be simultaneously true and false might indeed be puzzling, but it need not be contradictory. One possible rejoinder is that a single statement may be literally false and yet metaphorically true if we agree that a single expression may perform a dual linguistic role, failing in one for the sake of succeeding in the other. But what does it *mean* to say that some statements are *literally* false and yet metaphorically true? On many traditional theories of metaphorical meaning, this tension between literal falsity and metaphorical truth remains unresolved. If metaphors are regarded as elliptical counterfactuals, however, their literal falsity is analogous to the (necessary) falsity of a counterfactual's antecedent; and since this is, in itself, insufficient to determine the truth value of the entire counterfactual, we should expect that the literal falsity of the metaphor is equally insufficient to determine its metaphorical (i.e., its counterfactual) truth value. Beardsley's notion that a metaphorical sentence may be simultaneously true and false loses its paradoxical appearance with this insight.

One further connection between metaphor and counterfactuals remains to be noted. There are cases of "competing" counterfactuals, where it would seem impossible to choose between possible consequents. A standard instance is the following: "If Bizet and Verdi were compatriots, both would be French" and "If Bizet and Verdi were compatriots, both would be Italian." Here there appear to be no background assumptions (barring pure chauvinism) that would coerce our judgment in one direction rather than the other. A similar example, introduced by Chisholm, is this: "If Apollo were a man, then either (1) he would be mortal, or (2) one man would be immortal," and again there is no reasonable ground for preferring one alternative to the other. Now, just as these (purely hypothetical) counterfactuals present undecidably competing alternatives, metaphors may generate reversible counterfactuals. "Juliet is the sun" may yield not only: "If Juliet were a celestial object, she would be the sun," but also "If the sun were a person, it would be Juliet." The metaphor seems equally compatible with either reading: there are, again, no apparent background assumptions that would tilt the scale decisively in one direction or the other, a Julietlike sun and a sunlike Juliet being about equally possible, equally implausible, and equally appealing. Thus, reversibility is to metaphor what competition is to counterfactuals.

Parenthetically, it is worth asking whether this property of reversibility might be another way to account for what I. A. Richards and Max Black have identified as the "interpenetration" of the terms in a metaphorical expression—a relation wherein the transfer of association and significance is mutual and reciprocal. Beardsley describes it as "a two-way movement in metaphorical interpretation."[12] "If to call a man a wolf is to put him in a special light, we must not forget that the metaphor makes the wolf seem more human than he otherwise would."[13] Or, rephrased counterfactually: "If the wolf were some other animal, he would be human."

Finally, then, there is much to be gained by thinking of metaphors as elliptical, literally implausible, yet significant counterfactuals. Elliptical because the grammatical form of a metaphor seldom, if ever, assumes the overt structure of a counterfactual. Literally implausible because the reconstructed antecedent cannot normally be supposed true or even probable against the background of normal nomological assumptions. And significant, nonetheless, for its bite, its novelty, its aptness, perhaps even its truth, which are, however darkly, grounded in—not translated by—those perpetual "paraphrases" we feel compelled to construct to affirm our understanding. And an understanding of metaphor, unlike the understanding of more pedestrian expressions, requires a high tolerance for the conjunction of the hypothetical and the unlikely: in short, for the imaginative.

Notes

Grateful acknowledgment is due to Judith Tormey and Peter Kivy, who contributed substantially to the argument, and to Jack Glickman for bringing John Gardner's description of "Smoke" to my attention.

1. Monroe C. Beardsley, "Metaphorical Senses," *Nous* 12 (1978): 3–16.

2. L. Jonathan Cohen and Avishai Margalit, "The Role of Inductive Reasoning in the Interpretation of Metaphor," in *Semantics of Natural Language*, ed. Donald Davidson and Gilbert Harman (Dordrecht, 1972), p. 722. See also the essays in *Metaphor and Thought*, ed. Andrew Ortony (Cambridge, 1979), and *Critical Inquiry* 5 (1978).

3. See Stanley Cavell, *Must We Mean What We Say?* chap. 3, (New York, 1969), and Ted Cohen, "Notes on Metaphor," *Journal of Aesthetics and Art Criticism* 34 (1976): 249–59. The examples dealt with here are deliberately simple. The parsing of complex metaphors is difficult on *any* theory of metaphorical meaning and consequently contributes nothing substantial to choosing among competing theories.

4. See Donald Davidson, "Truth and Meaning," *Synthese* 17 (1967): 304–21.

5. Nicholas Rescher, *A Theory of Possibility* (Oxford, 1975), pp. 173–74.

6. Ibid., p. 174.

7. J. L. Mackie, *Truth, Probability, and Paradox* (Oxford, 1973), pp. 109–10.

8. Why select "If the fog were animate" as the appropriate antecedent here? Why not just "If the fog were something other than it is"? The answer lies in recognizing that the metaphor itself suggests, if it does not explicitly give, the relevant reference class. "Isolde is the brightest star," for example, clearly limits the reference class to stars, and "Elisa is a diamond" suggests that stones or minerals or the like form the framework for selection. Other metaphors, of course, will tolerate or invite more expansive and amorphous reference classes, but none is so vague as to yield a wholly unrestricted antecedent. In general, the selection of an antecedent will determine one's interpretation of the metaphor.

9. Cavell, *Must We Mean What We Say?* pp. 78–79.

10. Max Black, "Metaphor," *Proceedings of the Aristotelian Society* 55 (1954–55), 273–294.

11. Ina Loewenberg, "Truth and Consequences of Metaphors," *Philosophy and Rhetoric* (1973): 40.

12. Beardsley, "Metaphorical Senses," p. 13.

13. Black, "Metaphor," p. 291.

15

On Hardy's Badnesses

SAMUEL HYNES

During the twenty years that Monroe Beardsley and I were colleagues, we collaborated on a number of projects, from a joint letter to the *Times Literary Supplement* to a book-length study of our college's policies. But there was one joint venture that we never managed to complete, though we talked about it a good deal. It was to be an essay on Poetic Badness, and we only got as far as some elaborate graphs (though Beardsley, being more energetic than I am, did, of course, write his fine lecture on bad poetry in *The Possibility of Criticism*). My remarks here might best be regarded as my tardy contribution to our abandoned project, one more speech in the long dialogue with Monroe Beardsley from which I have learned so much.

My subject is related to Beardsley's "Bad Poetry" lecture but is different. He dealt—as no doubt an aesthetician should—with the general theory of badness; and he used as his examples poems of such extreme ineptitude that some critics might hesitate to call them poems at all—works, for example, by Julia Moore, "The Sweet Singer of Michigan," and contributions to the *Poetry Anthology*, one of those vanity collections in which all the contributors are also subscribers. Whereas I mean to consider only one poet—and that one widely regarded as the greatest English poet of this century.

When you discuss the badness of a major poet, you are taking up a tender subject, as I know from experience. Twenty years ago I wrote a book on Hardy's poetry in which I rather stressed the fact (which seemed to me obvious) that not all of Hardy's poems are excellent. I have been scolded ever since for my lack of positive critical thinking, and by some of the weightiest of Hardy's admirers—by Philip Larkin, for instance, who "trumpeted" (his word) "the assurance that one reader at least would not wish Hardy's *Collected Poems* a single page shorter, and regards it as many times over the best body of poetic work this century so far has to show."[1] And the most recent survey of Hardy criticism is still complaining of my "unwillingness to endorse Hardy's greatness."[2] Still, I am unrepentant. I do not doubt that Hardy was a great poet, but I also think that he was peculiarly prone to write bad poems, and I see nothing irreverent or wrong in saying so: surely it is never the function of a critic simply to endorse greatness. "If way to the Better there be," Hardy wrote in a poem, "it exacts a full look at the Worst"; in his case, at least, that seems a reasonable position from which to begin a critical examination of his work.

A full look at the worst will not take us far, though, until we develop some ways of deciding which poems *are* the worst. On this basic question Hardy himself will be of no use at all, since he seems to have been entirely lacking in self-criticism. The *Collected Poems* show this lack very clearly: the book contains virtually every poem Hardy ever wrote, and there were no exclusions from later editions, no sober second thoughts. Apparently Hardy liked everything he wrote and kept it all (another evidence of that is the way, in his later years, he would dig up early poems and include them in his new collections). But more than that, Hardy seemed peculiarly unable to recognize what the unique, excellent, Hardy-ish qualities in his poems were. He did not often comment on his own works, but the judgments he did make were exceptionally fallible, and such poetic principles as one can abstract from his critical remarks are, when applied to Hardy's poems in general, usually wrong.

Consider, as examples, the following self-judgments. First, a remark on "When I Set Out for Lyonnesse": the poem, Hardy said in a letter, "showed something of the song-ecstasy that a lyric should have."[3] I am not entirely certain what "song-ecstasy" is, but Hardy must have meant the qualities of musicalness and strong feeling that have traditionally been associated with the word "lyric"; it is the sort of remark that you might find in any turn-of-the-century review of current poetry. Applied to "Lyonnesse," Hardy's remark does have a certain vague appropriateness, but he seems also to suggest that these are necessary conditions of lyric poetry. If that is true, then either most of Hardy's poems are not lyrics, or they are unsuccessful ones. But this is a point that Hardy evidently did not perceive, since he went on calling groups of his poems "Love Lyrics," "Lyrics and Reveries," and "Late Lyrics." That is, he seemed to go on believing that "song-ecstasy" defined a category to which most of his short poems belonged. And that is simply not the case.

Another example of his judgment comes from a letter to a friend, written in 1901 shortly after the publication of Hardy's first book of poems, *Wessex Poems*: "As you have been re-reading my books I shall ask you when I see you what you think of my opinion that 'Her Death and After' and 'The Dance at the Phoenix' . . . are two as good stories as I have ever told?"[4] Here Hardy is judging two of his poems simply as narratives; and, indeed, the two poems do have some of the characteristics of Hardy's short stories. But not many critics would argue that Hardy was an important, or even a very good, short-story writer, and it might well be argued that the qualities that these poems share with the prose stories are in fact weaknesses. This may seem paradoxical—after all, we are talking about a man who was a great novelist as well as a great poet—but it is nevertheless true: he was not good at short narrative, whether in prose or in verse; and he was if anything rather worse at versified narrative, simply because the verse form offered him opportunities for additional kinds of badness.

What these two self-judgments have in common is a conventional sense of what a poet is: he is a singer, and he is a storyteller. Much of Hardy's poetic energy went into performing these conventional roles, as a glance at *Collected Poems* will show; without the songs and the stories, it would be quite a slender—but marvelous—book. And he was also a conventional poet in other ways: he wrote many occasional poems—poems on the deaths of Queen Victoria, Swinburne, and Meredith, and war poems for both the Boer War and the First World War. He also wrote what one can only call "poetic" poems: poems that seem to exist mainly to show the poet's technical virtuosity (and which Hardy later labeled "Sapphics" and "Onomatopoeic" when critics overlooked his demonstrated skills). In all these instances, Hardy was behaving like a *poet*, as his generation understood the role (that, I take it, is what "conventional" means): this Hardy was not only the contemporary of Alfred Austin and William Watson; he was their fellow.

"What we really object to in a so-called 'bad' literary work," Beardsley wrote, "is a peculiarly incongruous combination of oversimplification and disorganization that is fatal to the integrity of the work."[5] I would argue that this sort of fatality occurs in Hardy's poems most commonly when he is conventionally and self-consciously being "the poet": in his narratives, in his public poems, and in his virtuoso pieces. This is not the common view of Hardy's poetic limitations; that view, indeed, takes the opposite position, that Hardy was worst when he was *least* conventionally poetic. Richard Ellmann, for example, writing recently in the *New York Times Book Review*, chides a critic for approving lines of Hardy's verse "that blend cliché and ineptitude." "The problem is crucial in Hardy," Ellmann continues: "He claimed to have been awkward to avoid being mellifluous, but other means of avoidance were possible. Awkwardness is in him sometimes a kind of inverted narcissism— see how unbeautiful I am!—and a serious impediment to articulation."[6] But it seems to me that Ellmann is here describing not Hardy's badness, but the central properties of his excellence: that the "narcissism" (which I would call "inwardness" or simply "privacy") creates the essential Hardy relation to reality, and that the "awkwardness," if it is an impediment to articulation, is a necessary impediment, and creates the essential Hardy relation to language.

We have here a provisional theory of Hardy's badness: let us test these propositions by looking at some bad poems. First, "My Cicely," a narrative that Hardy fancied enough to recommend as a poem for performance, stressing especially the sound effects. In the poem the speaker, who has thought his West Country sweetheart dead, learns that she is alive (it was someone else of the same name who died) and rides from London to Exeter to be reunited with her. He finds, however, that she has married beneath her and has become a barmaid; so he rides back to London and persuades himself that it really was his love who died. So much for the plot; here are a couple of stanzas to demonstrate the verse form:

> "Alive?"—And I leapt in my wonder,
>   Was faint of my joyance,
> And grasses and grove shone in garments
>   Of glory to me.

> "She lives, in a plenteous well-being,
>   Today as aforehand;
> The dead bore the name—though a rare one—
>   The name that bore she."

A reader with an attentive ear will notice that these two stanzas rhyme (so do the twenty-nine that follow, all on the same -ee sound), and that they are written in an elaborate and unusual meter: clearly "My Cicely" is one of Hardy's virtuoso pieces, as well as a narrative.

But what, exactly, is *bad* about "My Cicely"? Well, first of all it is a clear example of what Beardsley calls the disproportion of insensibility.[7] The speaker rejects his beloved because life has made her older and, to his mind, coarse; and this is a crude and inadequate response to the situation. At the end he acknowledges that some people think him odd for pretending that the living woman is the dead one, but the poem itself confirms his rejection:

Frail-witted, illuded they call me;
   I may be. Far better
To dream than to own the debasement
   Of sweet Cicely.

But it is not far better, and the poem, by saying so, reveals a fundamental lack of humanity. This is essentially a moral judgment of the
poem, though Beardsley has tried to make it an aesthetic one by
calling it "disproportion." Not being a philosopher, I do not share
Beardsley's concern for philosophical tidiness, and I would prefer to
keep the moral questions in moral terms: indeed, it seems to me
necessary to keep in mind that one kind of poetical badness is *moral*
badness.

    But if "My Cicely" is a morally flawed poem, it is also bad in
strictly aesthetic terms. One might employ a number of other Beardsley terms to give names to some of its most striking aesthetic weaknesses: "privative," "disruptive," "reductive," "too muchness," "too
littleness"—the poem is guilty of all of these. It lacks metrical variety and interest, for instance; Hardy was proud of the way he had
made the meters imitate the action of a galloping horse, but if you
stop to think of it, galloping is a pretty monotonous rhythm, and
that is what the poem has. It contains details that work against
unity (the scenic and historical particulars along the route, for example, which Hardy thought enough of to illustrate in the first edition). It is oversimplified in its treatment of a complex human relationship. It contains too much geography, and too little feeling.

    All of these failings would be flaws in any poem, but there is
one other element in "My Cicely" that is a peculiarly Hardyan
weakness: the poem enacts an *action*—the journey down, the meeting, the return—and Hardy simply could not do actions in poems.
It was not a matter of being unable to control narrative movement
in verse, but something more complex: an inability to find actions
that would adequately express his sense of the world, an inability to
make his actions symbolic. Why Hardy, whose novels move so powerfully and symbolically, should have been unable to do this in his
verse I am not sure: it may have to do with the fact that he wrote
virtually all of his poems after he had ended his novel-writing career;
or that they are the poems of late-middle and old age (a time of
retrospection and meditation, not of action); or that his philosophic
understanding of the human situation had changed. But whatever
the reason, the fact is clear: he could no longer shape causal, sequen-
tial actions into poems without reduction and distortion.

It would be easy to compile a substantial list of Hardy's narrative poems to support this conclusion: "Her Death and After," "The Dance at the Phoenix," "The Supplanter," "The Rash Bride," "The Vampirine Fair," "The Re-enactment," "The Satin Shoes," "The Turnip-Hoer," "The Bird-Catcher's Boy," "Burning the Holly"—examples leap to the mind. And they come from every one of Hardy's eight volumes of verse, for he never stopped writing narratives, and he never stopped writing bad ones.

On the other hand, it is extremely hard to find examples of really *good* narrative poems. Even those few excellent occasional poems in which you might reasonably expect action—poems like "The Convergence of the Twain," which is, after all, about the sinking of the *Titanic*, and the few good war poems ("'And There Was a Great Calm,'" or "In Time of 'The Breaking of Nations'")— are in fact meditative and static. The only exceptions to this general judgment are a few of his ballad-tragedies ("The Trampwoman's Tragedy," "A Sunday Morning Tragedy"), where Hardy was sufficiently supported by a tradition to succeed.

Narrative verse, then—the poet-as-storyteller—is one kind of Hardy badness. Aggressive lyricism—the poet-as-singer—is another. The easiest way to explain what I mean by this category is simply to quote a few striking examples:

> I've never gone to Donaghadee,
> That vague far townlet by the sea;
> In Donaghadee I shall never be:
> Then why do I sing of Donaghadee,
> That I know not in a faint degree?

> Once engrossing Bridge of Lodi,
>   Is thy claim to glory gone?
> Must I pipe a palinody,
>   Or be silent thereupon?

> When up aloft
> I fly and fly,
> I see in pools
> The shining sky,
> And a happy bird
> And I, am I![8]

These are all examples of sound effects that are awkward or monotonous or mechanical—effects that seem unmediated by Hardy's great poetic intelligence. Not that he was not an extraordinarily skillful metrist—he was: there are more than 700 different verse forms among his 900-odd poems, and most of them are handled with great finesse. But sometimes one feels a disjunction between the ostensible subject of the poem and the particular lyrical virtuosities that Hardy has hit upon (why *that* cadence, *that* rhyme-scheme for a poem about not going to Donaghadee?), and this disjunction is likely to be most apparent where the musical effects are most insistent. It often seems as though Hardy, having arbitrarily committed himself to an elaborate formal pattern, is determined to complete it, at whatever cost to other, more important elements in the poem: he is ostentatiously, publicly *being a poet* by striving for conventionally poetic effects that are contrary to his true gift.

I suggested, in commenting on Richard Ellmann's remarks, what I thought the true nature of that gift was: that it was a mode of inward discourse, an impeded, unmellifluous articulation of private feelings. The good poems are made of the two constituents of private experience: sense data and consciousness itself. Hardy was an acute and precise observer of the physical world, and especially of small-scale nature—insects, drops of water on a gate, a leaf falling—no doubt because the world he *saw* was all the reality that he was sure of. He took the recording of the actual as a central poetic act and would defend even a trivial poem with the argument that it had actually happened (as he did with "In the Days of Crinoline").[9] The great examples of this faith in the confirming authority of actuality are the poems concerned with the death of his first wife and his recollections of their life together—the "Poems of 1912–13" and related later poems. "I myself (naturally I suppose) like those best which are literally true" he wrote to a friend just after *Moments of Vision* was published, though he added that these poems "perhaps are quite unattractive to readers, and may have little literary merit."[10] But clearly, for this kind of private poetic act, attractiveness and literary merit were not considerations that troubled him.

One way to describe Hardy's best poems is to say that they are all spoken with a private voice. The teller of the tales is a storyteller; the voice of the poetical lyrics is a singer: in both cases a sort of public role is assumed. And so is an audience: telling and singing imply persons spoken or sung *to*. But the good, private Hardy poems address no one, except the self. And this is true even when Hardy is speaking in a voice not his own: when he speaks from a woman's point of view, for example, as he does in the fine "Bereft." In the universe of these poems, there are the particulars of nature, and there is a self, but there is nothing and no one else.

Often the essential poem seems to have pre-existed in actuality, a kind of *objet trouvée*, and Hardy's creative act has simply been the recording of it. He told his friend Edmund Gosse, for example, that the scene of "Autumn in King's Hintock Park" as he actually witnessed it was a poem, though he might not have gotten it down properly on paper, and he went on to describe exactly where it had taken place. In telling Gosse all this, Hardy was not simply identifying his source: clearly he believed that a poem's roots in actuality somehow sustained it.

But though the poems are rooted in the actual, they do not readily reveal its meaning: there are, as Ellmann observed, impediments. These reveal themselves in the articulation of the subject, but the causes are deeper than style. The best poems have a hovering mysteriousness about them. No doubt this is in part a consequence of the private nature of the discourse. Insofar as Hardy is expressing private feelings, he is naturally (given his nature and his time) reticent; insofar as he is addressing himself, he does not need to be explicit, since a mere glancing allusion to an occasion of suffering or loss will recover the whole experience: remembered pain, as any adult knows, is responsive to the slightest reference. But the mysteriousness is more than simply personal; it is in Hardy's world, which withholds the satisfactions of order and meaning—the impediment, that is, is *out there*. In Hardy's world, feelings exist, but they exist independently of meaning; the subjects of his poems are those feelings, including most prominently the feeling of the absence of meaning.

One further thing needs to be said about the good poems: they are not actions. They occur after the event—most often after an experience of loss—and what they are concerned with is not the experience itself (they are not narratives), but the states of mind that follow from, and endure, loss. i could offer many examples but will content myself with one minor one, not much noticed by Hardy's critics, but entirely characteristic.

The Division

Rain on the windows, creaking doors,
    With blasts that besom the green,
And I am here, and you are there,
    And a hundred miles between!

O were it but the weather, Dear,
    O were it but the miles

That summed up all our severance,
There might be room for smiles.

But that thwart thing betwixt us twain,
Which nothing cleaves or clears,
Is more than distance, Dear, or rain,
And longer than the years!

"The Division" is a modest, minor poem, but it contains the elements of Hardy's best work—for example, the 1912–13 elegies. It says, as elegies do say, that loss is one condition of existence, and the impossibility of doing anything about it is another. And that is *all* it says. It has nothing to say about the questions that might reasonably occur to one, given the situation: What caused the division? What can be done about it? That is, it is not concerned with action, with the place of the poem's situation in a narrative line. Nor is it concerned with consolation: it simply expresses the feelings appropriate to irrecoverable loss, as a condition of human existence.

"The Division" is not a particularly awkward poem, but it is nevertheless an "impeded" one. It says very little, it is not vividly metaphorical, and its language seems strained without being "poetic"—as though the poet had to make do with a small and randomly selected vocabulary, not especially appropriate to the occasion. It has, you might say, a slightly strangulated quality: it is working as hard at *not* saying things as most poems do at being eloquent. In all of these ways, it is a representative *good* Hardy poem.

And how do the good poems relate to Hardy's *bad* poems? I can think of a number of possible theories of the relationship. You might say that in the world of poetry, as in the world of morals, badness is a corruption of goodness, and that Hardy's bad poems simply show a misuse of his gifts. Or you might say that goodness is a transformation of badness—that Hardy managed somehow to raise what were essentially the wrong principles to excellence. Neither of these in fact seems to me to describe Hardy's case. It comes nearer the mark to say that in his work badness is an absence of goodness, a *departure* from his true gifts. Certainly it is true that the essential properties of privacy, mystery, and impeded articulation are lacking in the really bad poems, though you could put this the other way round, too, and say that the properties of storytelling and song are missing from the good poems.

The point, clearly, is that Hardy was two poets. One believed that poetry is an imitation of poetry, that it takes public and conventional forms, that it is, in short, *literature*. When Hardy wrote in this mode, when he consciously attached himself to the literary high culture of his time and became the Last Victorian, he was a bad poet: not just relatively unsuccessful, but awful. The other poet took poetry to be an ordinary but private activity, like meditation, or day-dreaming, or despair. This poet had no audience, and no immediate precursors: he wrote in an English tradition, but I think largely unconsciously, drawing on folk poetry and hymnology and the Bible, and on the natural world, as other English poets had done before him, but not for literary ends, not to be a *poet*. His great precursors were anon., Hodge, and God.

The poems of the public, literary Hardy are mostly bad poems. They withhold nothing: indeed, they often give us more information, and a fuller interpretation of themselves, than we want ("My Cicely" is a dire example). The poems of the private Hardy, the good poems, tell us almost nothing: like life, they frustrate our desire for explanation. The bad poems have plots; the good ones (like "The Division") suggest nonexistent plots, but withhold them. There is a difference of reference, then, a different sense of "aboutness" in good and in bad poems. The aboutness of the bad poems is likely to be a story, or sometimes poetry itself; the good poems are about states too vague, or too impeded, to be paraphrased.

To say all these rude and negative things about Hardy's bad poems is not to say—as Larkin seemed to fear—that one wishes all the bad ones destroyed. Far from it: Hardy would not be Hardy without his bad side; it explains much about him and his ambitions, and by contrast it illuminates the private consciousness out of which the good poems came. Hardy was right: a full look at the Worst *is* necessary. He did not mean that phrase as a critical principle, but it will do for his case.

Notes

1. Philip Larkin, "Wanted: Good Hardy Critic," *Critical Quarterly* 8 (1966): 179.

2. Richard H. Taylor, "Thomas Hardy: A Reader's Guide," in *Thomas Hardy: The Writer and His Background*, ed. Norman Page (London, 1980), p. 255.

3. Viola Meynell, ed., *Friends of a Lifetime: Letters to Sydney Carlyle Cockerell* (London, 1940), p. 285.

4. W. M. Parker, "Hardy's Letters to Sir George Douglas," *English* 14 (1963): 221.

5. Monroe C. Beardsley, *The Possibility of Criticism* (Detroit, 1970), p. 110.

6. Richard Ellmann, "The Story of Modern Poetry," *New York Times Book Review* (27 April 1980), p. 34.

7. Beardsley, *The Possibility of Criticism*, p. 102.

8. The poems quoted are "Donaghadee," "The Bridge of Lodi," and "The Robin."

9. C. Day Lewis, "The Lyrical Poetry of Thomas Hardy," *Proceedings of the British Academy* 37 (1953): 163.

10. Letter to Florence Henniker, dated 7 February 1918; in Evelyn Hardy and F. B. Pinion, eds., *One Rare Fair Woman* (London, 1972), p. 179.

Tragedy and Comedy

16

The Quality of the Comic

GEORGE MCFADDEN

Like most authors who have attempted it, I have found that writing about the comic is no laughing matter. Plato's Socrates took the nature of the ridiculous (in the *Philebus*) as an important and exemplary problem, and even Bergson's urbane little book on laughter is much more serious than it seems at first reading. The topic of the comic is, in fact, notoriously difficult. Freud was at pains to say so and to belittle the extent of his own findings, though he has so far been the most successful researcher into jokes and humor. The success of Bergson and Freud, furthermore, arises from the ability of each to involve his treatment of the comic in his thought as a whole, so that it comes before us supported at many points by a theoretically consistent view of things.

Needless to say, this essay has no such extensive contribution to offer. I have tried, however, to make what I think is an original insight into the nature of the comic more permanently valuable and more genuinely applicable by incorporating it into the terms of Edmund Husserl's phenomenology—to me the most effective body of thought for the discussion of aesthetic values. In varying degree, this philosophy counts such distinguished contributors to literary studies as Max Scheler, Martin Heidegger (and many of his disciples), Maurice Merleau-Ponty, and Jacques Derrida. The fullest contribution to date has been that of Roman Ingarden, author of *The Literary Work of Art* and *The Cognition of the Literary Work of Art*, on which I rely for a theoretical underpinning. The most important feature of Husserl's phenomenology for me is that, unlike some other ways of doing philosophy current in America and Britain, it retains an interest in such notions as quality, essence, and belongingness—even if only to criticize them skillfully, as Derrida does.

Roman Ingarden's understanding of the basic phenomenological approach, though it coincides with Husserl's, may surprise some readers. Instead of beginning with a defined conceptual field or model ("a most unphenomenological way," Ingarden says), "one should begin with the very object of investigation; one should attain its immediate experience manifesting itself in the phenomena and only then fit one's concepts . . . to the data that have been obtained." Instead of relying on a given model, the literary critic (even more, I should say, than the investigator into the philosophy, the theory, or the sociology of literature) should aim first at a "faithful reproduction . . . of what is given to us in experience and with which we concretely commune both cognitively and emotionally." As for validation of one's results in this kind of investigation, proof will come when other readers "find a verification . . . by referring to immediate experience, which is achieved by contact with appropriately selected examples . . . regardless of previously constructed concepts."[1]

In these brief quotations there are several terms that have been strictly tabooed by the recent critical thought associated with Derrida and Roland Barthes. Faithful reproduction, reference, appropriation, they point out, are clearly recognizable as preconceptions that go to specify Western culture; recourse to immediate concrete experience itself is another such preconception. Such deconstructions, whether or not one accepts their polemical implications, do in fact constitute a very useful critique of Husserlian notions of fulfillment, essence, belonging, and immediate presence. My view, however, is that Ingarden (who is alert to the need for a critique also) offers a workable set of ideas for the literary critic who wants to do justice to fictionality and reality both, who is not prepared to desert Western culture, and who would like to write about literature without constant recourse to the models of Freud or Saussure or Mendeleev—but who is critic enough to recognize merit in Barthes and Derrida just the same.

For this essay, the necessary elements in Ingarden's theory are, first, his description of literary qualities (or "aesthetic value qualities"), and, second, his careful analysis of fictionality, on one side, and of the reader's response to fictional writing on the other. My understanding of the comic is that it is a quality of a certain class of fictively constituted objects. Purely linguistic or verbal analysis will therefore fall short of describing it. For descriptive purposes it is necessary to investigate the content of the fictive constitutions that have this comic quality in common and to seek by means of renewed, direct reading experience, of both outstanding and mar-

ginal examples, for a deeper and more accurate insight into the nature of the comic quality variously exhibited in them.

My term "content" (frequently used by Husserl to mean the
object to which intentional acts are directed) is also under a taboo
that absorbs content and form into meaning units called "literary
devices." As if they did not derive their actual efficacy from the
time and space of the fictive world wherein they emerge, literary
devices are sometimes supposed to exist in an imaginary armory or
combinatoire. This separate existence in a formal organization is
supposed to be necessary in order to give meaning to the devices,
and the fact that both author and reader have a shared formal
knowledge of this linguistic totality is supposed to make literature
possible. It is at least equally sensible to believe, as I do, that what
author and readers share is an acquaintance with the world gained
through living in it together. I find many good reasons that need
not be gone into here for preferring the totality (if that is the right
word) of shared experience to the totality of language and its repertory of devices—at least for literary criticism. If criticism is thereby
prevented from being an exact science, one can nevertheless continue to work toward making it more scientific than it is now.

"Comic" and "Quality"

When the word "comic" appears by itself as a substantive in
this essay, as it often does, the reader may expand it into a phrase:
"the comic quality" or "the quality of the comic." The usage is familiar in English (as in other languages), especially in discussions
involving aesthetics. The term "quality," however, is difficult to justify in contemporary discourse. It can hardly be taken in the old
sense of "substantial quality" or separable property or attribute, as if
it had a life of its own; I shall not be talking of "the comic spirit."
Rather, the comic is a quality, as the color red is a quality. Stage
comedy, Chaplin films, Wodehouse stories, exhibit different shades
of the comic quality, as there are different shades of the color red.
The comic is not to be identified with any one art form, and especially not with a single art form called "comedy." It is a quality of
many art forms, whose number will continue to be augmented. In
his Third Investigation, Husserl explains that a quality is associated
in "moments of unity" with "sensuous intuitive wholes . . . present
to outer or inner sense," and he finds qualities equivalent to what
von Ehrenfels called "form-qualities," Meinong, "founded contents," and Riehl, "moments of unity"; Husserl's alternative term,
"figural moments," is perhaps most fitting of all to convey what is

meant by speaking of the comic as a quality: it is one of the figural moments of a literary work of art.[2]

To state my primary insight in terms that will become more clear, the comic quality is a characteristic mode of aesthetic consciousness. Its characteristic comic matter is "that peculiar side of the act's phenomenological content that not only determines *that* it grasps the object but also *as what* it grasps it, the properties, relations, categorial forms" that the cocreative acts of author and reader attribute to the content of a literary work of art on which the consciousnesses of both find more or less the same focus. The definitive matter of the comic is an objectivity such that we sense it as (or interpret it as) having the properties of continuance as itself and freedom in relation to a continued threat of alteration; and this matter is conveyed in a particular form of literary art, whether of the genre of comedy, of satire, the novel, or some other art form.[3]

My understanding is that, according to Husserl, all thinking takes place in objectifying acts, and that quality and matter are two moments or inner constituents of such acts. The matter and quality of the comic are not separable as parts of the object, but are open to analysis as aspects of an integral act. When we think of something as comic, therefore, we do not divide its content into quality and matter unless we are carrying out a phenomenological analysis. Further, Husserl's term "act" does not imply a corresponding special activity such as "the aesthetic faculty," but merely abbreviates the concept of "intentional experience" that he explains as "any concrete experience that 'refers' intentionally to an object." To go further in explaining intentionality, he adds, one can only cite examples. In our case, we cite examples of concrete aesthetic experience referring to works of literary art marked by comic quality.

Finally, to show that Husserl's conception of quality and matter is peculiarly adapted to the description of the multifarious forms of the comic, we find him not only confirming the possibility of "combining any quality with any matter," but also defining matter as what is constituted in an objectifying act (with various act qualities), whether posited (believed, affirmed) or not. We must think of an act quality, therefore, as "having real reference to an object . . . through intimate *liaison* with a presentation," including the presentations of feelings and of "mere imagination." Making use of such broad concepts, our phenomenological inquiry may extend to the most extreme forms of black, absurd, and surrealist comic writing.

Instead of using the otherwise ambiguous term "matter" in this limited Husserlian sense of the object of mutual, intersubjective acts of creation by the writer and cocreation by the reader, I shall use the special term "objectivity" as the name for that imaginative structure in which the "figural moment" of the comic inheres, or is constituted. As with a funny story, an "objectivity" needs to be offered by the teller and imaginatively constituted by the hearer before the joke can be "seen." This polysyllabic term, though not a winning one, comes more trippingly on the tongue than "objectification" or "objectivation." Its German equivalent (*Gegenständlichkeit*) was used by Husserl and Ingarden, and my term is the one adopted by the latter's translators.

The Limits of Theory

When I venture to speak of my theory of the comic, I use "theory" in a sense far short of Husserl's requirement of "grounded explanation"; in fact, I wish to avoid any suggestion of "explaining" the comic. To explain would require me to establish laws, like the law of cause and effect, or of action and reaction, or of economy of forces, whereas in dealing with works of art I recognize the truth of Kant's insight that they are free and therefore give themselves their own laws in an exemplary manner only. They are not rule-governed members of a system or order of constructs that might be drawn from a structural model. My "theory" is the statement and definition of, and an extended commentary upon, an eidetic intuition: that is, an insight into the essence of a literary quality that has not hitherto been looked at in this way.

In one sense at least, my theory is more rigorous than others that are being offered: it is not composite. My focus on the essentially comic is more unitary than that of the classic superiority theory. Distorted as it is toward what is merely laughter-causing, the superiority theory as it was stated by Hobbes and others is (at least for us) hopelessly involved in the hegemony of superior subject and inferior object. In addition, Hobbes requires the extraneous temporal aspect of suddenness. His "sudden glory" is a very partial perception of the *contra expectatum* of classical rhetoric, which Kant later made into an even more limiting element of his account of the question; for the comic can strike us anew, whether we laugh or not, long after the element of surprise has gone forever.

A recent example of the composite approach to defining the comic, Robert Bechtold Heilman's *The Ways of the World: Comedy and Society*, proceeds by establishing several characteristics as more or less shifting parameters of what the playgoer and reader find in stage comedies: elation, acceptance of the world and its fundamental disparateness, liberating play.[4] Heilman's study is an unusually well-written book that obviously comes out of much experience and an excellent critical judgment. It is thoroughly researched, too; its analytic summaries of a large number of contemporary theorists are very helpful. In his descriptive procedure, however, and in eschewing the language of any philosophical school, Heilman bars himself, I should say, from the kind of insight I aim at. Our two approaches function as discovery techniques in quite different ways: Heilman's aims to include several rather incompatible theories, each with ambiguities of its own, within a general statement that can be accommodated to the existing variety of comedies. This procedure, I believe, fits Thomas S. Kuhn's description of the theory that is a background of normal science within a professional group, but at just that time of crisis when a breakthrough to a new, less composite theory is badly needed. Whatever else it may be, my theory is simple and direct enough to offer the basis for such a breakthrough.

I have not tried to explain the comic as the cause of a certain result (e.g., laughter), or the result of a particular cause (e.g., an intersubjective relation of superiority and inferiority). For any object that takes shape in a work of art, or in the literary works of art that we are concerned with, continuance-as-itself is an activity that necessarily takes on the character of spontaneousness, of self-directedness and self-governance, or of self-determination, as we might say. This is definitely the case when the self-continuance is opposed and yet successfully maintains itself. In a work of art, the opposition is manifestly marked so as to constitute a threat directed specifically at the self or kernel of the object, or objectivity (as I shall now continue to call it), rather than at some peripheral or nonessential aspect of it. There is then an overall reinforcing of the component self. What I shall go on to show is that a link has been created between self and freedom. These characters of self, self-maintenance and continuation, spontaneity and independence, on the side of the purely aesthetic perception of what is comic, have been attached to our ethical, social, and personal sense of freedom. And freedom has become the most important of all values during that epoch that can easily be recognized as beginning in the American and French revolutions. Since there is no clear sign among artists and critics today that some other chief value has superseded freedom, I see no necessary reason to agree with those who posit, somewhere in recent years, an epoch-making transformation equal to what occurred in the eighteenth century.

A Modified Historical Approach

What we call, in the arts, the Romantic period opened with a new perception of the literary genres and the qualities that marked them, and especially with a new perception, and a new theory, of the comic. I am going to argue that an integration of comic theory as it was articulated by Schiller, Coleridge, Hazlitt, Hegel, Kierkegaard, Nietzsche, Bergson, and Freud is not only possible but (one might almost say) necessary if we are to understand what appears to be the eventually complete transformation of pre-Romantic comic forms by Kafka, Céline, Beckett, and many others still writing today.

In committing myself to a modified historical approach, I am mindful that for any literary objectivity to manifest itself as such in fiction, there must be an ethos, that is, a mode of behavior convertible into human value terms, usually the terms of a "substantial" or "natural" concrete ethic (especially if the work is to have many readers). The concept of a concrete ethic (in Hegel's sense) is necessarily historical. Yet though historical change constantly occurs, it only shows itself clearly over a span of many generations, so that at any one moment social behavior appears as if permanent and, indeed, simply natural—except for the moments (again, in the Hegelian sense) when it undergoes revolutionary change. The contrast of two vast periods—from Plato to the eighteenth century, from the American and French revolutions till now—though it is too gross to satisfy historians, is at least a useful critical limitation of an historical kind. It establishes a working diachronic base; with it one can see an emergent transformation of value feelings, including strictly aesthetic ones, belonging to comic perception and comic response.

The classic superiority theory of the ridiculous, though it failed to account for several masterpieces of ancient comic writing, was thoroughly involved in the ethos of theater comedy by means of specific class divisions and social conventions that were promoted to the status of universal laws of the dramatic genres and the decorum of the stage. During the eighteenth century, it is generally agreed, a revolutionary change occurred that altered ethos on the stage as well as off. Just as we can mark the moment of this social change with the Revolution in France, we can mark the reversal of the former comic hegemony in the enormously successful *Marriage of Figaro* by Pierre-Augustin Caron, self-named de Beaumarchais. In this comedy, instead of two plots maintained as separate, hierarchical structures, one conducted by upper-class and the other by lower-class players, we have an acknowledged complicity among classes and actions. Instead of marking its upper-class figures with urbane wit and perfect manners, *The Marriage of Figaro* makes Count Almaviva a callous predator, humiliatingly dependent upon his valet. Figaro, on the contrary, is everything magnanimous and fine that the old comic ethos would have tied to nobility: but now the recognition-and-reversal scene prefers to show him to be by birth simply a good bourgeois. As for the Count, he is to get back where he belongs, into bed with the Countess, like any decent citizen with his wife.

Furthermore, it makes sense to see the emergence of humor, too, against this moment of social and political revolution. The emergence of English humor was recognized all over Europe as a strikingly novel development in a sphere where novelty is rare but immensely significant—human feeling. "Humor" and "humanity," whatever their background in the vernaculars of Europe, were both terms loaded with new and closely associated meanings bearing upon the new ethos. Friedrich von Schiller (another bourgeois who earned his "von") expressed the impact of the new ideas of humor as a value quality in this remarkable comparison: "Thomas Jones," he observed, "pleases us much more than Grandison." [5] The reason? Fielding's Tom Jones is more natural than Richardson's Sir Charles Grandison; and nothing produces this difference so much as the fact that Tom is treated humorously, Grandison seriously.

Deconstruction and Reconstruction

It has become evident to me (after the fact, actually) that my procedure agrees, up to a point, with the deconstructive method first made clear in the work of Jacques Derrida. I go back to a neglected text, Plato's *Philebus*, for my fresh start, and I observe that Plato presents certain aspects of the comic problem more clearly than anyone else during the next two millennia. In his emphasis on the mixed pleasure-pain experience of laughter, however, Plato opened the door to the inadequate understanding of the comic as essentially limited to the laughable and the ridiculous; this reduction Aristotle's writing promulgated much more specifically, in the form of an opposition between tragedy as the genre of high life and comedy as the dramatic form belonging to a lower or mediocre life. The deconstructive move is to reverse the opposition, by preferring the comic over the tragic and finding more worth in so-called ordinary life than in high life. And here the critical procedure is in obvious accord with developments in literary history.

The Essence of the Comic

When we return to a beginning and ask what is the comic, none of the familiar answers prove quite satisfactory. Not that they are all wrong, but they are inadequate if we intend to form an idea of the comic that will reach its essence. The most natural reply, "the comic is that which causes laughter," was rejected by Aristotle long ago, and for good reasons. Anyone can see that there is only a partial overlap in the appropriate use of the term "laughable" and the proper meaning of our term "comic." Still, if not laughter, then smiling, or at the very least a sparkling in the eyes, or an enlivening of the expression on one's face, is a spontaneous accompaniment of the comic experience. "Deadpan humor" or dry wit is no exception to this rule, but is itself a branch of the comic that uses assumed insensitivity as a foil. In the presence of the comic, failure to respond to it is comic.

The comic appears to be neither a simple experience, nor simply a response to a certain kind of experience. It is complex, at least in that it includes both an experience of something that can be called funny or amusing and some kind of gesture, expression, or formulation that marks it off and begins to make it communicable. Such "communication," of course, need not be in writing or addressed to anyone besides oneself; all that is absolutely necessary is a seizure or comprehension of the amusing moment so as to make it in some degree noteworthy and memorable. One could be entertained for hours by the sight of children or young animals at play, but if one never had a particular momentary sense of certain of its aspects falling into a particularly characteristic structure, the experience would be pleasant or enjoyable but not ever comic.

The essence of the comic thus includes a positing and structuring aspect when "what-is-funny" may be grasped with enough definiteness to be recalled or retold; it has acquired anecdotal permanence, if not continuance or duration. But the more important question still remains. It concerns the essence of that which is grasped as funny or amusing and which is made to continue. I shall be content to seek for an answer that will prove adequate to our sense of the comic as it has been perceived during the last two centuries. Modern people have found that the characteristic feeling of fun or joy that identifies the comic arises from their sense of the activity of a being that is notably engaged in being-itself, in self-activity, self-assertion by utterly characteristic behavior, in self-maintenance, self-definition, self-sustenance. This sense, of course, would be very weak or would vanish if the being *merely* maintained itself; such monotony would be boring or would simply pass without our notice. The comic prominently includes, therefore, an aspect of the changeable, actually posed as a threat of alteration to the self-continuing structure. It is essential that this threat be present, and also that it be successfully resisted by the self-governing process of the comic structure itself rather than by factors external to it.

Within the Romantic frame of mind, which sees political in-

dependence as a necessary aspect of fully human existence, the term
"self-governing" serves to disclose an actual, and perhaps universal,
requirement for the comic: freedom. To us, and since the mid-
eighteenth century, self-government is no mere metaphor for freedom, but a necessary condition of it, humanly speaking. The associations of the comic with spontaneity, liberation from inhibition
and constraint, unblocking, vital movement, and ease and grace of
behavior all point to freedom as an indispensable component.

The essence of the comic, therefore, is founded in a being that
shows the power of continuing as itself, substantially unchanged,
while overcoming a force or forces that would substantially alter it.
Both continuance and change are necessary to the comic; but the
impulse to change, as soon as it appears, is taken up into a kind of
rhythm of test and proof, as a form of challenge or stimulus to the
comic entity. The comic itself, in its kernel, is so much itself, so
characteristic, that it stands out, draws attention to itself, invites or
actually begets some counterforce, be it rivalry, mere conformity to
averageness, or sheer inertia. This force takes shape as it is poised
in the light of the comic, as a threat or as an opponent in some
contest or gamelike activity, either of which serves to bring out the
unchanging identity even more. What the comic overcomes is peculiarly visible in the light of the comic, so that the latter has a
creative aspect to it: it seems to provide its own objects for fun-
making. This active, independent, and productive power goes along
with freedom, and it always marks the genuinely comic.

The Concept of Literary Genre

Before going further, however, we must face the problem of
distinguishing the explicitly comic in literary works from the accompanying but universally aesthetic qualities of freedom, self-
sustainedness, and spontaneity. Since we are trying to confront the
question at a time when old, well-defined literary genres have ceased
to retain much explanatory value except for historical purposes, we
shall look for terms in the context of a modern literary theory. I
choose Schiller's, believing that it emerged along with explicitly
Romantic literature and also helped give the lead to its development. The basis of his theory is Kant's opposition of the human
mind to nature. Schiller's analysis of the alienated stance of the
modern writer is indispensable if we are to bring the problem of the
comic to a contemporary focus.

Schiller realized that once the writer saw nature as something
other than himself, he became free of nature as a universally determining source or model, but at the same time he lost his feeling for

nature as the human home. His resultant sense of loss provoked the most powerful of all "Romantic" feelings. Its name, *Heimweh*, dates from Schiller's youth as a word in German, and it was soon converted into the learned term familiar to the world, "nostalgia," by a backformation using the Greek *nóstos* (journey back to one's home) and *álgos* (pain, distress). The term is highly appropriate, recalling the *nóstoi*, or sad wanderings, of the Greek heroes after their victory at Troy, for they sought homecomings that most of them never achieved. In an irresistible movement, loss by human beings of their natural home was converted to a sense of loss of their innocence and their simple happiness in childhood. We should call this dominant feeling, I am convinced, "nostalgia for the naive." Provided we think of nostalgia as having its positive, recreative side as well as its distressful one, nostalgia for the naive is the most persistent identifying mark of literature written during the last two hundred years.

Schiller used this development of alienation from nature and of nostalgia to uncover a new structure of the literary genres. He also described two different kinds of writer, with opposing temperaments and sensibilities to match. The new situation appears most clearly in Schiller's description of the opposing genres of elegy and satire. In elegy we have the artistic overcoming of alienation in the form of a beautiful lament for a once-existing harmony of the human in nature, especially in the setting of classical Greece. Or we have the idyll, which in easy disregard of actuality treats that harmony of human and natural as if existing "now." For the latter treatment, however, we need a new kind of writer, the idealist. He seeks to reunite mind and nature in the ideal (not the real historical past or the seriously imagined future).

Similarly in satire: its two kinds are the "sublime" and the "mocking" (or "playful"). The basis for the distinction is the kind of feeling involved. Sublime satire employs tempestuous, even tragic, passions. It is serious—either punitive or pathetic—in its demands. It works powerfully upon the will, driving to put an end to the disjunction between what is and what ought to be. On the other hand, playful satire (which Schiller clearly prefers) often treats a morally neutral subject; yet it avoids the trivial because the beautiful soul (*schöne Seele, bel âme*) of the poet redeems and supports his material.[6]

At this point in his account of the specifically new genres, Schiller enters into a digression amounting only to two paragraphs wherein he discusses tragedy and comedy. Like sublime satire, tragedy arouses strong passions and hence (if only temporarily) it limits freedom. Comedy, on the other hand, never suspends freedom but perpetually asserts it—not least because the comic writer need admit no dependency at all upon substantial, fateful ties to state, society, and history. He is free to move at will in his imagination, free to *play* with these "substantialities" and to call his readers to an equal freedom. What he must do, however, is remain himself and be always at home in his own beautiful soul (or sensibility, or vision, as we should say), preserving a lively vigor that provides and sustains his themes with inner resources of his own. He must beware of pathos and oracular meanings, and "look serenely about and within himself to find everywhere more coincidence than fate, and ought rather to laugh at absurdity than to rage or weep at malice."[7]

Making the most of this account, we can conclude that the comic is in a special relation to freedom. Other genres of art cannot do without freedom, but comedy is the only genre continually to assert it. Furthermore, though no genre may be adequately defined by a simple quality, comedy is the only one wherein freedom gives the tone in a predominating way to the complex quality that emerges from the work as a whole. This statement can be made while admitting that one should not attempt to base "rules" upon such a determination, but only point to freedom among a set of "exemplary" conditions, as Kant proposed. The kind of freedom that is exemplary for art, according to Schiller, differs between the naive writer and the reflective one and between the idealist and the realist. Likewise among the genres, which in modern times tend to be satire, comedy, elegy, and idyll, there are differences in the kinds and extent of freedom.

Finally, Schiller would seem to be the first writer on art to introduce the notion of a "fall," in the manner of Roland Barthes's division between "works of our modernity," which are "writable," and the bygone "classic" works, which are only "readable." There is an important difference, of course: Schiller's "fall" is an historical one in the main, although he does insist that "reflective" geniuses have written in the age of the "naive" and that "naive" writers can still exist in a world that has lost its naiveté. Barthes's "modernity" is more like an ever-shifting present, a rather arbitrary canon including Sade, Flaubert's *Bouvard et Pécouchet*, and Mallarmé because they still have something new to offer to the reading and writing community of which M. Barthes finds himself a member. Schiller, on the other hand, was professor of history at Jena at the time of his aesthetic inquiries, and he wrote in direct response to the events of the Revolution in France—in all of European history, surely, the most plausible septennium (1789–95) for an actual "fall." Schiller's fall, nevertheless, like that of Adam and M. Barthes, involved human freedom above all. When human beings fell out of nature and began to look at all the rest of the world as "other," they became free and responsible in essential ways, unsuspected before the *novus ordo seclorum* we celebrate on our paper money.

My thesis is that the concepts and terms with which Schiller described the new order of writing are still valid. They account for both the systemic state of and the ongoing transformations within literary work and literary studies today. This means, I believe, that we are still in the cultural epoch widely known as the Romantic period. The extraordinary turbulencies of the last thirty years may prove to be threshold phenomena of a breakthrough in our progress to an entirely new epoch, but similar disturbances have already occurred (around 1830 and 1910) without putting a closing bracket to the stage of the Western consciousness that Schiller described in two critical masterpieces, *Letters on the Aesthetic Education of Man* and *Naive and Sentimental Poetry*. (Lest this last claim seem forced, it should be pointed out that the Hegelian dialectic, Marxist "alienation," the all-importance of artistic "culture," and other essential components of our continuing world view were already present seminally in Schiller's texts, especially the latter.)[8]

The Comic in Modern Literature

Let us proceed, then, with an inquiry into the conditions that are exemplary for the comic in modern literature, trying first to explore the content of Schiller's concepts and to determine (not too aggressively) the applicability of his terms to works that are of interest to us now. A convenient text will be the material from Kant and Schiller collected and commented upon by R. D. Miller in his *Schiller and the Ideal of Freedom*.[9] First, let us reaffirm Kant's insistence upon exemplary, rather than rule-governed or constrained, generation of art and the experience of works of art. Kant, as Miller says,

> is concerned to safeguard the principle of freedom in aesthetic experience . . . from the restricting influence of all 'interests,' all concepts, and all purposes, so [that] the necessity which is a feature of aesthetic experience is not imposed by a rule or a law. Kant calls this aesthetic necessity 'exemplary,' because we notice a certain regularity, certain effects which appear to be *examples* of the working of a rule, without being able to state what the rule actually is.[10]

We can ask, "What is the rule of Falstaff's character?" meaning its secret, its "idea" or principle, its essence; but we cannot hope to supplant the insights of Dryden, Morgann, or Bradley about Falstaff with any final formula.

In an essay of 1793, "Of Grace and Dignity," Schiller developed in a highly significant way the need, as Miller puts it, to "reconcile the freedom of man, as an independent rational being, with the freedom of nature."[11] On the one hand grace is restricted to human beings, but on the other hand, for their own sake, human beings are led by grace in themselves to go further and set nature free. Here Schiller very clearly puts forward the principle of preserving the natural and liberating it from inhibitions, one of the most important clues for our grasp of the comic.

Aesthetic Freedom and Comic Redemption of Power

Moreover, and at the heart of his response to the demands of those terrible years, in "Of Grace and Dignity" Schiller established a metaphoric union between the aesthetic and the political. Miller sums it up: "Just as a liberal government refrains from treating individuals as a means to an end, but respects their individual freedom, so man with his aesthetic sense is concerned not to interfere with the freedom of nature."[12] Schiller sees the aesthetic as a way of redeeming power: instead of being mere violence against aggressive enemies, passive subjects, and inert nature, power becomes a freely flowing energy within a community governed by mutual respect.

Schiller described his own age as torn between the perversity and the lack of nature of the refined classes, with their moral rootlessness, and the rawness, coarseness, mere nature, of the lower classes and their superstitions. Schiller also talked of ancient Greece as a naive state of ideal harmony between nature and reason, which too soon declined. After the Greeks, an artificial political structure of lifeless mechanical parts replaced an organic community, and the human was neglected in the specialized pursuits of each man.[13] In Schiller's protest we have seeds that fell on fertile ground, not in Matthew Arnold alone, but in Marx, in Nietzsche, in Bergson, in Freud. Schiller's way of meeting the needs of his own chaotic era was through totality of personal character, where principles and feelings united, and where the victorious forms of art served as examples (but not as programs or manifestos) and helped individual human beings to solve the problem, posed so sharply by the Terror in France, of a disintegrating modern community ripe for an intellectual tyranny. This urge toward freedom from compulsion and violence was bound to promote the comic, as Schiller saw, and to

undercut the tragic except as an historical mode, a genre fit for re-
vivals rather than premieres.

Schiller identifies, as the beautiful task of comedy, the promo-
tion of what he calls "*Freiheit des Gemüts*," a concept that may be
said to include freedom of mind, soul, and natural disposition. But
he says it cannot be identified with moral freedom, the particular
quality tragedy is concerned with. Comedy can only be identified
with aesthetic freedom. Tragedy is concerned with death; in it the
life formed by art is cut off and terminated in order for greatness to
be achieved in a final, catastrophic manner. But in his comic writing, where the poet remains himself, at home in a world of his own,
the forms he gives life to are made free, without effort and always.[14]
What Schiller gives us as the aim of comedy is in itself a definition
of aesthetic freedom: "Its purpose is uniform with the highest after
which man has to struggle: to be free of passion, always clear, to
look serenely about and within himself, to find everywhere more
coincidence than fate, and rather to laugh at absurdity than to rage
or weep at malice."[15]

In comic writing the two opposed kinds of mentalities that
Schiller sees as marking the reflective epoch, the realist and the
idealist, can find agreement, for the disproportion between real and
ideal can be dissolved in what we call a sense of humor. Overcoming victoriously what otherwise might crush them, both kinds of
person are then found laughing rather than raging or weeping.

Conclusion

The theoretical structure of the comic quality, as sketched out
so far, may be illustrated in a simple and direct fashion with a short
passage from Book 2 of *Gulliver's Travels*. Gulliver, a voyager of considerable self-sufficiency and aplomb, has been taken up as a pet by
the giant Brobdingnagians. He entertains them with tricks of skill
that include handling a small boat, which he has built himself,
in the equivalent of a bathtub. In chapter 5, in one of the many
adventures brought on by his smallness, he has to deal with a
giant frog:

> Another time, one of the servants, whose office it was to
> fill my trough every third day with fresh water, was so careless
> to let a huge frog (not perceiving it) slip out of his pail. The
> frog lay concealed till I was put into my boat, but then seeing
> a resting place, climbed up, and made it lean so much on one
> side that I was forced to balance it with all my weight on the

other, to prevent overturning. When the frog was got in, it hopped at once half the length of the boat, and then over my head, backwards and forwards, daubing my face and clothes with its odious slime. The largeness of its features made it appear the most deformed animal that can be conceived. However, I desired Glumdalclitch to let me deal with it alone. I banged it a good while with one of my sculls, and at last forced it to leap out of the boat.

In accordance with the theory, we may say that Gulliver himself is a comic figure. He steadfastly remains himself, a sober, cleanly, self-reliant seafaring man, coping with an extraordinary set of threats arising out of his size, itself a characteristic feature of his ordinary humanity. On the other hand, the frog is very much a frog, behaving exactly as we know a frog would do. The appalling effect of "the largeness of its features" upon Gulliver can readily be imagined, but the whole scene is made into pure fun by the slapstick, yet soberly efficient, self-assurance of the hero. "I banged it a good while with one of my sculls" strikes, in its combination of exaggeration and understatement, the great chord of English deadpan humor. All we have to do is to imagine the scene vividly, and it is unforgettably comic. One might apply the theory further and suggest that Book 2 of the *Travels* is comic throughout, because both self-maintenance and the threats against it are kept up. This is somewhat less the case in Book 3. In Book 4 the theory leads us to decide that Gulliver, as a character, ceases to be a comic figure in himself: degraded by the experience with Houyhnhnms and Yahoos, he loses not only his self-assurance and self-reliance, but his sense of belonging to the human race. Nevertheless, his new character helps Book 4 itself to function in a sublimely comic way. *Gulliver's Travels* as a whole shows us, one might say, an essentially comic truth: that human nature remains itself only while it freely resists distortion to the extremes of big and little, strong and weak, clever and stupid, immortal and mortal, master and servant, mind and body, superman and beast. We are creatures of the middle state in life.

Notes

1. Roman Ingarden, *The Literary Work of Art*, trans. George G. Grabowicz (Evanston, Ill., 1973), p. lxvi.

2. Edmund Husserl, *Logical Investigations*, trans. J. N. Findlay, 2 vols. (New York, 1970), 1:442. See Section 4, original division.

3. In this and the two following paragraphs, I have drawn upon Husserl's Fifth Investigation, sections 20–22, 30, 32, 38, and 41–43: see

pp. 589–, 597–600, 617, 620, 641, and 648–51 in vol. 2 of Findlay's translation.

4. Robert Bechtold Heilman, *The Ways of the World: Comedy and Society* (Seattle, 1979), pp. 47ff.

5. Friedrich von Schiller, *Kallias*, letter of 23 February 1973; in *Sämtliche Werke*, ed. Gerhard Fricke and Herbert G. Göpfert, vols. (Munich, 1962), 5:425–26.

6. Friedrich von Schiller, *Naive and Sentimental Poetry*, trans. Julius A. Elias (New York, 1966), p. 119. Elias gives crossreferences to the text edited by Oskar Walzel in the *Sämtliche Werke*, Säkular-Ausgabe, 16 vols. (Stuttgart and Berlin, 1904–1905), vol. 12; see pp. 195–96.

7. Schiller, *Naive and Sentimental Poetry*, p. 122; Walzel ed., p. 199, with "*Bosheit*" for "malice."

8. See the comments of Thomas Mann in "On Schiller," in *Last Essays*, trans. Richard and Clara Winston (London, 1959), pp. 15–. Elsewhere, according to Elias (in Schiller, *Naive and Sentimental Poetry*, p. 1), Mann referred to it as "the greatest of all German essays."

9. R. D. Miller, *Schiller and the Ideal of Freedom* (Oxford, 1970).

10. Ibid., pp. 73– (my emphasis). Miller refers to the *Kritik der Urteilskraft*, ed. Georg Reimer, in vol. 5 of the collected works published for the Royal Prussian Academy of Sciences; see p. 236. Miller's valuable study was first published in a limited edition in 1959, and then republished by the Clarendon Press with a foreword by Sir Isaiah Berlin, praising it as "by far the clearest, most accurate, and intelligent account of the intellectual relationship between Kant and Schiller" (p. v), particularly in their treatment of freedom.

11. Miller, *Schiller and the Ideal of Freedom*, p. 102.

12. Ibid., p. 103; cf. "Über Anmut und Würde," in *Sämtliche Werke*, 5:460.

13. Miller, *Schiller and the Ideal of Freedom*, p. 109. See *On the Aesthetic Education of Man*, fifth and sixth letters; and *Sämtliche Werke*, 5:580–81 and 582.

14. Miller, *Schiller and the Ideal of Freedom*, p. 126; trans. in Schiller, *Naive and Sentimental Poetry*, p. 121; Walzel ed., pp. 197–.

15. Miller, *Schiller and the Ideal of Freedom*, p. 122; Walzel ed., pp. 198–99.

17

On the Tragic
A Confession and Beyond

STEFAN MORAWSKI

I

The literature discussing the idea of the tragic is already enormous. Perhaps the best way to approach this subject might be to compose a typography of the conceptions offered to date, followed by a critical analysis of those ideas of the tragic that have shown the greatest staying power. Another very helpful approach would investigate the historical determinants that have lent amplitude and meaning to this category of thought. Undoubtedly the determinants have altered over time, especially if one considers the whole duration of European history. The Aristotelian conception markedly differs from the Port Royal notion advanced by Pascal, and that from the modernist definition—"the tragedy of culture"—given by Georg Simmel. Not only are conflicting intellectual biases and bents involved, but also, and more fundamentally, we find different artistic practices in writing tragic dramas, different philosophical frames of reference, and, finally, different sociocultural formations leading to the irreconcilable tragic modes of experiencing and grasping the world. Yet another tempting, and rewarding, research direction would lead us to reflect on the whys and hows of the spread and flourishing of the tragic idea in some eras and its muting in others. Were the Middle Ages conducive or resistant to meditations on the problematic status of mankind? Does the Christian religion permit the view that man may be abandoned by God and left in the void? If Job is a paragon of tragic religious character, is his lot really tragic? On the other hand, what can we say of Kierkegaard's "leaps" from the quotidian world to God and back? If man can possess only *deus absconditus*, it may be that the Christian faith bears the imprint of a genuine tragedy. Max Scheler mentioned in his *Bemerkungen zum Phaenomen des Tragischen*,[1] and quite justly, that Raphael and Goethe were blind indeed to the sense of the tragic. Nonetheless, one is inclined to search for the reasons more broadly than in their individual relations to art and existence. For their ages too did not abound in the tragic vision. On the other hand, beginning with Hegel the issue became crucial—and around the turn into the twentieth century every artist and philosopher felt called upon to express himself on this matter. One need only look quickly at J. Volkelt's *System der Aesthetik*[2] to realize that the problem of the tragic was then obsessive. A subsequent wave of attentiveness came with the existentialism of Heidegger, Jaspers, and Sartre.

Each of these problems rewards inquiry, but my line of discussion will be entirely different, as my title indicates. I am not concerned with others' viewpoints here; here I will develop my own. Before I undertake this task, let me offer a few indispensable qualifications. Tragedy taken as a literary genre does not itself reveal what is tragic. On the contrary: it is the tragic that provides material for the tragedies. For this reason I shall not tackle the questions that were extensively treated by Aristotle in his *Poetics*, that is, the composition of the whole and the specific dramaturgy of tragic events (the *peripeteia*, recognition, pitch of action, etc.). Nor am I going to deal with the problem of the aesthetic pleasure that can be derived from a stage representation of disasters and the cruel turns of fortune in a hero's life. This theme spellbound many seventeenth- and especially eighteenth-century thinkers. A second premise that I have to stress is this: when I offer my "personal" understanding of what is tragic, "personal" does not imply entirely private or arbitrary. Just the opposite: the experience I have had (without which I could only be a distant observer of what constitutes the tragic) has to be rooted in a universally relevant human nature and human mind. Nevertheless, the tragic is no scientific notion that can be empirically verified, as greenness or roundness can be; nor can it be unanimously accepted, as the abstract idea of the triangle can be. It is dependent on a philosophical vision, on how one conceives the foundations of human existence and social ontology. This kind of approach must then be subjective, for it is based on feelings, conations, an intuitive and imaginative grasp of what we are as human beings. The subjective characteristics are, however, objectively founded because each philosopher appeals to the ontological structuring of man.

The premise I advance here explains the title of my deliberations: they cannot be other than a confession, and yet they reach beyond my individual experience and understanding inasmuch as they seem to proceed from the order of things. Of course, my own philosophy must necessarily remain at variance with other frames of

mind; but from this it does not follow, as might hastily be concluded, that the partners in discussion will never have a meeting of
minds. The partners' elucidations may be quite distinct as a result of
their applying divergent theoretical apparatuses; yet they will refer
to and be based on the same syndrome of phenomena.

I have a final qualification, which concerns the skeptical or
even the radically negative response to any conception of the tragic.
That such responses will occur is likely and to be accepted and reck-
oned with, as ranking among man's possible reactions to the world
and himself. What shall I say when X or Y rejects categorically the
idea of tragic human existence, while I have dared to affirm that it
is the very essence of what it means to be human? The answer will
be simple: either I am fundamentally right, and thus X and Y are
misguided by the outward appearances that distort their arguments,
or else their experiences are decisive and their reasons are stronger,
and therefore my stance is delusory because I have taken as universal a world vision that is of delimited range and weight. I see no way
of arriving at an ultimate solution to this stand-off. And this is precisely what I wished to emphasize when I said that in this domain
nothing is scientifically certain and validated.

II

When we scan the various historical interpretations of the concept of the tragic to note their recurrent threads, we repeatedly find
two notions that draw our attention. The first of these is the idea
that the tragic arises from an insurmountable incongruity between
the order of facts, on the one hand, and, on the other, the order of
values; in other words, an irreconcilable conflict of "is" and "ought."
The second is the idea that the tragic is the outcome of an inevitable clash between two values of the highest standing, leading to the
elimination of one of them. We need not, I think, see these two
approaches as mutually exclusive. I will contend that they are sup-
plementary and together provide the preconditions of the concept.
Or, more precisely, they point to the necessary condition of the
tragic, although they do not provide the sufficient condition.

The first of these notions stresses the biopsychic and social aspects of the human being. Although we are mortal, we live as if
immortality might be ours. Contingency makes havoc of our plans,
but we seek for the alpha and omega that no circumstance or even-
tuality could touch. Our human energies and potentials weaken
with advancing years, but it remains our chief goal to be fully creative for as long as we exist. The world about is nonsensical and

inimical, and still we build our lives on a principle of harmony, love, and friendship. History offers anything but the embodiment of justice, equality, and freedom, but we strive, desperately and, as it were, indefatigably, to realize these most highly regarded values. We know that evil is within us—selfishness, excessive ambition, jostling for prestige, competing with others for possessions and power, to have the upper hand and to be the frontrunner in the race for achievements and rewards—although the "ought" to which we lend lip-service bids us do just the opposite. We vainly do our best to remember that the Other is our brother in need; exaggerated ambitions are cancers in our bellies; prestige is a superficial distinction; competition means ultimately to seize power and gain victories that for the most part are insubstantial fluff; authority without charisma is pathogenetic; achievements (truth, beauty, ethos) are fugitive when their substance is spent as the mere means to an end, that is, some prize.

The existentialist approach drew the radical conclusions of the incompatibility of the factual and the axiological orders of human being. Nothingness is our lot, they say, and we have to transgress it at every moment, heroically. Our existential projects constitute the values that steer each life and instill it with meaning. The past does not matter; it is eliminated from the game by the very situation of living in the void. The present is under a permanent pressure of the inchoate, care-distracted, and anxiety-ridden mere *condition humaine*. The future exacts either passive resignation or our transformative activity. At the horizon awaits death. Heaven yawns empty. Even should God be our project, it is a tremulous one. Following Jacob Boehme (*Vom irdischen und himmlichen Mysterium* and *De signatura rerum*), we might subscribe to the deity as only the infinite *Urgrund*: that is, the absolute chasm and absolute silence that emphasizes our limitless freedom.

The thinkers who provide this conception of the tragic illuminate the problem to the extent that they stress the collision of aleatoric factors that crosses our plans and leaves them as the flotsam of the unknown. The *sein-sollende* opposition to mere factuality, as the German neo-Kantian philosophers called it, is highlighted. However, I do not accept the existentialist viewpoint that values derive solely from our individual projects, for the sociocultural world that we inhabit is rife with them. It is one matter to make a personal choice of a meaningful existence, and still another to create on each occasion, as it were anew, the axiological dimension. But the category of the universally human (or, in the existentialist vocabulary, *Dasein* as the ontological basis) compels us to assume some set and hierarchy of values. This is why I cannot agree that the above notion—the conflict of the human project with the factual emptiness of existence—touches the very essence of the tragic. Nor can I agree that death allied with nothingness makes of life a fundamental tragedy. Even the sudden decay of a person full of creative potency, of a young genius, does not seem to provide a sufficient indicator of the tragic nexus. I would instead call such an event highly dramatic and deplorable or lamentable: what the modernist German aestheticians describe as *das Klägliche* or *das Jämmerliche*. A melancholy, gloomy sadness (*Trauer*) arises when we are confronted, say, with the eternal departure of a loved one. But the tragic is something more.

The second notion concerns the clash of two irreconcilable values of the highest range; hence, one or the other has to perish. Love pitted against loyalty to one's people or state; friendship pitted against a dedication to truth that must be spoken; a strictly artistic vocation as against an active commitment to combat social evil; the temptation to cultivate esoteric, mystical experience versus the worldly duty to help people who suffer in one way or another: here is a sampling of the oppositions that occur too frequently and painfully to be disregarded. Of course, each historical and cultural context alters the set of conflicting values and their relative importance. But the underlying opposition belongs to all of human existence. And there are cogent grounds to believe that notwithstanding contextual differences, the same basic values recur when one is compelled to choose. Hegel made the point well in his *Aesthetics*[3] when he contrasted the ancient Greek and the modern European experience and grasp of the tragic. Granted, the idea of *moira* in Sophocles and Aristotle is no longer current; the ancient suffering of an inevitable fate is alien to us. Yet the chief tragic nexus of human existence is grounded in the conflict of almost precisely these values. Hegel was probably the finest exponent of the approach. All such values of high standing are of equal weight, lending to the conflict its sense of loss and genuine tragedy. The ethical powers embodied by the competing sides are similarly "blind" in mutually denying one another; accordingly no *Schuld* adheres to the outcome, and the victor incurs no guilt as the unilateral value is advanced. Let us refer again to the untimely death of a loved one. For this to be more than a dramatic event, for it to become tragic, requires, first, that our love, incarnated in the one that we mourn, be regarded as among the highest values of our existence. Indeed, should I not be able to endure this terrible loss of my beloved, the only substantive, logical consequence would be suicide. An alternative to suicide is to let the loss be forgotten until time extinguishes the grief. Neither case is tragedy. Should, however, I continue to live with the perpetual fresh memory of the beloved, should I persistently hold this value of mine to be supreme, and should I nonetheless pursue other values (biological *joie de vivre*, excitement in work, friendship, etc.), the human tragedy then takes form. I have become impaled by a conflict of values, whether or not I have consciously experienced it.

May we then conclude that the Hegelian viewpoint satisfactorily explains the tragic? I think not. For Hegel's solution to the problem presumes an Absolute Spirit in which all conflicting values may be reconciled and reharmonized or integrated. His perspective being panlogical, he located the tragic in individual and social history over and beyond the specific human existence. I do not reject his theses that conflicting values may be internalized in one person or different persons and that the *Weltzustand* (i.e., historicocultural oppositions and contradictions) is embodied through such individual mediations. I do deny, however, that the tragic can be cut off from intimate, immediate experience. Second, each individual, upon encountering the tragic, experiences the irreconcilable clash of values. This conflict has its place inside each of us; or, to put it another way, we dwell inside it. That is why the Hegelian *Versöhnung* appears by comparison to be a mystification. Indeed, what a tragedy-stricken person endures is an *endgültig dysharmonisches Gefühle*—a feeling of ultimate disharmony, in Max Dessoir's phrase. Third, no statement of this conception that merely points to incommensurate noble values will be satisfactory; instead, one must first scrutinize and decipher the antinomic nodes of human existence in order to grasp the full depths of tragedy.

III

Now to the core of the problem. What does constitute a sufficient condition for the tragic? Let us briefly summarize the irrevocable relations we experience vis-à-vis the world.

I–Thou

We seek to come together, not only by intermingling the Self with a chosen Other, but also by knitting a unity of the body and spirit. Love and friendship are our highest goal. As in the Platonic myth, the two halves set apart should regain each other and integrate as an intimate oneness. This aim notwithstanding, such moments of harmony are exceedingly rare and quickly perish. Sometimes the erotic frenzy provides the experience of uncompromised "being with." Alas! Man and woman are incommensurable subspecies, the cause stemming from the biosexual *habitus* of each. Alas, too! The best friends remain at some distance from one another. There is always a residue of the unique that erects a wall between I and Thou. We will always know that we are separate; the communication can never be complete, and, what is more, we have to defend and continually reconstruct our separateness. It is not a narrow love of Self that conflicts with love of the Other, nor is it a mere constancy toward myself that interferes with my friendship for X or Y. Rather, it is a syndrome, an antinomy of Selfhood-togetherness, that constricts these two opposing values of the highest standing.

I–Society

By "society" I mean any small social grouping (family, club, circle) or association of institutional character (church, trade union, political party), as well as the largest entities (nation, state). What I stated with regard to the I–Thou relationship can be asserted even more relevantly here. Each person looks for community and yet cannot yield altogether to the collective-cum-being. The closest affinity with one's fellow humans may be achieved in some rare circumstances. This notwithstanding, the grouphood of individual existence without any limitations seems to be unachievable. Each one lives menaced by sheer loneliness or by sheer gregariousness. The spectrum between these extremes is always problematical, infused by a tragic tension. Consider, for instance, the form of psychotherapy developed under the initiative of Kurt Lewin in the mid-1940s and advanced by Carl Rogers' guidelines for group encounters. The dilemma here rests on the idea of self-realization achieved through the most intimate, spontaneous interaction with others. Tearing off the masks, sharing the most private experiences with others, should bring the participant back to himself or herself. These values—the uncovered or regained selfhood and the spiritual commingling—converge but are never unified. The existence of the group always means, to at least some extent, the unfreedom of the individual. The same may be argued with regard to communal development.

And at this point we pass to another aspect of the I–Society relationship. All individuals yearn for a social order in which justice, freedom, and equality are more than cherished ideals and are practiced continually and creatively. Social realities belie the wish. Freedom is for the most part throttled or confined. Equality is undermined or restricted. Justice is mocked. Not a single system has been able to translate the lofty ideals of humanity into a full historical embodiment. Humanistic democracy is a convenient phrase but without any genuine pragmatic equivalence. The "American Dream" collapsed, as did the "Soviet Paradise." Notably, the tragic paradox is harbored not so much in the conflict of "is" and "ought" as in the principle of equality, which destroys the principle of freedom, or in the idea of uniform happiness, which eliminates both freedom and equality. Let me recall the prophetic We (1924), the antiutopian novel of Zamyatin, where the people are wholly satisfied under the benevolent yoke and paternal vigilance of dogooders, but exist as mere numbers, as sheer anonymities. Apparent counterparts of this apocalyptic foreboding are to be discerned in today's social systems: manipulation by the mass media or authoritarian control by the party headquarters, "equality" in the consumption of rapidly obsolescent consumer goods or in humiliating subordination to an administrative Leviathan, but in no case access to authentically equal rights for all human beings, and, of course, no freedom for all to fully realize their potential. In the so-called socialist countries, the counterfeit unanimity and the constant official lie make for an apathetic, corrupted, unhappy people; but it would be untrue to claim that in such societies, however bereft they are of civil liberties, the principle of social equality is only a slogan. In the so-called affluent or welfare states, happiness is much more a reality, but at the cost of a much more palpable inequality. Here the civil liberties are respected, and, nonetheless, one cannot confirm that the principle of freedom is available everywhere and to everyone within the Leviathan ruled by transnational corporations. Instead, people are submitted to patronizing manipulation by various institutions and the iniquity of diverse taboos.

In sum, no society provides a humanity-oriented, harmonious order. The tragic syndrome occurs in this framework: the clash between the values that are supposed to transform the idealized society into a fully humanistic whole but instead exclude or destroy one another. All the solutions are acceptable only in part, while all the strivings go toward total solutions. The disharmony I have outlined above is omnipresent; its extension—if I may buttress the analysis—is, for instance, the elemental clash between that instrumental strategy of humanity in whose service both science and technology have been enlisted, and the other values, such as religion, mythology, art. The Promethean thrust to master our environment, to rationalize, mechanize, and quantify our efforts, to exalt "the organization man," necessarily collides with the meditative mood, self-exploration, the commitment to getting in touch with reality instead of prevailing over things and people. We should finally add to this dark picture the current ecospasm: the victorious leap into interplanetary space and the triumphs of genetic engineering versus the increasing devastation of natural resources. In his essay in futurology, *The Third Wave*,[4] Alvin Toffler envisions an electronic household linked by computer-assisted channels to the world, but he minimizes the losses that could occur with this development. Should his forecast become reality, the environment of electronics and computers could displace the former primary environment of nature. The spontaneous response to nature itself could be lost. A tragic vision indeed, introducing our next nexus.

I—Nature

The individual displays a continual propensity to break through cultural determinations and uncover his or her inner nature, the authenticity of each human being. The same impulse also impels us toward the nature beyond us; in making contact, the individual may regain vital energies. Cultural barriers are intransigent, however. We cannot remove them. It may be that the hippie's life style is closer to nature than the straight person's. Nonetheless, to be a hippie is a cultural project. Even voodoo world views and techniques are social products. Moreover, we grow more and more helpless before a changing climate to which we do not know how to adapt ourselves. On the other hand, would we wish to lose our cultural milieu? If it vanished, we would also lose our most precious values. But of course the overthrow of the cultural context is a futile thought. In practice we know that our selfhood is embedded in a culture no less than in nature. And the two stimuli are incommensurate. The one downgrades the other. When they operate simultaneously, the equilibrium is unsure, menaced from either side. Ecospasm recalls us to the golemlike consequences of humanity's best technology, notwithstanding its intention to alleviate poverty, hunger, war, and disease. Individuals must live on the horns of a dilemma: the sources in nature must be exploited to the maximum, but they must also be preserved.

In the context of I—Nature, we could speak of a phenomenon that I hereby dub "psychospasm," or "axiospasm." In this framework the tragic is even more acute than it is in ecospasm. One can never become pristine again, plunging naked into the primordial realm of archetypes; there is only the irrefutable longing to. To be human means to transgress the animality in man, which, accordingly, is incessantly reborn and stifled. The individual's existence is made meaningful by the highest values of culture—by art, say, or by research, public service, religious activity, or love of family. The more engagement, devotion, and sense of realization are associated with the chosen value, the stronger becomes the streak of self-alienation. In challenging the world to be free within our choice, we end by falling into the trap of our own passion. Our own nature—the pole opposite to culture—exists for us as the potential and play of many (or infinite) courses of action. If I am a man of self-chosen destiny, I then become unable to avoid one-sidedness; I am imprisoned by the value or values that I chose and am able to act upon and develop. The tragic nexus embraces nature and culture in myself, rent internally. It means I shall never regain a totally integrated selfhood; I shall always submit myself to something, feeling uneasy and one-dimensional even when it is a free and passionate submission I make.

I – Transcendence

We are mundane beings, grounded in what our senses can perceive, our reason acknowledge, and our deeds constitute. But we fervently seek another dimension without which the mystery of existence seems negligible. The two axiological domains do not complement one another; they have different aims. If a human being is a fragile reed, then there has to be some firmer footing, some spiritual rock, and no fortress is more reassuring than a divine eternity. The maxims of religion, however, mystify our earthly status. We want assurance and reject it simultaneously. Redemption from turmoil and trouble is the goal, but we cannot assent to it because the price is absolute certitude or total abandonment, grace or disgrace. The tragic nexus in this context is twofold. The transcendence, which is indispensable in comprehending human existence, is downgraded or trivialized as we pursue worldly affairs. But we cannot live according to transcendence, because it would condemn us to be either an angelic or a damned being.

The paradox is that we live in the two antithetical dimensions, never taking full possession of either. The gospel of religion—never mind which—opens the door to thoughts of life and death, mortal time and universal time, hollow existence and the heroic efforts of humanity to defeat the senselessness that pervades daily life. The values of transcendence attain their highest realization when an individual acquires a holy dimension. Holiness surpasses the mystical experience, for the partnership with God is felt to be not enough: the holy person addresses himself to the brethren, illuminating them, offering love, inspiring them to goodness. The danger arises of becoming enslaved, not only by the church as an institution, but also by the holy service itself, by representing divine powers that assuage existential anxiety. One needs God but is afraid of an absolute greatness that demands humility. And we dream of becoming godlike and know in our hearts that it is impossible and, moreover, that if achieved it could offer only a static perfection.

Surveying all the above issues we may conclude that the tragic derives from *coincidentia oppositorium*: the human existence torn by antinomic values. Our choice among the values is necessitated by our status as frail creatures needing shelter and nurturance. Yet none of the options are self-sufficient and satisfying. This tragedy of choosing, which turns into the destruction of something vital and highly precious, is moreover intensified by the transformation of the prized value into an antivalue. Homeostasis and the achieved integration of the person through his or her value relations with the world entail the peril of a deadening existence. The social community meant to be totally harmonious and fulfilling becomes an anthill, a barracks society, or a concentration camp. Perhaps the bedrock of the tragic grounding consists of the insatiable impulse to become a peer of the almighty; to be bursting with animal vigor and also a person unique, godlike, a supreme participant in the cosmos. Perhaps it consists in the "ought" of merging all possible high values and causing them to support and strengthen one another, leading to the irresistible hope of forever joining freedom, equality, justice, and all the other values.

That hope is vain, for these values are fundamentally incompatible, never to be reconciled. Nonetheless, human beings cannot give up the striving for something more than a brute existence. Who wishes to be regarded as a mere pawn in an unintelligible game, to be ruled by one value exclusively and to remain a passive object in the ever-recurrent alienational processes? There slumbers in this person the fear of building an artificial, suicidal paradise. Yet he wants to be the architect of his own doom, and even the designer of the cosmic universe. Thus, he is a fighter against the irrelevant host of mishaps or lucky accidents that only apparently shape his destiny. He does not bow before the fickleness of time; he tries not to fear his death. Existence means constant anxiety, a darkness with but a few bright points that inexplicably elude one, a labyrinth with too many exits but none that afford genuine and profound relief.

Why then the defiance, the challenge thrown back at the fundamental knottiness and perplexity of being? We can grasp the reason precisely because of our tragic self-consciousness. My compatriot, Zygmunt Adamczewski, analyzed these motifs in his Heideggerian book *The Tragic Protest*.[5] The tragic vision implies, as he rightly says, no despair and no joy, no simple, univocal stance with regard to pessimism or optimism. I am not strictly existentialist-minded, but I am eager to consent to Adamczewski's statement that the tragic personality accepts and also denies the order of being. His "yes" and "no," expressed simultaneously, can be traced, as I see it, to the acknowledgment of the existential antinomies, as well as to a recurrent questioning of the either/or type of solution.

Hence, a tragic self-consciousness of existence is always grounded on the rift within oneself. What one renounces comes back like a boomerang, for it cannot be altogether renounced or foregone. This has been long observed; Volkelt described the experience of the tragic as the *Kontrastgefühl*. Dejection is mixed up with the sublime (the *Niedernickende und Erhaben-befreiende*). The first arises because we discover no good response to our condition and the world about us. The second is aroused because we are never dismayed or dazzled by the troughs or crests. Like the mythical Prometheus, humanity begins ever anew its contest with destiny, eternity, inchoate determinates: the choices that seem no choices at all.

IV

Why do I deal with the tragic as an aesthetic category, some may ask, when the tragic involves an existential truth and a determinate ethos derived from a view of life and what it ought to be? My reply is that the art of tragedy renders, in a condensed way, the essence of human affairs. From the advanced standpoint of the tragic ethos, there can be no demarcation line between the provinces of art and of life. Dostoevsky's *The Brothers Karamazov* reveals the polyphony of mutually destructive values in an incomparable manner. Consider Isaac Babel's *The Red Army Cavalry*: it takes the tragedy of the sociohistorical revolution as its main issue. In Graham Greene's *The Heart of the Matter*, man pursues a tragic monologue with and against divinity. The I–Thou game of antinomic love and distance finds a paradigm in Ulrich and Agatha of Robert Musil's *Man without Qualities*. Oedipus wages a duel with blind *moira* while he rises to tragic self-awareness. Hamlet is classically caught in the jaws of the axiological predicament: no choice of values can salvage him from the muddle he is in; only his death provides a dramatic solution. The I–Nature nexus was masterfully embodied by Malcolm Lowry in *Under the Volcano* in the self-devastating passion of the consul.

The latest avant-garde of art too bears witness effectively to these tragic motifs, even as it blurs deliberately the boundaries between art and life. For instance, the happenings of Hermann Nitsch's OM Theater are an effort to revive genuine human potential through a primitive ritualistic spectacle. This return to nature is celebrated by Marina Abramovich and Klay in their common-body performances, and it is also notable in many exhibits of "earth works." The artistic commune of Otto Muehl makes the I–Thou relationship central. Jerzy Grotowski's posttheatrical program focuses on the I–Thou antinomy and touches on the I–Society motif. The latter theme is profoundly dealt with in the Living Theater's activities.

Icarus is the model of the tragic character striving for more than can be accomplished by human beings. Max Scheler, it is true, cited Christ's redemptive death as the paradigm of the tragic event, but he was concerned with the *unschuldige Schuld* aspect, and not the absolute faith that proves unavailing, the aspect that concerns us here. Tragic, for us, is Christ the supreme martyr for all-embracing Love, who showed to humanity a road to truth that humanity has never fully trodden and gave a lesson that never became the individual-cum-social practice. It is in this figure and context that Christ has appeared in literature, drama, or the fine arts. And no wonder: for the best art, along with philosophy and religion, has always rebuked the unexamined life, which, as Plato said, is not worth living. It has provided the most effective testimony to the more valuable ideals.

I realize that everything I have written might be seen as pure speculation. Is it? I said in my introduction that my "confession" of an approach to the tragic has a grounding that others might confirm. One lays claim to universality: speaking for oneself, one presumes a validity for each human being. The counterargument—

that the majority of people do not experience what I have described—does not persuade, since I do not argue that all persons see and grasp the world in a tragic manner; I state only that all are potentially able to experience what I have, should they awaken from semiawareness and achieve a sensitive edge to their consciousness. If I am right, then nothing is more frequent than humanity's flight from an adequate response to this tragic nexus of existence.

A more telling argument might be made against me: I could be reproached for exaggerating the dark side of our existence. It is often urged that while there is much spiritual malaise in the world, the opposing forces are no less present. But such opinions will compel me to look at the foundations of the world view that is opposed to my premises and hypotheses. Let me repeat that the issue of the tragic is based on the philosophical or ideological orientation of the writer. So while I concede that other approaches have legitimacy, I insist on looking for such traits of the human ontology as gain acceptance by different and yet fundamental world views. It may be that my own and some different "confessions" could meet and overlap, and then at least some of my thought on the tragic could win additional defenders.

A third counterargument to mine is a friendly one. Granted what you advocate, it says, why should the self-aware carrier of the truth be tragic-minded? If he knows that all high values cannot be reconciled, a reasonable meta-attitude should then be able to ameliorate the constant rifts. Here is mellow advice: one should practice to become a stoic, distancing oneself from the tragic. But this is sorry advice, for the paradoxical status of the tragic experience lies precisely in the inability to distance oneself. In this case knowledge and feeling are unified in advancing a viewpoint and reflecting upon it.

The final counterargument comes from another side. Some discussants might charge that my concept of the tragic is quite wrong; that, say, Aristotle's idea of character and misfortune (the tragic fall) is more apropos. I would gladly defer to a better conception, but first let me hear from my adversary what existential-ontological reasons enable us to cope with the tragic experience in one aspect or another. Should my adversary rejoin that we should leave aside questions based on world view and deal only with the aesthetic meaning of the category, this retort too will require philosophical justification. To be sure, my discussant can refuse to justify it, but his silence is a dodge; it must disrupt the pursuit of an understanding of the ethos of life and art. Yet I might, up to a point, approve of his muteness if he added in commentary: "Perhaps the tragic should be left to feeling, imagination, and intuition; no discourse can do justice to it."

Notes

1. Max Scheler, *Abhandlungen und Aufsätze* (Berlin, 1915).
2. J. I. Volkelt, *System der Aesthetik* (Munich, 1910).
3. G. W. F. Hegel, *Aesthetik* (Berlin, 1835), Part III, Sec. III, Ch. III.
4. Alvin Toffler, *The Third Wave* (New York, 1980).
5. Zygmunt Adamczewski, *The Tragic Protest* (The Hague, 1963).

Response to the Essays

As the time for the completion of this volume drew near, the editor found himself shuttling, over a period of several months, between the hospital room of a seriously ill Monroe Beardsley and the telephone for lengthy conversations with most of the contributors. The book was not to be simply a collection of essays, but a collection scrutinized by Beardsley and responded to by his hand. Every participant in the project felt that his involvement in this dialogue with his friends was essential to the work. The publication was delayed in the hope that the dialogue would be possible. It is with deep appreciation and added admiration that the authors salute their colleague, who, still far from full recovery, summoned the energy to provide the following responses. With these remarks the work at last stands complete.

—John Fisher

18

Response to the Essays

MONROE C. BEARDSLEY

I agree with Frank Sibley that dramatic intensity, grace, and elegance are properties that "inherently" possess aesthetic value when found in artworks, but I attribute this to their being primary aesthetic qualities: grace, for example, is never a defect, I think, unless it interferes seriously with some other primary quality. But to defend this view against such a powerful attack by someone as sensitive to such qualities as Frank Sibley is difficult indeed, and somewhat rash, no doubt.

Unlike Sibley, I cannot believe that there are three types of aesthetic quality: those that are primary, those requiring fuller explanation, and those that are entirely neutral and require explanation in terms of primary qualities. Perhaps I am missing something here and will eventually come round to Sibley's position. Meanwhile I will probably continue to think that an artwork cannot have too much grace or dramatic intensity, unless these crowd out some other primary quality.

I must confess that Sibley's distinction between additive and interactive qualities gives me pause, and perhaps I ought to have paid more attention to this earlier. But I thought (perhaps mistakenly) that there was sufficient independence of the aesthetic qualities (though not, of course, of their *conditions*) to warrant the knife analogy.

There are a host of good arguments in Sibley's paper, and I wish I could deal with them as they deserve. For example, I am willing, despite its odd sound, to speak of a hint of wistfulness as being more or less intense—not that the wistfulness is less wistful, but that the hint is more pronounced, and this, I take it, is a good thing. Or, to take another example, the gentleness of a work's humor may be desirable.

There is one point that must be admitted: I have not succeeded in coping with the negative aesthetic qualities to my complete satisfaction, and perhaps this is the result of my "heroic" attempt to make my three basic criteria work. Perhaps I am misguided in this endeavor, but I hope to find a good answer someday.

I did not mean to suggest (though I may have done so) what Lars Aagaard-Mogensen seems to think I believe: that a simple quality—if there is such a thing—could ever be beautiful when it appears alone. To my mind it must emerge from a complex, though the quality itself is simple. I suppose I should have given more of an argument in support of my view, though since Plotinus "refuted" the stoics I do not believe it has been doubted much. I think that this emergence is essential to the experience of art. I connect it with the creativity of art and hold that works that lack it are uncreative.

I do doubt that "pure" colors are more beautiful than others, for otherwise an etching could not be beautiful at all—which I think it can be. On this point I may differ from Sircello.

On the simplicity of beauty, I agree that there are different kinds of beauty and have been puzzled about how this fact can be reconciled with the simplicity of regional qualities. My present view is that when we speak, for example, of the "wild beauty" of the middle part of Schubert's great C Major Quintet, we do not imply that the beauty is complex, but simply say more precisely what the quality is. But I may be wrong about this and Aagaard-Mogensen right.

I do not wonder that Aagaard-Mogensen expresses some doubts about my account of "human qualities," since I have given so little help on this score. I am convinced that there must be some relationship to human beings involved in metaphor, though not necessarily as close as the one Alan Tormey finds in his book on expression, and I am convinced that terms such as "beauty" have only a nonmetaphorical use. But if there is a contradiction here, I have not found it—not even if we add that "beauty" is commonly used for descriptions of artworks.

Göran Hermerén's thesis 3, "Interpretations as well as analyses and explications of works of art (paintings, poems, novels, etc.) (*a*) can always be checked, or (*b*) can only be checked, or (*c*) should always be checked, against the qualities of the work of art in question," as it stands, I should have thought to be undeniable, though perhaps not in the rather too simple version I propounded in *The Possibility of Criticism*. Certainly properties and interpretations of a given work must be checked against the text, pictorial properties, or whatever, before they are accepted. I deny that "every work of art is open in the sense that it can be described and interpreted in many ways"—that seems a bit much. Even if Adorno is right in holding that you cannot "derive" an artwork from its social setting, it does not follow that interpretations need not be checked against the text. Another form of argument is needed, such as those supporting the "intentional fallacy."

I am inclined to call thesis 4, "Works of art (a) do not refer to anything whatsoever—every work of art is a closed world without any connection with anything else; or (b) do not refer to any subjective or objective reality outside the realm of art—works of art refer only to other works of art," a definition of "ideal form." Concerning irony, I have merely insisted that there must be an internal clue that makes the work ironic—you cannot go by the social circumstances alone. Aside from these observations, I think that Professor Hermerén's analyses are to the point, and I am inclined to be in general agreement with him.

I do not feel that I am in disagreement with Ingarden about professional critics as much as is implied by Bohdan Dziemidok, since I am concerned with the *meaning*, not the *origin*, of their aesthetic judgments. I do not doubt that they are "employing learned, professional criteria" and producing "cool judgments," but I think their judgments are about the capacity of the work to arouse a certain experience, and here Dziemidok and I do not appear to differ—or to differ with Ingarden. (I wish I had thought of the interesting point myself!)

But as regards rights: the civil liberties of no reader can be taken away. Each reader retains his or her "right to reject" my judgment—except in the weak sense that all of us have a duty to be rational, and my judgment is supremely rational.

One need not be a phenomenologist to be against relativism. But Ingarden's two "premises" of relativism seem to me neither necessary nor sufficient for it.

Those radical innovators in the business of creating (and selling) artworks do not affect the issue, I think, especially when they ask us please not to evaluate their works at all. If they are producing outlandish works, then chances are that they are interested in social or cognitive or other values and should not be judged by aesthetic criteria at all—so I fail to see how their works are related to the argument.

I would like to agree with Ossowski, but I cannot admit two kinds of aesthetic evaluation, one in terms of origin and one in terms of effect. Nor do I see how this solves the problem. The first kind seems to be another form of intentionalism—or to lead to it. In short, the attempt to disconnect an "artistic" value from aesthetic value seems to fail because in the end the so-called artistic value seems to be dependent upon—indeed, reducible to—the aesthetic value.

I am very glad Stephen Barker has found in my discussion of Kant a hint pointing toward an interpretation that resolves the issue he so clearly formulates—although he has had to add a lot of his own ideas. I am also glad to be corrected on one point: that it is not all free play of the imagination, but only that which bears the aspect of a game, that constitutes the experience of beauty. The role of disinterested pleasure in all this has puzzled me for a long time, and Barker has gone a long way toward clearing it up. There is something rather narrow about Kant's baroque taste, but I believe Barker has singled out the explanation of the inexhaustibility of beauty, in Kant's sense. The concept of the "feel" of the phenomenon is a valuable one.

John Fisher has singled out the concept that has given me the most trouble in aesthetics. In my latest try at it, I have tried to combine what I believe to be the genuine insights of a number of persons, but I am all too aware that I have not succeeded. There are two things I have become sure of: that there is such a thing as aesthetic value, and that it cannot be defined except in terms of aesthetic experience. Therefore Kennick is right in thinking that I was trying at a definition.

Fisher is properly critical of various features of the latest attempt. But he is also generous. He is certainly right that a fully satisfactory theory of art has not been forthcoming. But I am not convinced that we need to explore the differences among our experiences of all the arts before we can get a general account of aesthetic experience.

George Dickie is certainly right that I passed too quickly over my point about the "moulding" of the artist's thoughts, and his distinction is a help. If the Romantic artist is conceived as one who does not absorb from his culture some notion of what painting (or plumbing) is, then I agree that there are no Romantic artists. But it seems to me that to state the thesis in this way is in effect to trivialize it, and I was trying to state an interesting thesis, even if it was inadequate, or maybe false, about the conditions that make something an artwork. I agree about Grandma Moses, but her work, I suppose, is not at issue, and that Duchamp's bottle of Parisian air is a work of art is to me doubtful. Once exhibited at the Philadelphia Museum of Art, it is undoubtedly institutionalized, in a fairly strict sense, but I do not think that this is sufficient to make it an artwork, or necessary.

If I have lapsed into a repetitive idiom, I can only observe that so many have criticized Dickie's view on this matter that perhaps there must be some important truth in it.

There has been a lot of talk about the "domination of the market" and "consumer sovereignty" as late phases of capitalism, and I guess there is plenty of evidence that forces are in motion that tend, as Charles Dyke says, to debase taste and reduce it to a level of mediocrity. But what we are witnessing now may be a passing fad, or fads, as evanescent as the economic forces behind them, and we must not forget that Cellini, Shakespeare, and Mozart worked in a "market economy," too. At least they had to sell their works, dicker with popes and princes for commissions, and so on.

Since I do not think that people "come equal to the market" anyway, it is little loss that "present-day society identifies no such role" as distinctive of the artist. About the "emargination" of the artist in present-day society, however, I can only agree with all Dyke has said, and I thoroughly agree, too, that the main problem is to make society safe for the artist, or more supportive of him or her. There is hope under socialism, but, as Dyke remarks, not under most societies that call themselves "socialist" today.

That, as I see it, is the extent of the "hopelessness" of my "dream"—a society where civil liberties will permit all forms of self-expression, where creativity is not abridged by any form of government or private censorship. I guess that is the liberal dream, too. In such a society, "the time and money required to become a Beardsleyan contemplator" will not be lacking to the unintellectual or the poor.

Nor, I think, must such a society consist solely of rationalists: it is enough that a relatively small number experience the good of art and enjoy it. That is all we have ever had to work with. And, to avoid elitism, there should be artworks of good quality that can be enjoyed by everyone. As for aesthetic education, all one can say is that it has never been tried—like nonviolence. In fact, the emargination of the artist begins in kindergarten, where children are taught to be consumers. On my view, *homo aestheticus* remains out of reach because we have not built a society ready for it—but neither has anyone else, past or present.

Contrary to Dyke, by the way, there are lots of books—some of them pretty good—on the teaching of literary appreciation. It troubles me that this teaching tends to be done down the hall from the teaching of writing, but that, I think, is the result of realizing that writing is hard—harder than reading—and requires special training. And so with painting and music.

I must say to Francis Sparshott that I do not think that there are any characteristics that a picture *must* share with what it represents, but I believe it must share something distinctive in the way of pictorial qualities or forms in order to be recognizable, and recognizability, rather than actual recognition, is the key notion here. Even the picture of Churchill as a bulldog must have something Churchillian about it. And though horse-pictures may vary enormously, they all possess *some* resemblance to horses in their own fashion.

The analogy between representation and overheard conversation is, it seems to me, a very good one and could be extended to fiction, as hints. In fact, this is a typically fertile Sparshott essay. I do not believe Sparshott pays Goodman more than a left-handed compliment, though, in praising his chapter on representation for its "elegance" and then referring to it as "an essay in formal logic," though it is correct to say that Goodman deals with representation only broadly there.

It is a special honor to read the essay by Paul Ricoeur among those that make up the present volume, and so it seems ungrateful to begin by disagreeing with him. Nevertheless, on the first page he appears to identify the interpretation of literature with the exposure of the "world of the work," whereas I think there is much more to interpretation than that. However, I agree with his succeeding claim that it is the "temporal character" of human experience that is the "specific stake" of narrative. I must admit that I do not see why circularity is involved in asserting a correlation between narrativity and the temporality of human experience, even if we allow that there is something paradoxical about the latter.

Ricoeur's phenomenological description of the experience of reading a "followable" story is replete with insights, but I must confess that I do not fully understand how this description solves the "central paradoxes that perplexed Augustine to near silence." It is true, and important, that when we know the denouement of a narrative we can see what led up to it, and in a sense reverse the direction of time; but it seems to me that this feat depends also on accepting the direction of time as possessing a certain inevitability.

There is something to the idea that there is a hidden "hermeneutic potential" in every life, a story waiting to be told; and the same is true of history as a whole. But it is doubtful to me that a "configuration" can be imposed upon, or found in, the texture of every life—an "order" that makes sense, in the sense of having a "theme," and consequently constitutes the substance of a viable narrative. Even the fragments of experience dished up to a psychiatrist may not fit together in a dramatic form, or why would we need to tell stories in the first place?

I think that Seymour Chatman has said about all the true things there are to be said about themes in literature. At least I am willing to go a long way with him. As we would expect from the author of *Story and Discourse*, his discussion is both thorough and lucid, and I am glad some of my own work was of use to him. About the only protest I would lodge is that, contrary to what is said in his paper, I do not want to include the explanation of dictionary meanings under "explication," and I have more or less abandoned the distinction, however valuable, between "explication," "elucidation," and "interpretation" and now let the last one do all the work.

I am glad to see, and say, that Alexander Nehamas is living up to the Nietzschean injunction because he has taken issue with me on an important point indeed. I am sorry to see that he runs themes and theses together. But I am all for the position, taken by Seymour Chatman, that themes are a special emergent level and have to be considered on their own terms. Unfortunately, as this essay so well argues, there is some difficulty in defining "plot" and distinguishing it from the work itself. I had thought, to use an expression of Nehamas's, that the plot consisted of the events that happened in the work to the people in it. As such, it could be abstracted and described, along the lines of various persons quoted by Nehamas. But I admit to some doubts after reading his essay.

In the essay in this volume by Ann Banfield, we have a splendid example of her continuing effort to make literary theory a more exact discipline by introducing exact and rigorous arguments based on the application of (largely, but not exclusively) Chomskyan linguistics to literary works. She has already demonstrated, in her essay "The Nature of Evidence in a Falsifiable Literary Theory," that "the syntactic evidence establishes the validity of [Benveniste's suggestion of] a category of narration stylistically distinct from discourse, but falsifies the claim that narration can contain no *I*." I, for one, could profit more from her discoveries. In the current essay, there is much to agree with, or simply accept, so careful and well confirmed is the argument.

I differ with her on only a few points. I think she makes a good case for the mutual dependence of competence and performance, but in my *Aesthetics* I did not want to put much stress on the concept of a *norm*, whatever language Wimsatt and I used in *The Dictionary of World Literature*. There is surely more to the concept of *competence* than that, and in any case my essay in the Lang volume shows that I would not agree that "style is one such idealization of the text," though this is approximately true, I think, of *a* style. There are probably several ways of "idealizing" style, as I am sure Ann Banfield would agree.

I must take issue also with the notion that some nouns have only "virtual reference." Banfield, it seems to me, is too confident when she says, "The epithet is not classificatory. There is no class of 'idiots' or 'bastards' whose members can be identified by common objective characteristics." I realize that this issue is controversial and that a proper defense of my view would require some space, but I want to flag the play, in any case, and say that it is my view that all evaluative terms have some classificatory function, even when used as epithets. This point is no doubt connected with the dubiousness of some of her examples: in (37), for example, I do not see why we cannot correctly say, "The book that was great was donated to the library, but the other kept." Or why we cannot correctly say, "That friend is beloved" (40). I expect my linguistic intuitions differ from hers on these points, though they mostly correspond; so much for "falsifiability"!

Because of my general ignorance of linguistics, on which Ann Banfield relies heavily for her evidence, I have consulted my colleague Muffy Siegel, who has pointed out to me (if I understand properly) that Banfield is somewhat hard on Kuno because the phenomenon he discusses is part of a much wider one in which all intentionalistic terms (such as "believe," "know," and others) participate, and no way is provided for drawing a line between those that, in context, affect the linguistic status of the subject of the clause following the intentionalist term, and those that do not.

The subject of Alan Tormey's essay has long interested me, and his solution is ingenious. I do not know if Kate Smith is a turquoise beetle. Metaphors are elliptical counterfactuals, says Tormey. I, on the other hand, regard them as a unique fact of language, whereby credence-properties of objects are transformed into connotations of words. The first problem I find in Tormey's theory is that of finding the right reference-class. Let us agree that Juliet is the sun. Does this mean that if Juliet were a celestial body she would be the sun? Or does it mean that if Juliet were a double star she would be the sun? This problem gets difficult when fish or animals of various species are involved: does "man is wolf" compare man (for this is essentially a comparison theory of metaphor) with wolves, or with all animals, or what? I do not question the truth of metaphors *or* counterfactuals, but their interpretation.

Another difficulty I find with the theory is that it seems to me to pose unanswerable questions. What would happen if Juliet were the actual sun? I do not know. The entire solar system would have to be different. The distinction between serious possibles and merely hypothetical ones goes some way toward clearing up these problems, but something remains.

One thing that stumps me—but here my puzzles have been partly anticipated in the paper—is how the theory is to be applied to such well-known metaphors as those from Shakespeare's sonnets ("When to the sessions of sweet silent thought," for example) without introducing extraneous ideas or images. This is a problem even if the theory works for Carl Sandburg's "Fog"; and—to return to an earlier point—how do we know that the line is to be construed as "If the fog were animate . . ."? Why not "If the fog were a fish . . ."?

I must say that Samuel Hynes has added a great deal to my faltering and obscure attempt to define bad poetry in the fourth chapter of *The Possibility of Criticism*. His analysis of Hardy's poetry convinced me completely, and I am only sorry that an invitation from Wayne State University compelled me to go ahead with that project and to write *The Possibility of Criticism* without waiting for the completion of our very interesting discussions of this topic— not that our discussions would ever have been complete on this or any other critical topic, for we carried on an endless conversation, the results of which are to be seen throughout the book.

I have to take slight exception to his introduction of an Yvor Winters–like moral argument, which I was trying to avoid in favor of a purely aesthetic explanation of poetic badness, not that I would denigrate the moral nature of literature, but at the time, as today, I regarded the critic as well equipped to detect disproportions within the poem, but (saving present company) no expert on morality. I wanted to give the critic his proper work, but Hynes has shown me that the critic may be unusually sensitive to moral considerations, and his forthcoming edition of Hardy's poetry is bound to make this even more evident.

George McFadden's essay is remarkable, it seems to me, among its other qualities, for its perceptiveness about the relation between freedom and comedy. I agree wholeheartedly that no genre of art can do without freedom, but comedy is the only genre continually to assert it—as McFadden says. I confess that I was somewhat daunted by the first few pages of the essay, but I learned a lot from the pages that follow.

The only place where I take issue with him is where he defines the comic as the quality of a fiction and thus ignores purely verbal humor. As a devoted reader of P. G. Wodehouse, I will accept this limitation of the subject to be discussed, but I do not think an adequate account of humor can be given with this limitation.

If I recall correctly, Hegel said that *Antigone* represented a conflict of values, each of which had something to be said for it. Stefan Morawski apparently agrees with this view, if I read him right. Or at least he is close to it. This seems to me too narrow to cover all the cases of tragedy. But what seems to me remarkable is how he has broadened the Hegelian formula with the help of phenomenological existentialism to the point where it fits the facts, and therefore I find it quite convincing. The question in my mind is whether or not the proposed concept is too broad, and on reflection I am inclined to think not, though to tie the tragic quality to the "problematic status of mankind" is stretching things a bit, and I am not sure that we have to go so far.

Despite his disclaimer, Morawski adds to the conflict between "is" and "ought," and it is hard for me to see how these are reconciled. "Is" and "ought" imply an opposition between clear-cut duties and inclinations, whereas Antigone was faced with a conflict of duties.

To end this book with a consideration of tragedy would perhaps be too gloomy, were it not that Morawski manages to find a certain amount of triumph in tragedy. That is a discovery that others too have made. I am with him, and them, and it remains only to emphasize again what a pleasure it has been to read these essays and to comment upon them, though, if the authors had the last word, I am sure that they could say much in their own defense.

Index

ADAMCZEWSKI, Z., 289

ADORNO, T. W., 35

Aesthetic: attitude, 72; education, 121–25, 301; experience, 53–68, 69–85, 86–96, 119–21, 265, 273, 300; judgment, 53–68, 69–85, 299; object, 88–89; qualities, 3–20, 21–34, 263, 297, 302; response, 88, 92; terms. *See* aesthetic qualities; value, 3–20, 35–49, 53–68, 89–90, 247–59, 299

Affective fallacy, 90–91

ARISTOTLE, 88, 146, 152, 155, 182, 186, 190, 192, 268–69

Art and society, 35–49, 99–108, 109–30, 131–46

Artworld, 105, 114–16, 129–30

ASCHENBRENNER, K., 61–62

Attention, 194–95

AUGUSTINE, 150–51

Autonomy of art, 35–49

BARTHES, R., 163, 262, 272

Beauty, 3–20, 69–85, 298

BECK, L. W., 85

Beholder, 92

BERGSON, H., 261, 267, 274

BLACK, M., 243–44

BLEISCH, D., 92

BLOCKER, G., 39

BOOTH, W., 182–83

BRUFORD, W. H., 173–76

CASSIRER, H. W., 73

CAVELL, S., 242

Characterization, 131–46

CHISHOLM, R., 244

CHOMSKY, N., 201, 204, 209, 213–14, 229

Closure, 175

Comic, 6–7, 261–77, 305

Consciousness, 133–36

Contemplation, 116–20, 165–66

CRAWFORD, D., 73

Creation, 103–05

CRITES, S., 157

Criticism, 3–20, 111–14, 149–60, 161–79, 180–97, 247–57, 261–77, 305

CULLER, J., 161–63

DANTO, A., 129–30

Deconstruction, 202, 262, 268–70

Depiction, 141–44

DERRIDA, J., 261, 268

DEWEY, J., 54, 88, 92–94

DICKIE, G., 61, 88, 93, 129–30

Disinterestedness, 72

DUFRENNE, M., 142–43

Effects of work of art, 35–49

ELIOT, T. S., 92

ELLMANN, R. 249–50, 253

Elucidation, 162, 303

Empathy, 207–30

Existentialism, 278–92

Explication, 162, 303

Fiction, 149–60, 161–79, 180–97

FILLMORE, C., 205, 227

FISH, S., 91–92

FISHER, J., 60–62, 65
Freedom, 266, 270–75, 281, 284–86, 305
FREGE, G., 210, 219
FRESCO, M., 39
FREUD, S., 28, 158, 261, 267, 274
FRIED, M., 145
FRYE, N., 185
Functionalism, 89–90

Generality, 3–20
GOMBRICH, E., 38, 47
GOODMAN, N., 132–33, 136, 141, 194, 302
GOTSHALK, D. W., 54
GRAFF, P., 60–62, 65
GUYER, P., 73

HANSLICK, E., 39
HARDY, T., 247–57
HEGEL, G. F. H., 267, 282–83
HEIDEGGER, M., 261
HEILMAN, R. B., 265–66
Hermeneutics. See Interpretation
HILDERBRAND, D., von, 55
HOBBES, T., 265
HUME, D., 110
HUSSERL, E., 261, 265–66

Imagination, 71–76, 79, 149–60
Imitation, 186
Ingarden, R., 40, 56–60, 64, 91, 191, 195, 261–63, 299
Institutional theory, 99–108, 114–24
Intention of artist, 38, 93–94, 264
Intentional Fallacy, 35, 90–91, 202
Interpretation, 73, 149–60, 161–79, 180–97, 201–34, 298–99, 302
ISER, W., 92

KABURAKI, E., 235–46
KAHLER, E., 190
KANT, I., 69–85, 134, 153, 265, 270–73, 300

KAPLAN, A., 138–39
KENNICK, W., 88
KERMODE, F., 154, 156
KMITA, J., 61
Knowledge and cognition, 29, 71–76, 105–06, 133–36, 154–59
KRISTELLER, P., 37
KUHN, T., 266
KUNO, S., 235–46
KURODA, S.-Y., 205, 207, 212

LARKIN, P., 247, 256
LATTIMORE, R., 187
LEWIS, C. I., 54
LEWIS, D., 145
Liberalism, 99–108
Linguistics, 201–34
LOEWENBERG, I., 243

MacDONALD, M., 186
MACKIE, J., 240
MARGOLIS, J., 68
MARX, K., 274
Marxism, 35–36, 197, 273
Meaning, 38, 91–92, 149–60, 161–79, 180–97, 201–34, 235–46, 261–77, 299
MERLEAU-PONTY, M., 261
Metaphor, 4–7, 28–32, 235–46, 304
MILL, J. S., 121
MILLER, R. D., 273–74
MILNER, J. C., 205–09, 217
MINK, L. O., 153
MORAWSKI, S., 41
Munro, T., 54
Myth, 180–97

NAJDER, Z., 64–66
Narrative, 149–60, 161–79, 180–97, 248–49, 302
New Critics, 35, 91–92
NIETZSCHE, F., 155, 180
Novel, 180–97

Objectivity, 91, 265
Ontology of art, 131–46, 280–83

Origins of art, 99–108
Ossowski, S., 53, 62–66

Panofsky, E., 94
Pepper, S. C., 54
Perception, 134
Perrine, L., 165–68
Pitte, F. P., van de, 84
Plato, 268
Play, 79–83
Pleasure, 79–80, 83, 88
Plot, 149–59, 180–97, 303
Polanyi, K., 111
Possible worlds, 141–44, 236
Prall, D. W., 54
Praxis, 99–108
Psychologism, 56, 60
Purpose, 77–80

Qung, Phuc, Dong, 205–07

Reader, reading, 91–92, 149–60,
   161–79, 180–97, 262–63, 302
Recognition, 131–46
Reconstruction, 268–70
Reference, 39, 131–46, 149, 163,
   201–34, 264
Relativism, 58–59, 70–72, 88,
   92, 69–85, 86–96, 99–108,
   299
Religious experience, 87–88
Representation, 131–46, 302
Rescher, N., 239
Resemblance, 131–36
Revelation theory of art, 169
Richards, I. A., 244
"Romantic" conception of art,
   99–107
Romanticism, 266–68, 300
Ross, J., 205–07
Rules, 75–78, 124–25, 265,
   273–74

Sartre, J.-P., 145
Satire, 261–77
Schafer, R., 158
Schapp, W., 158
Scheler, M., 261, 278–79
Schiller, F., von, 268–75
Smith, B. H., 175
Sorber, E., 142
Stein, G., 184
Style, 203, 230
Subjectivity, 91–92, 128
Symbols, 131–46

Taste, 70–71, 110–14, 301
Text, 149–60, 161–79, 203
Theme, 149–60, 161–79
Thesis, 161–79
Tomkins, J., 91
Tragic, 6–7, 305–06, 278–92
Transcendence, 287
Truth, 235–46

Uehling, T., 73
Unity, 92–93
Upensky, B., 216–17

Value, 4, 90, 93–94, 99–108,
   116, 280–83

Wallis, M., 54
Warren, A., 181–83, 185
Weiand, J., 102
Weitz, M., 39
Welleck, R., 181–83, 185
Werkmeister, W., 35
Whitehead, A. N., 86
Wilde, O., 44
Wittgenstein, L., 84
Woolf, V., 91
Wölfflin, H., 36–37

Ziff, P., 29

This volume was designed by Vic Schwarz, composed by G & S Typesetters in Goudy Old Style on a Mergenthaler Linotron 202, printed by Thomson-Shore on Warren's Olde Style Wove, and bound by Thomson-Shore in Holliston Crown Linen and Ecological Fibers Rainbow Texture, with Rainbow Antique Endleaves.